Shakespeare and the Catholic Religion

by

Carol Curt Enos

DORRANCE PUBLISHING CO., INC.
PITTSBURGH, PENNSYLVANIA 15222

ISBN # 0-8059-4768-X
Printed in the United States of America

First Printing

For information or to order additional books, please write:
Dorrance Publishing Co., Inc.
643 Smithfield Street
Pittsburgh, Pennsylvania 15222
U.S.A
1-800-788-7654

Dedication

This book is dedicated with love and thanks to:

My husband Paul, for his steadfast support through some difficult health problems and some discouraging times—and for his valuable insights on the many revisions he read;
Our daughters, Mischa and Heather, for their encouragement and enthusiastic support;
Our sons, Curt and Kevin, for helping me stay anchored in reality;
My mother, Helen Curt, for a lifetime of encouragement;
and finally, to my late uncle, Albert Ginest, whose bequest enabled publication.

Contents

Illustrations

William Shakespeare

Author's Preface

It is both odd and regrettable Shakespeare left no written record of anything he did, hoped, loved, valued, or believed in. Most peculiarly not even his plays, which have so deeply impacted our lives in countless ways, are in his own handwriting. His nebulous figure wavers tantalizingly behind his plays, never quite coming into clear focus despite numerous attempts to define him as a personality. We have been left with a gigantic puzzle that resists assembly into a recognizable form, because key pieces have been lost or effaced forever. We have no knowledge of his political views or his allegiance or resistance to Queen Elizabeth and King James. We assume he was not happily married, but that is merely an assumption. Only fragile shreds of information situate him as a citizen of Stratford in his retirement. We know nothing about his reaction to government censorship of his plays or about legal restrictions which may have inhibited his being totally forthright in his plays if he expected them to reach the stage. The years between his birth in 1564 and the first mention of him in connection with the London theater world in 1592 are virtually blank. Ironically, we can only guess at his religious orientation, even though he lived during a time when being a declared Puritan or Roman Catholic was a life-or-death matter.

If he was a Catholic or a Puritan, in defiance of the requirement that all citizens conform to the state church, his plays will certainly not yield that information in an obvious form, because unorthodoxy in religion signaled disloyalty, and the stage censor would have dutifully quashed the play. A skilled playwright, however, just might have been able to write ambiguously enough to beguile both the censor and the monarch with a smokescreen of praise that disguised fundamental questions such as the morality of kings or queens, the validity of the claim to rule by divine right, the legitimacy of certain claims to the English throne, and the ethical behavior of kings—all set, of course, in the dim, distant past to obscure any challenge to the present regime. Whether or not it was Shakespeare's intention to write in this manner, his plays can frequently be interpreted from diametrically opposed vantage points. Determining why he structured his plays so they could convincingly and appealingly speak to the adherents of opposing ideology, as well as attempting to discover how Shakespeare was aligned in the various controversies his plays depict, seem to be critical questions to address to understand the plays.

With these questions in mind, I propose to reassemble some of the social context in which Shakespeare lived and worked in an attempt to identify trends, pervasive views, or merely intuitive extrapolations, based on available and recurrent factors, to reveal Shakespeare's character. Distinguishing the contingencies and requirements of his dramaturgy from his actual beliefs may not be possible in the absence of any prose record left by him in essays, diaries, or letters. As I see it, we have two options: we can try to extrapolate from the plays what can logically be attributed to Shakespeare himself, and/or we can examine in minute detail the lives and interests of his friends in the London theater world, in Stratford, and possibly in Lancashire, to look for clues that reveal something about his interests or his involvements. Some view the question of Shakespeare's religion as being strongly colored by the religion of the researcher. In this context, it is relevant that I was brought up as a Protestant in a Protestant environment. I hope my method is what Leah Marcus envisioned when she noted, "We need to bring back, among many other methodological tools of the old historicism, an idea called the Author's Intent or putative intentionality. . . . If Shakespeare avoided the appearance of intentionality, it was at least some of the time by design" (42). In attempting to restructure Shakespeare's particular contexts, it seems wise to look first at the larger picture of English politics which were a part of his world.

Acknowledgments

Although this book is not a direct outgrowth of the National Endowment for the Humanities summer seminars and institute I was privileged to attend, all three experiences enriched my understanding of the Renaissance context in which Shakespeare moved as well as sharpened my understanding of selected plays. I wish to express my deep appreciation to Professor Andrew McLean of the University of Wisconsin-Parkside, director of the 1990 NEH summer seminar of Shakespeare's *Henriad,* for his interest in my work and for all that he did to make the seminar stimulating and scholarly. Also, I am indebted to Professor Barbara Millard of La Salle University, director of the 1994 NEH summer seminar, "Shakespeare and the Creative Act: *Othello* and *Hamlet,*" for contributing her own expertise and for fostering a high level of scholarship. Finally, I wish to thank Professor Al Rabil for the intensive and supremely scholarly 1995 summer institute, "Worlds of the Renaissance," sponsored by the NEH and the Renaissance Society of America.

I am grateful, also, to the Bodleian Library for allowing me access to their collection in the spring of 1989 when I first began to see how the threads of Shakespeare's story led to the probability he was a Catholic in a newly Protestant land.

Special thanks go to Professor Margaret Arnold of the University of Kansas, who guided me to the completion of the master's thesis, which is the basis for this present work. Professor Arnold offered positive and valuable advice long distance from her office at KU and returned my manuscripts with lightning speed to Erlangen, Germany, where my husband and I were spending his sabbatical from KU and my leave of absence from the public school system of Lawrence, Kansas. I am also grateful to Professor

Richard Hardin and to Professor Doug Atkins of the University of Kansas for their careful reading of the manuscript and their insightful comments. The graduate committee at KU very kindly made special dispensation for me to write the thesis in advance of taking the course work, for which I thank them.

Finally, I am indebted to Leo Daugherty, Professor Emeritus of Literature and Linguistics of Evergreen State College and Thomas Merriam, Ph.D., for involving me in the Lancaster University and Hoghton Tower Conference (21-24 July 1999) and for their valuable comments regarding evidence of Shakespeare's Catholicism. Thomas Merriam kindly introduced me to Peter Milward, S.J., the noted scholar who has written extensively on Shakespeare's Catholic background and on the Catholicism in Shakespeare's plays. I have benefited enormously from Father Milward's careful and close reading of the manuscript.

Once again, my husband Paul, deserves my thanks for the photographs of the Saxon maps of Shropshire and Lancashire. The maps were reproduced by the kind permission of the Duke of Devonshire and the Chatsworth Settlement Trustees.

The ideas expressed in this book, however, are my own and should in no way be construed to reflect the thinking of any of those who have contributed to my understanding of William Shakespeare's plays or his political and religious orientation.

The Catholic Problem in English History from Henry VIII to James I

The Roman Catholic Church in England was variously outlawed or suppressed from the time of Henry VIII's break with the pope in 1534 to the middle of the nineteenth century.1 Catholics living in England were not fully entitled citizens even as late as 1829, as shown by Leys:

> For 270 years, from 1559 to 1829, Catholics in England were deprived by law of their full rights as citizens. Although for part of this time their disabilities were shared by others who dissented from the national church, the Catholics were under the ban of specific laws and excluded from concessions. They formed a minority of a very unusual kind. A group within a nation which is distinct in fact, if not in law, from the bulk of the people is not uncommon; but generally such minorities are made up of men of a different race, or living in certain areas, or pursuing a particular aim, political or social. The English Catholics, however, came from every class and were scattered all over the country; only their religion divided them from their fellows. (1)

---

1   The stigma associated with Catholicism lingers and may account for the fact that Shakespeare has persistently been regarded as a patriotic exemplar of Tudor loyalty, while the evidence he very likely was a Catholic has largely been ignored or perhaps suppressed.

In addition to legal deprivation, from 1570 until Queen Elizabeth's death in 1603, Catholics were ridiculed for worshipping idols, repeatedly charged with attempts on the queen's life, and convicted and executed barbarously as traitors. By the end of the queen's reign, 187 seminary and Jesuit priests (Pollard 376), fifty-six laymen, and three women were executed; and probably far more died in prison (Leys 48). In some cases, during Queen Elizabeth's reign, records were altered and destroyed to protect wealthy families or to obscure the strength of the opposition to the government. These distortions are enormous obstacles to sorting out actual facts about Catholics and their activities in Elizabethan England. They should be considered as factors, however, which can obscure the evidence related to William Shakespeare's religious affiliation. When we read his plays, we must constantly bear in mind their backdrop of religious turmoil that followed Henry VIII's break with the Roman Catholic Church.

Prior to Henry's establishment of the Church of England, being a Christian in England automatically meant one was a Roman Catholic. With the introduction of the Protestant religion, however, English citizens were required to make dizzying religious shifts in rapid succession, which in some cases occurred in the span of a single lifetime. They first were required to transfer their spiritual allegiance from the Roman Catholic Pope to Henry VIII as spiritual head of the church. At Henry's death, they were stringently "purified" by Edward VI. Following Edward's death, his half-sister, Mary, rigidly reimposed the Catholic Church in England. Finally, a kind of compromise between Henry VIII's and Edward's versions of Protestantism was struck by Queen Elizabeth and subsequently perpetuated by James I. The consequent, sudden expectation that English citizens would reverse their religion to conform with that of the current monarch was the source of grave concern and controversy related to the very serious—and eternal—state of their souls.

Confronted with the dilemma of having to choose between allegiance to their king or queen or damning themselves for eternity, it is little wonder there were numerous shades of conformity to the state religion, as well as outright, dangerous opposition to it. Depending upon the religious orientation of the king or queen at a particular moment in time, both Catholic and Protestant priests endured unspeakable suffering and tortured deaths to bear witness to the "rightness" of their religion over the other. Protestant heretics of Queen Mary's time were mercilessly tied to the stake to perish by fire. Catholic heretics in the reign of Henry, Elizabeth, and James watched, fully conscious, as butchers carved up their bodies. Each martyr viewed his death as testimony to the validity of his religion and expected to win souls to the faith through his sacrifice.

The most disruptive of these religious reversals, because it was so entirely unprecedented in English history, was Henry VIII's break from Rome to establish his new church. In addition to fear that the change imperiled his soul, the average citizen was confronted with daunting changes in his life from these religious shifts. Each upheaval first required citizens to make fundamental adjustments regarding whether the Pope or the English monarch was the spiritual head of the church. (Elizabeth attempted to lessen the impact by calling herself the spiritual governor.) Those who lived through the destruction and confiscation of Catholic Church property by Henry VIII and his son, Edward, were confronted with the loss of schools as the monasteries collapsed, the need to provide for spinster female relatives who could no longer find refuge in a nunnery, and the necessity to accommodate returning ex-monks who were ill-equipped to survive outside the church. In 1536, under Henry VIII's surveillance, citizens were confronted with the Ten Articles which were intended to be a compromise between the king's new church and the old Catholic Church. This compromise reduced the seven original Catholic sacraments to only three: penance, baptism, and good works (Elton 153). In spite of the changes and reduction in the sacraments, Henry VIII's church was so similar to the Catholic Church that many Catholics were willing to conform to the point of at least attending the services, for the Mass, so crucial to Catholic worship, had not yet been converted into the Communion, although Henry VIII had contemplated such a move before his death in 1547.

There were confusing shifts in other areas as well. Collection of taxes, formerly handled by the church, was now taken over by representatives of the king. Additionally, court cases that had traditionally been tried in church courts were transferred to civil or royally appointed courts.

During the six short years of Edward VI's Puritanical reign (1547-1553), it was increasingly difficult for Catholics to practice their religion because fines and surveillance became steadily more restrictive. Those who had conformed to the state church only to the extent of attending public service while at the same time remaining secret Catholics were faced in 1550 with Calvinistic changes, which made conformity less palatable. The Catholic priest, viewed as having been endowed by God's grace to offer sacrifice, was transformed into the more earthly Protestant minister whose duties were to preach and teach (Bindoff 162). The Second Act of Uniformity was passed on April 14, 1552, sanctioning punishment, including excommunication, for those who failed to attend the state church on Sundays and festivals (164). Catholics who had heretofore refrained from attending public church services, opting to practice their religion privately in their own homes, were now at risk. And finally, the dramatic move Henry VIII had been contemplating went into effect: the Catholic Mass, in which bread and wine were believed to be transformed into the body and blood of Christ, was replaced by the symbolic Communion ritual performed at a simple table rather than an ornate Catholic-style altar.

By the time of Edward VI's death on July 6, 1553, of complications from measles, smallpox, and consumption, Catholics and Protestants in England were even more sharply divided. It can be assumed that the entire citizenry, not only the Catholics, anticipated some relief from Edward's Puritan rigidity when his half sister, Mary, outwitted the plot to put Lady Jane Grey on the throne, taking it for herself instead.

Optimism soon foundered. Because of Mary's compulsive determination to restore the old Catholic religion throughout the land, those who had conformed to Henry VIII's Reformation were required to make a religious about-face or be classified as heretics. The Catholics, however, could at least find some comfort in being allowed to practice their religion openly again. All of the treason laws of Edward VI's reign were repealed (168), and mass was legally reinstated. The queen was not successful in restoring confiscated monastic property, but familiar Catholic iconography, ceremonies, and practices reappeared in the churches. The queen's greatest ambition from the outset had been to re-establish England's religious obedience to Rome, an ambition she achieved in 1554 when England was absolved by the Pope and reconciled to Rome. Protestant resentment was inflamed by the stringent methods imposed upon Protestants to conform to the Catholic faith; during Mary's reign, 300 Protestants in four years were burned at the stake (Trevelyan 230). In addition, Mary's unpopular marriage with Philip II of Spain linked English Catholics with Mary, Queen of Scots, and the political objectives of Spain, simply because they shared the same religion.2

Resentment toward the Catholic religion and Catholics was exacerbated by Mary's commitment to the alignment of England against Spain's enemy, France. The war of 1557 against France was expensive, requiring forced loans to meet the costs, in some cases inciting popular agitation which was put down by martial law, and resulted in the loss of Calais, England's last foothold in France. While Calais had lost its importance as a trading center and was costly to maintain, its loss in many ways was regarded as a blow to English national stature (Bindoff 180, 181). In the final analysis, the relief Catholics experienced in the short-term restoration of their religion was more than outweighed by their own discontent, which was exacerbated by the hatred toward Catholics that had grown as a result of Mary's persecution of Protestants. At her death on November 17, 1558, the emotional lines between the Catholics and the Protestants were even more sharply drawn.

---

2 This religious tie between Spain and the Scottish Queen was to have long-lasting and often dire consequences later for Catholics who became entangled in plots to unseat Queen Elizabeth and restore the Catholic faith in England through armed invasion by Spain. Even if one concedes that what appeared to be Catholic plots were sham plots instigated by Lord Burghley, it is nevertheless true that the Park Hall Ardens participated in the Somerville Plot and members of the Catesby family, linked through marriage to the Park Hall Ardens, were involved in the Gunpowder Plot.

Henry VIII

Anne Boleyn

Mary, Queen of Scots
Photographs by Carol Enos. Portraits housed in the Czartorycki
Collection, The National Museum, Krakow, Poland, ul. sw. Jana 19 31-
017, Krakow, Poland.

Queen Elizabeth and Religion

For a time there was some question as to which religion Queen Elizabeth would follow. She had been raised in Henry VIII's church, which was very similar to the Roman Catholic church in structure and tenets, even to the point of retaining the Catholic-style mass. She next conformed to Edward VI's Protestant church, then made a feeble attempt to return to the Catholic Church under Mary, and seemed to prefer the Catholic-style ritual to the Puritan plainness. She finally followed the safer, moderate Protestant way, largely because Elizabeth's claim depended upon Parliament's recognition of the legitimacy of her birth. Her father had broken with the Catholic Church just in time to marry Anne Boleyn and to make the birth of Elizabeth legitimate, thereby forever linking Elizabeth with the institution of the Protestant Church of England. Her claim derived not only from Henry VIII's will, which named Elizabeth as a successor, but also depended upon the ratification of the will by a Protestant parliament. Disappointed Catholics hoped the new queen would retain the Catholic religion as the state religion or would at least allow religious toleration. The queen herself indicated that she preferred not to "make windows into men's souls." However, faced with the mounting political and religious ambitions of Philip II to regain the crown as well as to re-establish Catholicism in England, combined with rising opposition exerted from the Catholic See in Rome, and the aggressive segment of the English Catholics, the queen was forced to confront what proved to be irreconcilable religious differences. A further complication was that Mary, Queen of Scots, a legitimate rival for the English throne, provided useful leverage for both the Catholic side as well as for Queen Elizabeth's ministers to manipulate the political scene from 1568 to 1587.

Even though Queen Elizabeth's claim was based on Henry VIII's will and approved by Parliament (Bindoff 185), a major complaint of Catholics was that she was not a legitimate sovereign because the Catholic Church did not recognize Henry VIII's divorce from Catherine of Aragon or his remarriage to Queen Elizabeth's mother, Anne Boleyn. In addition, the fact that Elizabeth's very own half-brother, Edward, shortly before he died, had set aside his father's will to declare Elizabeth illegitimate (Elton 213) added fuel to the Catholic charge that Elizabeth was a bastard and a usurper. Catholics maintained the throne should go to the next legitimate heir, who was Mary Stuart, Queen of Scotland. In spite of hints from Rome intended to woo England back into the Catholic fold by suggesting the Catholic Church might be willing to declare Henry VIII's marriage to Anne Boleyn legitimate if Elizabeth were to maintain the Catholic religion in England (Elton 269), she pragmatically chose to side with the Protestants. A combination of factors made this the safest way to power: a predominantly Protestant parliament, increasing Protestantism among the citizens; and foremost, her awareness that her claim to the throne depended upon a Protestant interpretation. The change in Queen Elizabeth's title from "Supreme Head" to "Supreme Governor" did little to mollify ardent Catholic opposition, which arose from being required to recognize the queen as the head of the church.

In addition to these real and imagined threats from the Catholic quarter, Elizabeth was faced with troublesome opposition from Puritans who criticized her conception of Protestantism. Since the time of Henry VIII, Parliament had become increasingly autonomous in its relationship with the king while it also was becoming an important tool on which the Crown relied to translate its will into legislation. Because of Puritan pressure from powerful members, Queen Elizabeth found that Parliament complicated her effort to reach a moderate settlement on religion. In effect, Puritan opposition became as troublesome as the Catholic threat. Parliament's position stood upon a precedent already set which authorized subsequent Parliamentary action in church matters. One very important precedent was the act of Parliament which ratified Henry VIII's will in recognition of Elizabeth's right to succession. Parliament additionally pointed to its role in regard to the Act of Six Articles and in the acceptance of the Prayer Book of 1549. Why should Parliament now be forbidden to express its opinions? Faced with what appeared to be an undermining of her power, the queen was even more resolved to maintain control of the Church because she had to curb the church convocation, the law-making body and the means to administer the law through the ecclesiastical courts. As the confrontation between Parliament and crown escalated, strident Puritan complaints against abuses in the English Church began to echo earlier complaints of the Protestants against the Catholic Church. The abuses of waste, favoritism, and dispensations smacked of papism, they charged. They insisted on purifying the state church of every vestige of the Catholic Church such as the wearing of vestments, the use of the liturgy, and the ritualistic ceremony. The scope of the argument spread to whether or not there should even be bishops in the church. This was a direct threat to the queen's power; she needed to retain the church hierarchy, for her power emanated from her position as the Supreme Governor of that hierarchy. Religious questions could not be disentangled from political questions, and Parliament proved to be so troublesome that the queen called it into session only thirteen times in her forty-four years compared with twenty-nine sessions in the preceding years of Tudor rule (Bindoff 213, 214).

Major changes instituted during Queen Elizabeth's reign were that the Prayer Book of 1552, introduced under Edward, was restored with some modifications; the Uniformity Bill was passed by April 28, 1559; and the Supremacy Bill by the 29th (192, 193). All but one bishop refused to take the Oath of Supremacy and were deprived of their sees, but not one was executed. The question of religion seemed to be settled, but then Henry II, King of France, died in December of 1560.

The Problem of Mary, Queen of Scots

In July of 1559, upon the death of Henry II of France, Mary Queen of Scots, and Francis II became king and queen of France. She was seventeen years old, and he was fifteen. Earlier, on the death of Mary Tudor, Henry II of France had quartered the arms of England on the bearings of Mary and Francis, recognizing Mary Stuart's claim to the English throne. The French already had a foothold in Scotland where Mary's mother, the French Marie de Guise, was acting as regent for her daughter. To counteract the French Catholic threat through the proverbial back door to England, Elizabeth's government covertly supported Puritan opposition in Scotland in various ways. Publicly, before Francis's death, the English government had sent negotiators north to arrange the Treaty of Edinburgh, which appeared to help the Scots oppose French troops that had been sent in, but a major objective was to defuse Mary's claim to the English throne. Terms of the treaty stipulated that Francis and Mary were to relinquish the Royal Arms of England and were to recognize Queen Elizabeth's title. Mary refused to ratify the treaty and still had not done so at her death twenty-seven years later, but the French government accepted the treaty (Jenkins 88). Mary's refusal to ratify it was pretext for Elizabeth's refusal to issue a passport for Mary's safe conduct through England in 1560, when, on the death of Mary's mother and husband within a few months of each other, Mary had to return to a Scotland already rumbling with religious friction. Well before Mary returned, her mother, Marie de Guise, acting as regent, had contended with vigorous Calvinist opposition, so the stage was set for strife for Mary when she returned "home."

The fiasco-riddled marriages, murders, and mayhem of Mary's eight years in Scotland have been told too many times to require recounting here.

Her unseemly behavior led the Scots to pursue their queen until she was forced to flee the country. Instead of returning to France in 1568, which seemingly would have been a safer move, Mary chose to seek refuge in England, expecting assistance from her cousin, Queen Elizabeth, to help win back her Scottish throne. Mary's choice to flee to England seems illogical from our vantage point, but she actually had no other choice. France snubbed Mary by failing to condole with her on the death of her second husband, Darnley, an indication France regarded her as implicated in his murder. Scotland had run her out of the country, so Mary had little recourse but to flee to her cousin, expecting to be treated as a fellow queen and expecting Elizabeth's help. She did not anticipate being locked up in England for twenty years, but because of the complicated intertwining of religion and politics, Queen Elizabeth could not afford the risk of freeing Mary with the likelihood that she would gather aid and troops against England. Even though Mary's claim to the English throne through Henry VIII's sister, Margaret, had some of the same weaknesses that worried Queen Elizabeth about her own claim, it was a valid one and a constant threat to Queen Elizabeth. In addition, through her father, Mary was properly descended from Scottish royalty. The most important difference to Catholics, of course, was their recognition of Mary as legitimate. Queen Mary's twenty years of incarceration in England polarized the country into opposing religious camps, the divisiveness escalating with each reputed plot by Catholics to free her.

The first of these conspiracies against Queen Elizabeth involved the duke of Norfolk in the Northern Rebellion of 1569, the only really serious rebellion in the entire forty-four years of her reign. Norfolk, the queen's powerful and wealthy cousin, had become an eligible widower in 1557. A secret plan to free Queen Mary developed which centered on a marriage between Mary and Norfolk, with the backing of Spain. A part of the plan entailed Leicester's urging Elizabeth's Council to recognize Mary's claims to the English throne and then restoring her to the Scottish throne. Even though he approached the Council without Elizabeth's knowledge, the Council nearly went along with his plan to help Mary (Pollard 289). Initially, Robert Dudley, Lord Leicester, was loosely linked with the Norfolk group for his own ulterior reasons. Lord Burghley opposed the match, however, and Pollard suggests that Leicester sided with Norfolk, in part to spite Burghley (". . . on this account he [Leicester] belongs to the Queen of Scotland's party" [Pollard 283]), while at the same time using this situation to pay back an old grudge he held against Norfolk. (See my discussion of *Twelfth Night*.) Norfolk was cautiously apprehensive about what Elizabeth's reaction to the proposed wedding would be if she learned of it before all the plans were in place, but Leicester convinced him she knew about and favored the match (284). A more likely scenario was that Elizabeth did not know and would not have approved, and Leicester knew it but was purposely framing the duke to pay him back for their earlier disagreements. Norfolk, however, gullibly believed that Leicester was helping him as a trustworthy friend. Once Leicester had set up the trusting Norfolk, he then had to protect himself from the queen's wrath, because he knew she would inevitably learn of the plot and uncover his role in it. His ploy was to feign illness and win her sympathy by calling her to his bedside and confessing the whole story. She forgave him, but she was not about to allow Norfolk and the Scots queen to marry, especially without her sanction (Jenkins 161).

She confronted Norfolk on September 5 and absolutely forbade the marriage. Norfolk was now in a precarious position with 20,000 men waiting in the wings for his signal to begin the rebellion and Spain poised on the side, ready to join in at the propitious moment. As he wavered, consulting friends about how he should proceed, the queen summoned him to court. Paralyzed with fear at the summons, he pretended to be ill and did not obey. Unfortunately for both the duke and the rebels, the plans had progressed too far to pull back, for the Northern earls had been in contact with the Spanish ambassador, and they believed aid from Spain was on the way. The original plan had called for Northumberland and Westmoreland to lead forces south toward Hartlepool, and once the Duke of Alva landed his troops (he failed to arrive entirely), Norfolk was to join them from the south, and then the Queen of Scots was to be set free. After much indecisive dither, Norfolk finally decided to obey the queen's summons to go to court, and he vainly tried to ward off the insurrection by sending word to the earls that they should postpone the rebellion.

By the time the earls learned the duke was not going to join them, they realized they had already crossed the Rubicon and to return was as dangerous as to go on, because they knew the queen would not pardon them for what they had done to this point (Pollard 293). On November 14, 1569, they ravaged Durham Cathedral and demolished all symbols of the English church. The English Bible and the Book of Common Prayer were torn to shreds, and the communion table was destroyed. They brazenly held a Catholic mass there with all of its ritual (Pollard 294). The next crucial step was to free Mary from her jailer, the Earl of Shrewsbury at Tutbury, but Queen Elizabeth had foreseen that possibility and had her removed swiftly to Coventry. The failure to capture Mary assuredly doomed the uprising. The ground swell of support the earls anticipated did not materialize, and, finding their situation hopeless as government troops advanced toward them, they began a retreat.

After the rebellion was crushed, more than eight hundred rebels were put to death. Most of the victims were of the lower classes following their lords in the old feudal way under the banner of religion. The wealthy, landed nobles were imprisoned rather than executed to enable the crown to confiscate their wealth. The duke of Norfolk was sent to the Tower in October 1569, and the queen showed surprising generosity by releasing him in August. She had ample reason to be angry at the cost of having to gather troops to put down the rebellion in the first place, but it was especially galling to have her attempts to tolerate the Catholic religion go unappreciated.

This rebellion was essentially a Catholic rebellion with its roots in England north of the Trent, an area that had remained much more feudal and much more Catholic than the rest of England and which posed a constant threat of rising again. The names of the powerful lords who rebelled against Queen Elizabeth in this failed Northern Rebellion call up the ghosts of the lords who supported Henry IV's "usurpation" of Richard II's throne, a segment of English history Shakespeare depicted in Shakespeare's *Henriad*. (See my discussion of *Richard II*.) One possible subversive reading of Shakespeare's plays about Henry IV and Henry V is the depiction of what Catholics regarded as Queen Elizabeth's lack of appreciation for their support of her early on—that friends who lend their support to a king in his bid for the throne are very often thrown to the wolves by the same king once he is safely in power. Did the Henry plays intentionally draw a parallel between Henry IV's turning against the Percies in the same way the Northern earls felt Queen Elizabeth had turned on them, denying the support they had given her in hopes she would allow them to practice their religion freely? Peter Milward regards Shakespeare's interest in the Wars of the Roses between the Yorks and the Lancasters as being related to the 1569 Rebellion and to the theory that Shakespeare spent his early years in Lancashire (42). He points out parallels between the rebellion of the archbishop of York in the two parts of *Henry IV*, which are reminiscent of the Northern Rebellion (82) and what Catholic lords of the North regarded as outright betrayal by Queen Elizabeth. They had supported her in the early stages of her accession, hoping she would declare for Catholicism or would at least allow religious toleration. Instead of toleration, the Catholics were steadily and increasingly repressed.

In this northern backwater, the new Elizabethan Protestant reforms had not yet taken a firm hold, which meant the area was a prime target of Catholic priests who sent "seditious" material from Louvain, stirring up resentment against the English government (Pollard 278). Northern recalcitrance became progressively linked to Mary, Queen of Scots, who had been assured in 1566, even before she fled to England, that "the papists in England were ready to rise when she would have them" (281). Queen Mary's cause, the priests' cause, and Spain's designs on England became fused. By various routes she was led to believe she could count on a Spanish invasion of England via Ireland to free her (281). Catholics who were primed for such an invasion probably would have seen a parallel between Henry IV's usurpation of Richard II's throne and what Catholics regarded as Elizabeth's usurpation of Mary Stuart's rightful place on the English throne. Similarly, just as Henry IV's usurpation brought on the Wars of the Roses, so might the civil war—which the Northern Lords had expected to initiate—ensue as a consequence of Elizabeth's usurpation of Mary's throne. However, the whole enterprise fell apart the moment they were outsmarted in their attempt to free Mary.3

The Catholics who sided with the rebellion, some of whom supported it financially or by taking up arms, could legitimately blame the pope as much as Queen Elizabeth for failure of the uprising to achieve its objective. The pope had moved too slowly and was in part responsible for the hesitancy of people to join the rebellion. If the pope had supported the rebellion from the beginning by issuing the Bull of Excommunication at the moment of the uprising, the rebels would have had a chance for success. As it was, when Pope Pius V finally excommunicated Queen Elizabeth on February 25, 1570, after the rising had gone down in defeat, the excommunication was of no help in soliciting support but only resulted in the queen's imposing harsher restrictions on Catholics. It also forced the English Catholics to choose between queen and pope. The Bull stated that:

> . . . peers, subjects and people of the said kingdom, and all others upon what terms soever bound unto her, are freed from their oath and all manner of duty, fidelity and obedience . . . commanding moreover and enjoining all and every, the nobles, subjects, people and others whatsoever that they shall not once dare to obey her or any of her laws, directions or commands, binding under the same curse those who do anything to the contrary. (Jenkins 170)

Emotions on both sides were aflame, and each side denounced the other with a flood of pamphlets and sermons.

The effect of the failed rebellion on Mary, Queen of Scots, was that she was from this time on aligned with Spain against England and less tied to the interests of France. The balance of power among the three great world powers had now shifted in such a way that England and France were uneasy allies who regarded Spain with suspicion. A further ramification was that over many years, as a part of the Anglo/French alliance, Queen Elizabeth kept the dukes of Anjou and Alençon on the string with the hint of possible marriage which would cement the alliance against Spain.

Unfortunately, the duke of Norfolk, who had envisioned himself as the potential bridegroom of Mary, seemed unaware of his narrow escape from death which was attributable solely to the leniency of Queen Elizabeth.

---

3   It is intriguing to contemplate what kind of reaction was stirred up in nearby Stratford when Mary, Queen of Scots, was transferred to the relative security of Coventry, only twenty miles away. Little five-year-old Shakespeare must have been affected in some manner by the excitement of the attempt to liberate Queen Mary, the awe and fear that the rebellion stirred, and the resentment over the frightful punishment of those who were captured in defeat.

Upon his release from the Tower, he was required to sign an oath of loyalty to the queen as well as swear to have no further dealings with Mary, Queen of Scots. So much for his oath, which he very quickly broke. Later he explained it was not valid because he signed under coercion (Jenkins 187). Early in 1571, he was back in touch with Roberto Ridolfi, a Florentine banker who had had a hand in the 1569 rebellion. The objectives of Ridolfi's plan have a ring of familiarity: capture Queen Elizabeth and the Council; free Mary, Queen of Scots; place her on the English throne, and restore the Catholic religion in England. Mary was a valuable pawn at this particular time because the French were considering a marriage between her and the duke of Anjou while they simultaneously continued to proffer him as a marriage partner for Queen Elizabeth (even though he was twenty and Queen Elizabeth was thirty-seven). A possible English alliance was more attractive to the French, so, realistically, Mary had to content herself with dealing with Ridolfi and Norfolk.

The nature of the Ridolfi Plot is still murky, and it may have been a sham plot initiated by the government to force the Queen to act against Norfolk. It initially called for a reinforcement of arms from the duke of Alva in the Low Countries, but, perhaps because he did not have much confidence in the plan anyway, he claimed he had none to contribute. To his credit, however, Alva did try to warn the pope and Philip II that this plot to invade England was not a realistic one and that it would probably not succeed. Philip agreed with Alva's assessment of the situation and said Spain would join only after Elizabeth had actually been killed, whereas "the Papacy hailed it [Ridolfi's scheme] with enthusiasm" (Bindoff 212). The English government claimed to have uncovered all the details of the plot through various means: by spying, and through Ridolfi's bungling. It was obvious Norfolk was deeply implicated in the plot and that he was definitely linked to an attempt to kill Elizabeth, so this time there could be no leniency. He was tried and convicted on January 14, 1572. Still the queen vacillated on his execution. He was finally beheaded on June 2.

The Northern Rebellion, the Ridolfi Plot, and the Bull of Excommunication solidified opposition to Mary, Queen of Scots, and caused an already predominantly Puritan Parliament to clamor for her death. The clamor reached a deafening pitch after Sunday, August 24, 1572, the day the Massacre of St. Bartholomew began. The massacre started in Paris when thousands of French Huguenots, gathered to celebrate the marriage of Henry of Navarre and Princess Margaret, were pulled into the streets by Catholics and brutally slaughtered. The killing frenzy spread to the provinces, and within eight weeks, 12,000 Protestants had been exterminated. This served to show every good Protestant in England how savage the Catholics could be, and Mary, Queen of Scots, was the focus of the ensuing terror. The Paris massacre seems to have originated with Catherine de Medici, who originally had used the Huguenots as a counterpoise to the

Guises, but who was now determined to get rid of the Huguenot leaders because of their interference in her influence with the king (Jenkins 199). The magnitude of the reaction was beyond anything she had imagined and showed how deep-seated the religious antagonisms were. All of this was done in the name of religion, of course, and, it was assumed, under the approval of God. The pope struck a medal to commemorate the blessed event. The Spanish ambassador praised the massacre in a letter to Madrid:

> While I write, they are casting them out naked and dragging them through the streets, pillaging their houses and sparing not a table. Blessed be God who has converted the Princes of France to His purpose. May He inspire their hearts to go on as they have begun! (199)

To English Protestants, this kind of talk meant such a massacre of Protestants by Catholics could also take place in England if the Catholics were not eradicated there.

Because of seemingly aggressive and varied opposition from the Catholics and because rumors were rife, the queen feared an international Catholic League had been formed under the leadership of Spain with the aim of reinstating Catholicism in England and deposing her. Opinion is divided as to whether such a league actually existed and whether Mary, Queen of Scots, joined it. Fraser says unequivocally that there was no such league for Mary to join (293). According to Pollard, on the other hand, the Catholic League "spread with the blessings of Philip II and the papacy until it included nearly the whole of catholic France [1576]" (342). Pollen terms it a "bogus league," a "figment," and "the fable of the papal league" (xviii). Whether or not a well-organized plan was in operation, the real or supposed threats of other plots were perhaps the most destabilizing form of resistance. While not one succeeded, the rumors and evidence of them supplied by the government instilled great fear. The Catholic Church appeared to back the assassination plots and to absolve any perpetrators from sin. The opinion of Pope Gregory XIII on assassination was stated by the Cardinal Secretary Como in December 1580:

> Since that guilty woman of England . . . is the cause of such injury to the Catholic faith and loss of so many million souls, there is no doubt that whosoever sends her out of the world with the pious intention of doing God service, not only does not sin, but gains merit, especially having regard to the sentence pronounced against her by Pius V of holy memory. (Jenkins 261)

With the apparent sanction of the pope, plots proliferated, undeterred by the failure of the two earlier—and pathetically ineffective—plots in which the duke of Norfolk had been involved, the 1569 Northern Rebellion and the Ridolfi Plot of 1571.

Closer to "home," Shakespeare's mother's family, the Ardens, were implicated in three later plots against the queen: the Throckmorton plot of 1583, the Somerville/Arden plot of 1583, and the Parry plot of 1585. In addition, the Arden family was later on the fringes of the Gunpowder Plot against King James I, and a John Arden participated in the Essex Rebellion of 1601. Shakespeare's family was not, however, directly implicated in the Babington Plot of 1586—the plot that was to prove fatal to Mary, Queen of Scots—although there are strong indications Shakespeare was acquainted with some of the participants. (See my chapter on the Ardens.) To isolate Shakespeare in his figurative ivory tower, removed from the faction and disagreement that surrounded him is to lead us further astray from what the plays meant to him in their contemporary context.

Queen Mary saw herself trapped as a virtual pawn to be used by both her friends and her enemies. While the Catholics used her as the figurehead for Catholic causes, Walsingham simultaneously used her as a tool to entrap Catholics. He fanned Elizabeth's fear about plots that frequently sprang up around Mary, hoping to push Elizabeth to agree that Mary must die. Walsingham finally seemed to have succeeded in his aim with the Babington Plot, the intricacies of which may never be unraveled. There are convincing clues Walsingham purposely orchestrated much of what appeared to be anti-government Catholic activity as a device to entrap Mary and to stir up hatred against Catholics.

A pathetic illustration of the religious dissension was that Mary could not even count on support from her son, James Stuart, who had been raised by Scottish Protestants to distrust his own mother. For years, Queen Mary misread James, expecting him to help free her from her captivity without realizing how brainwashed he had been by the Scottish Calvinists to regard her as the enemy because of their royal and their religious differences. Mary had been forced to abdicate in 1568 when she was held captive at Lochleven, but she had since revoked her abdication. She considered herself the true queen of Scotland, as did most of the Catholic governments abroad. If she were the true queen, James's claim was invalid, and this was the key factor in their rivalry. She needed his support, however, if she were ever to escape from her captivity. As a ploy to enlist James's help, she offered to share the throne with him in 1581 in an "Association." This brief time, when it looked as if James might favor the Catholics and go along with his mother's Association, coincided with the general Catholic revival in England, which was brought about by the arrival of Campion and Parsons on the English mission. A further encouragement was the Catholic influence exerted on him by his handsome cousin, Esmé Stuart (made duke of Lennox), whom the Guises had sent to sway James to the Catholic faith. The duke of Lennox was nearly successful in enlisting the aid of Spain, the pope, and the duke of Guise in the religious struggle in Scotland, but this religious rebirth was stillborn when James was kidnapped by the Protestant Scots in

August 1582. He escaped within a year and once again offered to join Mary's Association. This time Philip of Spain refused to support James and Mary, and James never again agreed to the project (Pollen xvii).

In spite of her isolation, Queen Mary managed to stay abreast of politics in England and abroad, but her maternal feelings toward James clouded her perception of him. He had begun to realize he was better off with his mother in prison than if she were freed. In 1584, after sixteen years of incarceration, Queen Mary was desperate to appease Queen Elizabeth in order to be freed. She offered to renounce the Pope's Bull of Excommunication, as well as her claim to the English throne, but Elizabeth, too, realized she was better off with Mary in prison because there was little chance she could gather followers and troops as long as she was locked up.

During the first few years of her imprisonment with the Shrewsburys at Wingfield Manor, Chatsworth, and Sheffield Castle, Queen Mary's life was relatively comfortable except for the fact that she was not free. She had a small court, a pension from the French government, was served by a Catholic priest disguised as a reader, was allowed to hunt and to go to the baths at Buxton, held dinners and theatrical performances, and was allowed small luxuries such as wine in which to bathe. Acting groups attached to households of the local Catholic lords were called upon to perform for some of the queen's festivities, and if Shakespeare was in one of these acting groups at the Hoghtons, Heskeths, or in the household of Ferdinando Stanley, he quite likely would have performed before her. This pseudo-royal life ended, however, with the assassination of the prince of Orange in the spring of 1585 (Pollen xxiv).

Because international politics and religion went virtually hand in hand, relationships between Protestant England and Catholic Spain and France had reverberations reaching Queen Mary even in her isolated captivity. The Protestant Prince of Orange, William I (the Silent), had been leading the rebels in the Netherlands against the Spanish governor, the duke of Alva, who was ruthlessly imposing Spain's will and religion on the country. The assassination of the prince of Orange placed Queen Mary in great jeopardy from that time on. The Spanish government had placed a price on his head when it pronounced a ban on Orange (Pollen xix), and when he was killed in July 1584, the Catholics, in particular the Jesuits, were accused of assassinating him. An account by Hayward of alleged Jesuit involvement in Orange's death provides a sample of biased accounts of Catholics that were popular in England in the later 1800s:

This bloody villain [Balthasar Gerard, assassin], meditating this murder, had been with a Jesuit at Treves: to whom he confessed himself, discovering to him his wretched design. Who kept him in their college, taking the Jesuit's counsel and direction, as this villain did confess boldly. (309)

If such vitriolic ranting against the Jesuits persisted in England as late as the l800s, how acidic must it have been when the events were actually taking place? And how has it blinded scholars over the years to recognize clues to Shakespeare's Catholicism?

Queen Elizabeth and her counselors drew a parallel between William of Orange and her as protectors of Protestantism against the machinations of the Catholics. What happened to William of Orange could also happen to Queen Elizabeth, and, to guard against such a fate, a Bond of Association was devised to protect her. An additional objective of the Bond was to entrap Mary, the gist of which was, "that all who took it should persecute to the death that person *in whose favour* any plot should be formed against Elizabeth's life" (Pollen xxv). This put Queen Mary at risk for any plot in her name whether or not she was a participant or even aware of the plot.

It now was necessary to place Mary under tighter security. Because the Earl of Shrewsbury had recently been accused by his own wife of overly intimate relations with Mary, and because his religious convictions were suspect, the government ordered Mary to be removed from his comfortable care and placed in that of Amyas Paulet at Tutbury in January 1585. Tutbury and Paulet were well suited to each other—cold, forbidding, and gloomy. Both were particularly noisome to Queen Mary who had earlier been detained at Tutbury and hated its drafty, smelly halls. Paulet's strict, Puritanical behavior towards her reflected his disapproval of her religion, as well as his personal dislike of her. He seemed to take pleasure in imposing every restriction on her, reminding her of her fallen state. Perhaps it was as a result of Mary's complaint to the French court of her treatment and accommodations that she was moved to Chartley on Christmas Eve of l585 (See my discussion of *Twelfth Night*), for it was at the instigation of the French court that she was moved. However, Jenkins suggests the move to Chartley was maneuvered by Walsingham as a plot to entrap Mary as well as to discover Spain's intentions to invade England by intercepting and reading her letters in and out of the castle (Pollen 290).

Pressure had been mounting from the Puritans to execute Mary, but Queen Elizabeth recognized the danger to herself in executing an anointed queen. Perhaps for self-preservation, more than out of compassion for Mary, Elizabeth procrastinated about deciding the fate of her cousin queen. Walsingham realized Mary would have to be caught in a plot against Queen Elizabeth's life blatant enough to leave Elizabeth no choice but to have Mary executed. Thus he set up a communication conduit via the beer delivery man that directly implicated Mary in the Babington Plot.

Antonia Fraser identifies two separate strands to the plot. One was to kill Elizabeth, and one was to rescue Mary (566). Both strands were to be backed by a Spanish invasion and supported by a rising of English Catholics. The two parts of the plot were so riddled with Walsingham's spies that at times the conspirators were unknowingly led by the agents into paths

Walsingham had devised. A key government spy was Gilbert Gifford, who seemed to be a renegade in an otherwise staunchly Catholic family. Gifford arranged through the French embassy to get mail to Mary secretly, although the secret was already known to Walsingham and was part of his plan. Every letter to and from Mary was decoded, read, and copied before it reached its intended destination, which meant the government knew every move being plotted.

By 1586 many Catholics had forgotten or were too young to know about Queen Mary's suspected complicity in the death of her husband, Darnley, and her subsequent marriage to the suspected murderer. For most Catholics she symbolized the fate of the Catholic religion in England, and her release from prison would have meant that England might once again be Catholic. Most of the young men who worked with Anthony Babington in the Association to assist the fugitive Catholic priests moved to the next stage of helping to free Mary from prison, manipulated at every stage by Walsingham's agents. From Mary's isolated position, the seeming lifeline thrown by Babington must have appeared to be a possible and carefully planned plot. She had given up hope of receiving any help from James, and to show her disavowal of him, she later assigned the English crown to Philip II of Spain if James had not converted to Catholicism by the date of her death. She had to face the bitter finality of the end of the Association with her son in March of 1585 when James and Queen Elizabeth signed a treaty of alliance with a subsidy for James paid by Elizabeth.

By some accounts, Anthony Babington's devotion to Mary began when he served as a page for her in his youth. He and his fellow conspirators, all of respectable, upper-class Catholic families, somewhat unrealistically believed they could depend upon military aid from Spain and on a Catholic uprising in England to help them free Mary. Envisioning Shakespeare in such a context opens a wholly new facet of Shakespeare's life if the theory he was in Lancashire during his teen years proves to be true. If he was there, he might have been acquainted with at least two of the participants: John Savage and Charles Tylney. Sir Edmund Tilney, Master of the Revels, the queen's appointee who passed judgment on the fitness of plays performed in London, was probably a cousin of Charles Tylney. John Savage was related to Thomas Savage, a trustee for the construction of the Globe in 1599. Both relationships are discussed in "Shakespeare and the Hoghton Will." Two other participants, Edward Jones and Henry Dunne, quite possibly were related to actor Richard Jones and to poet John Dunne, although there is no confirmation of any relationship. The fourteen idealistic young men were hanged, drawn, and quartered on September 20, 1586, after the plot was "uncovered."

Mary, Queen of Scots, seemed to have had a premonition the Babington Plot was her last chance for freedom, for she said if it did not succeed she "would be buried in a dark prison for ever and ever" (Fraser 576). In spite

of connotations of death in the phrase, she probably did not seriously enter-
tain the idea of execution. Queen Elizabeth herself could not face the awful
magnitude of killing a fellow monarch, so it would have been natural for the
Scottish queen to have considered execution an improbable consequence.
The collusion with Babington was to be, however, the final phase of her life.

By August 1586, Queen Mary had written the so-called "gallows" letter
that incriminated her in the plot to assassinate Queen Elizabeth. By the
middle of August, the Babington group had been rounded up for trial, and
the entire plot was revealed. Mary was taken to closer confinement on
August eleventh and systematically deprived of the trappings of royalty,
reminiscent of Shakespeare's depiction of the deposition of Richard II.
Mary herself saw the parallel between her downward trajectory and that of
Richard II. (See my discussion "Of Deposition and Usurpation.")

Queen Mary was transferred from Chartley to Fotheringhay by a pro-
cession of country lords over four days, September 21-24. At Fotheringhay
she was to be tried under the Act of Association of 1585 by a commission
stipulated in the Act—twenty-four peers and privy counselors (Fraser 592).
If found guilty of having conspired to pretend to the English crown, she
would be subject to execution (592). She at last realized, however, the trial
was a charade and that it was a foregone conclusion she would be put to
death. Now fully aware she could not escape execution, Mary's great hope
was to have a meaningful death as a martyr to the Catholic faith, so her fate
would continue to influence affairs in England by inspiring civil war to
restore her religion there. An additional comfort was that a public trial and
news of her execution would have an international impact. Shakespeare's
Julius Caesar and *Richard II* can be read as later reminders of the martyred
Queen, renewing the faith of Catholics who attended those plays.

Mary was allowed neither counsel nor witnesses and had to speak in her
own defense, a situation reminiscent of the trial of the Jesuit priest, Edmund
Campion, for both were at an extreme disadvantage as they faced batteries of
legal advisors who were well supplied with written records and legal counsel.
The trial opened on Wednesday, October 15, 1586. Mary's secret correspondence, orchestrated by the government in the early stages of the Babington
Plot, the main evidence against her, was read to prove she had plotted against
the life of Queen Elizabeth. She claimed she had never planned to usurp the
English throne but rather had always maintained her right to inherit it at the
proper time—in other words, after Elizabeth died a natural death. She insisted on her ignorance of the plot, emphasizing that her only concerns were to
obtain her freedom and to support the Catholic religion in England.

On October 25, 1586, the government commission met in the Star
Chamber in London and pronounced Mary, Queen of Scots, guilty of having conspired to kill the queen of England. The decision was not announced
to Mary until November 19. When she realized that the die was cast, she
asked the pope's permission to pass her claim to the English throne to Philip

II of Spain, an act reminiscent of Richard II's bestowal of the crown rights to Mortimer in Shakespeare's *Richard II*. Her purpose, although the effort ultimately proved futile, was to deprive James of succession to the English throne because he had refused to repudiate the treaty between Scotland and England, the one effort that might have saved her.

During her trial and in the last days of her life, Mary exhibited great calm and dignity. Queen Elizabeth's behavior, by contrast, reveals her doubt about the wisdom of executing Mary. In fact, she was unable to take on responsibility for such a grave move, and after prolonged procrastination, finally allowed herself to be "tricked" into signing the death warrant by using William Davison, Walsingham's undersecretary, as a scapegoat who "misinterpreted" her meaning. For public display, Davison suffered for his mistake with fines and imprisonment, but the punishment was lightened once the public saw that he was "guilty." The queen pretended to be indignant that the warrant had been acted upon without her consent, even going to the extreme of banning her faithful Lord Burghley from court for several months, but the charade probably convinced few that she was innocent of Mary's death.

On Wednesday, February 8, 1587, the queen of Scots, clothed in a red robe representing the color of martyrdom of the Catholic Church, was beheaded at Fotheringhay. Neither Mary's son nor Philip II of Spain, nominal head of Catholic Europe, had intervened to save her. Philip failed to act largely because he now had his own designs on the English throne, which he claimed through his descent from John of Gaunt.4 Philip's failure to support Mary probably influenced some English Catholics to fight against Spain when the Armada finally arrived in 1588—for most English Catholics sided with the majority of the country against Spanish domination under Philip. It seems likely that a larger percentage would have fought with Spain against England if the fight had been for the sake of Queen Mary.

The question of the morality and the legality of killing a king or a queen was the subject of much discussion throughout the country. Certain of Shakespeare's plays which deal with usurpation and the killing of a king, when read from the point of view of an Elizabethan Catholic, have parallels with the execution of Mary Stuart. If the fates of Julius Caesar, Richard II, and old King Hamlet in his plays are read as allusions to Mary's fate under Queen Elizabeth, Shakespeare appears to sympathize with Queen Mary, the victim. An aura of Catholicism hovers about these figures which seem deliberately fashioned to elicit sympathy. Decius Brutus's description of

---

4   Mary had bequeathed the English crown to Philip, and geneologists had traced out for him a hereditary claim through John of Gaunt. "He meant to take possession of England and give it to one of his daughters" (Jenkins 305).

Caesar's power in Rome after his death is very like what Mary Stuart envisioned happening in England as a result of her death. He becomes martyr-like through a death which:

Signifies that from you great Rome shall suck
Reviving blood, and that great men shall press
For tinctures, stains, relics and cognizance. (*Julius Caesar* 2.2.87)

The customs of preserving relics and of dipping cloths in the blood of martyrs, Catholic customs the government was trying to stamp out, were being perpetuated almost daily at the executions of the Catholic priests. Catholic religious imagery pervades *Richard II*, illustrated by the king's wistful recognition that he must trade his subjects for a pair of carved saints (*Richard II*, 3.3.148,52). Queen Mary's resignation was very similar to Richard's when she finally realized, because she could never regain the throne, the most influential recourse for her was to capitalize upon her death as a Catholic martyr. The plays seem purposely to make use of forbidden Catholic practices such as Richard's telling of his beads and old King Hamlet's suffering in a Catholic purgatory, a Catholic relic which had been outlawed. These figures are daring evocations of suppressed Catholic practices, but most of all are daring reminders of a Catholic queen who had become a martyr to the Elizabethan regime. References to historical kings and queens on the Elizabethan stage can be read as screened allusions to the contemporary regime. If Shakespeare was writing from a Catholic point of view, the allusions to contemporary figures would necessarily have been narrowly disguised to pass government censorship.

In retrospect, it seems Queen Elizabeth should have recognized the potential for disaster inherent in such a long imprisonment of Queen Mary, but she had few options once Mary got herself in such a predicament. Queen Elizabeth's choices were either to execute her or to set her free to challenge the English throne. At one point, there were negotiations to send Mary back to Scotland to be dealt with by her own countrymen, but the Scots wanted exorbitant compensation for executing a queen, an awesome task Queen Elizabeth could never fully confront (Jenkins 202). The result of the prolonged presence of Mary in England was that the repellent nature of her crimes gradually faded with time. An idealized picture of her as a beautiful, maligned, and wronged queen gradually evolved into the Catholics' view of her as almost a religious icon for Catholic discontent. She became the figurehead of various plots which involved freeing her, assassinating Queen Elizabeth, and putting Mary on the throne.

The Mission and the Tightening Noose

It may have been merely coincidence that 1568, the year when Mary, Queen of Scots, first sought refuge in England, was the same year William Allen established the English College at Douai in France. From the moment of Mary's arrival in England, the Catholics regarded her as a rallying point to muster support for their religion. She very likely figured in a plan to create Catholic schools and seminaries abroad to train priests who would then return secretly to England to save the dying religion. The prospect of freeing Mary Stuart and offering her as a legitimate rival to Elizabeth gave purpose and hope for success.

William Allen was from Lancashire and was related to the Hesketh family and also a good friend of the Alexander Hoghton family, two very important Catholic families whose surmised association with William Shakespeare, if valid, has enormous potential for enlarging our knowledge of Shakespeare. (Possible connections between John and William Shakespeare in regard to the Catholic activities in Lancashire and Cheshire are examined more fully in my discussion of the Shakespeares and the Catholic mission.) An outgrowth of the establishment of the Catholic schools abroad was the eventual move to infiltrate young Catholic priests into England to serve the many secret Catholics who were denied essential Catholic rites. The arrival of Robert Parsons and Edmund Campion in June 1580 initiated an "invasion" of young priests who began slipping into the country by the hundreds. The arrival of priests put the English Catholics in a dangerous situation, for those who received and succored these priests were taking an enormous risk.

As has been shown, restrictions on Catholics had already been steadily tightening in the decade before the onslaught of the mission. As a consequence of the Bull of Excommunication of 1570, life for the English Catholics had become dangerous and costly. One result was the law of treason had been extended to include any proved obedience to any Papal bull, as well as the joining or the reconciling of others to the Roman Catholic Church. To circumvent the Catholic charge that the extension of the treason law convicted a person on the basis of his religion, after 1575 the laws were scrupulously constructed so that the charges against priests and their abettors were charges of treason that could not be construed as condemnation because of religious beliefs. In spite of efforts by the government to disengage the question of religion from treason, it was clear to Catholics the objective was to stamp out Catholicism. Evidence that a priest was condemned to the gallows on the basis of his religion was demonstrated at his public execution. In the moments preceding their public torture which entailed being hanged, taken down while still conscious, disemboweled, and quartered, they were given the opportunity to save their lives by simply entering an Elizabethan Protestant church. Few accepted the offer of leniency.

Although the stated purpose of Jesuit and seminary priests who were sent on the mission was a peaceful one—perpetuating the Catholic faith— they were in many ways detrimental to Catholics. Their presence generated an insecurity, forcing the queen, pressured by her Puritan parliament, to impose increasingly stringent restrictions on Catholics. Before the arrival of the mission priests, the disagreement between Catholics and Protestants was principally over the use of the prayer book and the meaning of the Eucharist. For Protestants, communion was a symbolic service, whereas Catholics believed the bread and wine were literally transformed into the flesh and blood of Christ. However, because of the threat posed to the government by increasing infiltration of priests and the increasing danger imposed on Catholics sheltering the priests, tensions mounted, and each side became more entrenched in its own position, while plots against the queen increased in frequency after 1580. The increasingly bitter tone of Catholic arguments against the queen is illustrated by the altered tone of Cardinal Allen's messages. In 1581, before Edmund Campion was executed, Allen was conciliatory and emphasized the benign, persuasive, and attractive nature of the seminaries: " . . . many of the very flower of the universities have come over . . . have passed their long banishment in honest poverty, . . . we receive hundreds of their ministers [Protestant], . . . voluntarily flying from their damnable condition, and seeking after God" (Strype 94, 95). However, by April 1587, after the execution of Mary, Queen of Scots, in February and after the execution of many young priests, his *Admonition to the Nobility and People of England* urged them to support the Armada in order to:

> restore the Catholic religion and to rid them of Queen Elizabeth, that monster of impiety and unchastity who cannot be tolerated without the eternal infamy of our whole country, the whole world deriding our effeminate dastardy, that have suffered such a creature almost thirty years together to reign over our bodies and souls. (Jenkins 307)

Cardinal William Allen now joined with Cardinal Como, who, as we have seen, had bluntly stated in December 1580 that anyone who killed the queen would have the blessing of the Catholic church (Jenkins 261). Allen's priests were actually present in England, and if his men were to follow the Nuncio's recommendation, the government feared the queen would actually be deposed or assassinated. Shakespeare's staging of the assassinations of historical kings such as Old King Hamlet, Duncan, Richard II, and Henry VI can be viewed as addressing the threats of and fears about the assassination of the queen.

Some "conforming" Catholics were surviving by occasionally attending the Church of England services just to protect themselves and their property. Ironically, this comfortable, occasional conformity was made untenable by the Catholic church itself. Such conformity had been prohibited in the Papal Bull which Pius V issued in February 1570 (too late to bolster the Rebellion of 1569). This Bull declared Elizabeth to be a "heretic" and a "pretended queen" and absolved Englishmen of all allegiance to her. Catholics were "not to dare to obey her, and her monitions, commands, and laws . . . and all who do so are anathematised with her" (Simpson 86). This prohibition by the Pope was reiterated in a decision made by a secret Catholic Synod in London in 1580, which unconditionally prohibited any attendance at the queen's church. The Synod's move to prohibit conformity was fortified by instructions to the missionary priests to circulate religious literature that forbade Catholics to attend Protestant services (Mutschmann and Wentersdorf 12). This renewed prohibition against attending the English Church greatly complicated the lives of those secret Roman Catholics who were now subject to heavier fine laws and to property confiscation if they failed to attend the state church, or, if they continued to conform, were condemned by their own Catholic Church. Before his arrival on the mission, Campion expressed his concern regarding the plight of the English Catholic gentry to Pope Gregory XIII who mitigated the admonition to Catholics so that Pius's Bull was amended to read "That it should always bind her and the heretics; but that it should in no way bind the Catholics, while things remain as they are; but only then when public execution of the said bull shall be possible" (Simpson 141). This revision of the Bull served two purposes: it was a factor in the initial favorable reception of the English mission by Catholics, and it also afforded a degree of protection to the invading priests who could state, upon capture, that they regarded Elizabeth as their lawful queen (Jenkins 262).

This attempt to enable Catholics to survive and avoid forfeiting their wealth and property backfired in a sense when Elizabeth's government imposed new, harsher restrictions to force conformity. In 1581, Parliament passed the Act "to retain the queen's majesty's subjects in their due obedience" which resulted in penalties against Catholic citizens that extended beyond direct contact with a priest (Bindoff 238). A person could be convicted of *praemunire* if he merely possessed Catholic religious items. Even those Catholics who sought safety abroad in exile were subject to having their property forfeited to the queen (Pollard 370). Catholics were not allowed to hold government and university positions for which the Oath of Supremacy was required. Catholic families who would normally have had private tutors in their homes or would have sent their offspring to Catholic schools for their education were unable to do this because the closing of the monasteries resulted in the closing of the schools. Those who opted to shelter an illegal Catholic schoolmaster to educate their children privately were putting themselves in grave danger. The most severe restrictions were imposed later in 1593 when the laws passed went so far as to deprive Catholic parents of the right to educate their children at home or to move more than five miles from home (Mutschmann and Wentersdorf 20).

These restrictions were naturally the impetus for Catholics to devise various ways to circumvent the fines, confiscation of property, and imprisonment. They transferred deeds for property to relatives and friends so it appeared they owned nothing when the government came to attach their property. They devised complicated networks of Catholic support to assist each other with lawsuits and court summonses. A fellowship of young aristocrats escorted illegal Catholic priests to the homes of Catholics. Philip Caraman recounts how priests were hidden in secret, coffin-sized hiding holes when the government pursuivants came to search the premises:

> Braddocks is now a farmhouse. Two-thirds of the original mansion which stood in a fine deer park has been pulled down, but the remaining portion, the right wing of the old house, contains the hiding-place which Gerard describes. In the chapel Nicholas Owen removed the tiles from the fireplace and constructed a false hearth. 'Beneath this', writes Granville Squires (*Secret Hiding-Places*, ch. xxiii), 'he burrowed downwards into the solid brickwork. The place he made adjoins the large living-room below and is located high up and slightly to the side of the Renaissance fireplace. It was separated from this room only by the lath and plaster covered with a panelled wainscot.'

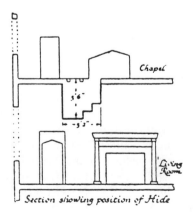

Section showing position of Hide

The big living-room is much altered and restored; the stone fireplace, however, is still there, though the heavy overmantel has gone. 'The chapel above', continues Mr. Squires, 'is unfurnished, but in good condition.' When I saw it first the Tudor arch of the fireplace had been blocked up for longer than the oldest inhabitant could remember, but when we broke into it the chimney was piled high with generations of birds' nests. Beneath this we found the hearth had been solidly replaced. It took two or three days to get it uncovered, but we were finally rewarded by being able to examine the hole . . . . (Caraman 277)

Wealthy families who sheltered their own, private resident priests often employed the services of the Jesuit priest Nicholas Owen, known as "Little John," an expert at renovating partitions and attics of houses to make tiny hiding holes in which the priests, laden with all of the items used in the mass, could flee when the house was searched by government pursuivants. There are hair-raising tales of priests who remained behind the false walls for days with minimal or no food and water, only to be captured in the end. Because the increased penalties for harboring priests made people reluctant to take the risk of providing shelter, the Jesuit priest, William Weston, who was eventually to be appointed superior of the English Jesuit mission after Jasper Heywood, drew up a list of those willing to provide safe hiding places (Morey 180). In spite of explicit government prohibition against it, some daring and committed families sent their children abroad to be educated at English Catholic colleges and seminaries. Many of the sons later returned secretly to England to serve as priests with full knowledge of what was in store for them if they were captured. The number of priests entering the country continued to increase, and the subterfuges English Catholics used to hide them seemed to be successful, for from 1574 to 1585, the number of seminary and Jesuit priests in England increased from only four to three hundred (182). The Catholics temporarily, at least, appeared to be outwitting the government.

After the publication of the Bull of Excommunication in 1570, the government had made a distinction between new Catholic converts and those whose Catholicism predated the Bull. It became illegal to be converted or to convert anyone to the Catholic religion. Compulsory attendance at the English Church was already in place, but the 1571 Parliament tried to add compulsory partaking of communion. The Queen wisely vetoed the bill (Bindoff 235). After 1581, all fines were enormously increased. The fines for not attending the English Church at least once a month was set at £20 (Jenkins 263). Anyone saying mass was subject to a year's imprisonment and a fine of £200. Anyone who was present at a mass was subject to a year's imprisonment and a fine of £100. A person who employed a Catholic schoolmaster had to pay £10 a month (Pollard 375). Also, it was made a felony to harbor seminary and Jesuit priests. The government enlisted the help of ordinary citizens by making it profitable to turn Catholics over to the authorities. The informer was to receive one-third of the fine paid by the criminal, making the wealthy Catholics especially at risk because of the potential profit to the informer (Leys 42). Because Pope Gregory XIII had made a concession allowing the priests to say they regarded Queen Elizabeth as their lawful queen even though the church had excommunicated her, the government devised a new means of determining guilt. The accused was asked "the bloody question": Would the accused defend the country against the pope if he invaded England? The defendant was not allowed to qualify his answer but was required to answer with a "yes" or a "no."

All of these restrictions and fines made otherwise sympathetic Catholics or Protestant friends reluctant to shelter the priests. It also increased the vigor with which the priests were hunted down, not just in the name of religion, but for the profit involved because of the bounty the government paid for captured priests. As shown earlier, the Bond of Association put into effect in October 1584 stated that in the event of an attempted assassination of the queen or of rebellion, the claimant to the English throne would be tried before a commission. If it could be proved the claimant had participated and had foreknowledge of the crimes, that person would be put to death (Jenkins 283). This was a transparent ploy to incriminate Mary, Queen of Scots, and those who were setting up the Scottish queen as the figurehead of plots against the English government. The Bond of Association eventually proved effective in 1587 when Mary, Queen of Scots, was tried and condemned to death under the terms of the Bond.

The government then turned its attack directly against the mission priests. A bill was passed in Parliament in 1584 ordering all seminary and Jesuit priests out of the country within forty days. The Act of 1585 made a priest who admitted to his priesthood under questioning automatically liable to the death penalty. As a way of sheltering the priests against self-incrimination under examination by the government, the Jesuits devised a technique of withholding part of the truth, called "equivocation." The first record of its use was in 1595 at the trial of Robert Southwell, and the practice gained notoriety in 1606 when the Jesuit superior in England, Henry Garnet, was tried and condemned in the aftermath of the Gunpowder Plot (Milward 61). The Puritans, of course, delighted in ridiculing the priests' obfuscation of the truth. The justification for equivocating was that there were times when certain actions were permissible because of the circumstances involved and that the priests could "equivocate" because not everyone deserve to know the truth (Morey 188). The Jesuit priest, John Gerard, defined equivocation:

> In equivocation the intention was not to deceive, which was the essence of a lie, but simply to withhold the truth in cases where the questioned party is not bound to reveal it. To deny a man what he has no claim to was not deception. (Milward 61)

Shakespeare's gatekeeper to Hell in *Macbeth* welcomes an equivocator to his domain because the equivocator had "committed treason enough for God's sake, yet could not equivocate to Heaven." This scene is usually interpreted as ridicule of equivocation and specifically of Father Garnet, but it can also be read as a pathetic cry bemoaning the hopeless situation of the priests for whom nothing was effective in saving them from the butcher's block. The ambiguous phrase, "committed treason for God's sake" can be interpreted to mean that the priests were willing to suffer the penalties of the temporal crime of treason for a higher reason, that is, for the sake of God.

Finally, a convicted recusant (a person who refused to attend the English Church) was deprived of all civil rights (Leys 39). Those wealthy enough to have several houses, or those with relatives or friends who were willing to shelter them, avoided the stigma of being proclaimed recusant and forfeiting the £20 fine imposed for not attending the English church at least once a month by changing their residence before the month was up (Morey 141). This made it difficult to check records of church attendance. Additionally, some simply refused to appear in court to face the charges against them. However, the government got around those evasions by restricting the movements of the Catholics and by putting pressure on local government-appointed sheriffs and recusant hunters to enforce the laws strictly. A new law in 1587 stated that if a person failed on the second summons to attend the assizes courts, he would automatically be proclaimed a recusant. The victims naturally regarded this procedure as an infringement of the English idea of right to trial because the person was declared guilty with no trial at all.

The Catholic Impetus in Decline

The death of Mary and the defeat of the grandiose Spanish Armada marked a shift in the Catholic counteroffensive, for both losses dramatically weakened the Catholic hope for the restoration of Catholicism in England. Because the average Elizabethan literally believed God intervened on the side of right, it must have appeared to many English Catholics that God was not on the Catholic side to have allowed such devastating defeats. As a result, the Catholic mission lost some of its appeal in England. Except for Edmund Campion, who realized he was going as a martyr, many of the early missionaries sent into England probably anticipated succeeding in their mission to restore the religion, and many of them must have anticipated living to glory in its success. After 1588, however, hope of success began to fade. The long years of financial and social penalties, the gruesome deaths the young priests suffered, torture, imprisonment in filthy prisons, and the strain of maintaining secrecy all took their toll on morale.

Eventually a fracture in the united front developed, which the government was able to exploit. Bereft of the guidance of William Allen, who died in 1594, the Catholics argued among themselves and split into factions which weakened their influence. The government found it advantageous to fan the jealousy between the Jesuit and secular priests that grew from their differing views on their roles and on the structure of the Catholic Church in England. Marian priests, those whose appointment predated the Bull, saw themselves as increasingly threatened by the rising tide of restrictions and punishments. Two factions developed: the Marian priests blamed the missionary priests for exacerbating their own problems, and the missionary priests regarded the secular priests as giving in to the government too easily. Morey identifies the differing conceptions of the nature of English Catholicism that were at the root of the disagreement: The seculars wanted to return to the structure of the medieval Catholic Church with an Episcopal government and rule by canon law; the Jesuits regarded themselves as missionaries with the task of evangelizing (200). In addition, the close ties Robert Parsons had with Philip II and Spain colored all of the Jesuits. As a group, they were generally referred to as the "Spanish party" and tainted with the suspicion they were willing to sell out to Spain. Parsons and Philip II, however, retained their old religious fervor and supported each other in the midst of a changing religious scene. The English secular Catholics were willing to work out a settlement with the government and felt they could accomplish it if the Jesuits would just leave England.

Secular complaints against the pro-Spanish Jesuits reached a peak in the College of Rome following what the Protestants regarded as an inflammatory tract Parsons published in 1594. In it, he supported the claim of the Spanish Infanta over the Stuart claim to the English throne (Elton 458), and Parsons' pronouncement clinched suspicion the Jesuits were in collusion with Spain to conquer England. A further ramification of the dispute developed because the last English Catholic bishop, Thomas Goldwell, had died in 1585, so that now there was no Catholic hierarchy, and the solution of the Roman authorities did not please the seculars. An archpriest was to be appointed to work with twelve assistants, and the archpriest was specifically instructed to consult with the Jesuits. Although the appointee, George Blackwell, was a secular priest, he was friendly with the Jesuits, making his appointment unpopular with the other secular priests, who saw themselves as still under the thumb of the Jesuits. In 1601, the seculars sent four priests to Rome for a hearing on the disputes, but the pope would not see them. A second appeal was more successful, and the archpriest was henceforth ordered to deal directly with Rome rather than with the Jesuits. This debilitating infighting was in sharp contrast to the friendly cooperation among the priests that had characterized the early days of the mission, and the disagreements weakened the Catholic cause as a whole.

England was still fighting Catholic Spain via the Netherlands and France, but the differences were less religious than economic. In the Netherlands, the queen continued to lure Alençon with the prospect of a possible alliance by affording him limited support. She never seriously regarded him as a future King of England, but rather used him as a tool in keeping the Netherlands from becoming a Spanish stepping stone to England and also as a tool to protect English commerce. In France, England supported the Huguenots, led by Henry of Navarre, who became Henry IV upon the assassination of Henry III in April 1589. The fact that England continued her support of Henry IV even after Navarre made an expedient conversion to the Catholic faith in July 1593 indicates that questions of religion took a back seat to economic and political gain. England's relationship with Scotland also underwent a subtle change which lessened its potential use as an entrée for invasion of England by either France or Spain because James VI was wise enough to realize that if he played along with the queen, she probably would name him as her successor. He had a few pangs of conscience immediately following his mother's death, but he soon fell into line with English expectations.

The lineup on both fronts was undergoing dramatic changes that shifted the grounds of disagreement. On the Protestant side, the two giants who had served both Queen Elizabeth and the Protestant religion died, and along with them died the great Puritan force Sir Francis Walsingham had exerted and the more moderate, but equally deep, Protestantism of Lord Burghley. Walsingham died April 6, 1590, and Lord Burghley died in August 1598. Leicester had died September 5, 1588, but while he was touted as a leader of the Puritans, Leicester was for Leicester, and, in some of his machinations, he even wooed the Catholics. Some of the religious fervor, which had been "the cause" for which wars were fought, now was replaced by economic and political concerns.

For the Catholics, there was a faint glimmer of hope on the horizon that stretched beyond Queen Elizabeth's reign. It was the possibility that the new King James would allow Catholicism to exist side by side with Protestantism, or even that he would declare himself a Catholic when he came to the throne in 1603. As will be shown, he had at times been open to negotiations with the Catholics, and a substantial number of Catholics anticipated the new king would offer some relief from the debilitating Elizabethan restrictions. However, in reality James desperately needed the support of the Protestant Parliament, so he cast his lot with the Church of England. Very soon after his accession in 1603, the recusant fines were once again in place, the laws against Catholics were strengthened, and the executions resumed. And, as might have been foreseen, the plotting against the monarch resumed. A few discontented Catholics engaged in the Gunpowder Plot on November 4, 1605, and once again, members of the Arden family were implicated in an anti-government plot—this time in an attempt to blow up the Parliament and King James I. The involvement of Shakespeare's family in such plots raises questions about how Shakespeare was affected and how he positioned himself in regard to some of his family members' subversive activity.

Shakespeare and the Mission Priests

It would be a mistake to think of Shakespeare as ignorant of the Catholic underground, which was at its height during his lifetime. While it is true the preponderance of the safe havens for priests were mainly located in the remote, northern shires, Stratford had its share of fugitive priests during Shakespeare's time. Shakespeare's Arden relatives are known to have sheltered priests, one of whom was Edmund Campion, who is recorded as having been at William Catesby's house at Lapworth, twelve miles to the north of Stratford in 1580 (Milward 44). Sir William had a distant family tie with Shakespeare's mother, for Sir William's wife was the sister of Edward Arden's wife. A priest, John Sugar, was captured near Stratford and executed in Warwick on July 16, 1604 (Mutschmann and Wentersdorf 67). Fripp tells of Stratford Alderman George Whateley (interestingly, the surname of the Anne recorded in Shakespeare's marriage license) who had two brothers, fugitive Catholic priests, who "hovered about Henley" (*Shakespeare's Stratford* 15). There was Robert Debdale, a Stratford grammar school scholar a few years older than Shakespeare, who was lured to Douai in 1575 by the former Stratford schoolmaster, Simon Hunt (Fripp. *Shakespeare Man and Artist* 181). Debdale became a priest and was eventually arrested and executed in connection with the Babington Plot in 1586 (182). The references to the exorcisms in *King Lear* may have had a connection with Debdale, who was arrested for his participation in exorcisms. These specific instances show how immediately Shakespeare must have been affected by the fear and suffering of both priests and those who sheltered them. The pitiable fugitive priests were not something remote and unfamiliar to Shakespeare. He had relatives involved in these daring escapades and probably knew, or knew of, captured priests who were friends or brothers of theater acquaintances, as well as citizens of

Stratford. When Shakespeare referred to the equivocation of Henry Garnet, he may have been referring to someone he knew.

Moreover, he very likely would have known of the school master, John Cottam's, brother, a Jesuit priest who was arrested on his arrival in Dover, having departed for England June 5, 1580, bearing a letter for Robert Debdale's parents in Shottery (Fripp, *Shakespeare: Man and Artist* 181). Cottam was arrested before he could go to Stratford, but it is clear Stratford was his destination. Shakespeare would also probably have known of Edward Arden's resident priest, Father Hugh Hall, who fled to the home of the Catholic William Underhill (New Place, later purchased by Shakespeare) in Idlicote. In 1574, the first three of the newly trained priests returned to England from abroad. One of these was Henry Shaw, perhaps related to John Shakespeare's Stratford friend, Rafe Shaw.5 These and other young men Shakespeare may have known personally were imprisoned and tortured, and some were hanged, drawn, and quartered.

Shakespeare's Park Hall relatives participated directly in the sheltering of priests and were involved in at least one plot in which a priest sought shelter in Stratford. Clopton House, just outside Stratford, was raided by the town bailiff on November 6, 1605, and "Romanist relics" were found. Father Hugh Hall, chaplain of the Park Hall Ardens, fled to Clopton House in 1583 to avoid arrest in connection with the Edward Arden/John Somerville plot. Clopton House was again connected with an anti-government plot when the conspirators in the Gunpowder Plot used it as a meeting place. Among those arrested in connection with this plot were Park Hall relatives of Mary Arden: Robert Catesby and Francis Tresham (Mutschman and Wentersdorf 68). At the time of the Gunpowder Plot, the same Hugh Hall, along with Father Henry Garnet, Father Superior of the Jesuits in England, took refuge with Thomas Habington at Hindlip Hall near Worcester. They managed to remain concealed in the priest hole during an eight-day search before they were finally discovered and taken off to eventual execution (68).When a John Arden escaped from the Tower on November 4, 1597, with the Jesuit, John Gerard (Caraman 128, 132), the Shakespeares must have experienced some

---

5   The relationships of the Shaws need research. Juline Shaw was a friend and neighbor of Shakespeare and a witness to his will (Fripp, *Shakespeare: Man and Artist* 401).   Stratford schoolmaster, Alexander Aspinall, married widow Shaw. Was he related to the Aspinall who was the steward of the kitchen for the Earl of Derby at Knowsley? Henry Shaw of Chester was at Douai in 1573.   Francis Shaw of Chester was at Rheims in 1579. Gabriel Shaw was a schoolmaster in the home of Bartholomew Hesketh, brother of Alexander Hoghton's widow (Honigmann 20). If these Shaws were related and interacted, this would have been another Stratford-Shakespeare-Lancashire connection.

anxiety, even if they did not actually shelter them. Both were picked up in a boat in the middle of the night by Richard Fulwood6 a relative of William Shakespeare's grandmother.

Other individuals associated with Shakespeare were involved in tactics to get around the government restrictions imposed on Catholics. There were plans, which never materialized, to found a settlement in North America as a refuge for exiled Catholics (Elton 350). An interesting connection with Shakespeare was that his patron, the Earl of Southampton, was an investor in both the Virginia Company and the Bermuda Company (Rowse 240). Shakespeare's *Tempest* was perhaps suggested by the fate of one of three ships which had set out to bring supplies to the colony in Virginia. Miraculously, when a storm blew the ship off course and she ran aground in the Bermudas, all on board were saved. Within several months, the ingenious crew had built a new ship and set out to join the others in Virginia. Although the colony eventually failed, to this point, a Catholic would have regarded this miracle as a stamp of God's approval on the Catholic settlement in the New World. Shakespeare's play evokes the New World atmosphere of freshness and wonder so vividly it is likely he heard eyewitness stories about it, most probably from Southampton, who was likely involved in both the religious and the commercial facets of the colony. Even though Edwin Sandys claimed to have won Southampton for the English Church, Mutschmann and Wentersdorf doubt that he had converted even as late even as 1613 when he joined the Virginia venture: "But in view of the fact that outward conformity was a *sine qua non* of participation in the Virginia venture—as in every other enterprise connected with the exploitation of the American colonies—it may again justly be doubted whether the conversion was genuine" (113).

---

6   The step-grandmother of Shakespeare had a daughter by her first marriage who married John Fulwood, November 15, 1561 (Stopes 39). John and Richard Fulwood (Richard is named above as a rescuer of John Arden) appear to be brothers (French 488). Robert Arden's first wife was a Palmer, and she was the birth mother of Mary Arden Shakespeare (Fripp. *Shakespeare, Man and Artist* 30). [French stated that her family had not yet been identified (466). Stopes states that she was either a Trussel or a Palmer (*Shakespeare's Family* 36).] Mary Arden Shakespeare, the seventh daughter of Robert Arden by his first wife, was then probably related to Adam Palmer of Stratford, overseer of the wills of Robert and his second wife, Agnes Arden. No children were born in Robert Arden's second marriage to Agnes Hill. Her children by her first marriage became step-siblings to Mary Arden and her sisters. Shakespeare would have thought of his step-grandmother as his grandmother because Mary Arden's mother died before his grandfather's second marriage in 1550.

As a tactic to bring about conversions, both the Catholic and the Protestant priests engaged in exorcisms to prove the validity of their faith, although Catholic exorcisms were more notorious and "attracted followers where Protestant clergy failed" (Morey 190). Edgar in Shakespeare's *King Lear* resorts to disguise and survives in conditions of great adversity in a way similar to the plight of the hunted priests who were pursued and persecuted by both the government and informers. Edgar babbles of "flibberty-gibbet" and other spirits called forth in actual contemporary exorcisms. It is just as plausible that Shakespeare heard the names of the exorcised demons from the priests as is the traditional assumption he read about them in Samuel Harsnett's *Declaration of Egregious Popish Imposters* (1603).[7] From 1580 to 1586, an association of young aristocrats, led by George Gilbert had shepherded the fugitive priests about the country. However, so many of the leaders had been executed in the Babington plot of 1586 that, without the protection of the association, the numbers of hunted priests whose lives paralleled Edgar's must have increased dramatically. Up to the time of the extermination of its members, however, the association had been very effective in assisting the priests.

---

7   "It is quite certain that Shakespeare had perused Harsnet's *Declaration* before writing *King Lear.* The verbal similarities, as presented by Kenneth Muir, are too many and too close to be ignored" (Milward.   Personal communication 10/11/99).

Interpreting the Plays from a Catholic Perspective

At least this much of the contemporary world and Shakespeare's position in it must form the backdrop to our understanding of his plays. The religious question was the most important issue during much of the time Shakespeare was writing, and that issue surely was suggested to the audience by some of Shakespeare's plays, whether or not that was his purpose. Furthermore, to really understand his plays, they should be read with the awareness of his family's Catholic background. It is not logical to divorce Shakespeare from the issues around him, which determined government policy down to the fine points of the everyday citizen's life. The traditional assumption that Shakespeare was concerned primarily with his art and did not engage in the religious controversies in the foreground during his life seems to me to close the door to a key route to understanding his plays. Religion was not something one could ignore in the sixteenth century, because it affected every phase of Elizabethan life. Personally, it was a matter of life and death; politically, it often determined government policy. Shakespeare knew members of his family, albeit distant relatives, who risked their lives for the sake of their Catholic religion.

Because studies claiming Shakespeare was a Protestant and a Tudor spokesperson are abundant and easily available, those studies will not be reviewed here. Scholars who have addressed the question of Shakespeare as a possible Catholic are definitely in the minority. John Dover Wilson, in *The Essential Shakespeare* (1920), suggested that Shakespeare's father was so strong in his Catholic faith he refused to allow his son to attend the local grammar school. E. K. Chambers in *William Shakespeare: A Study of Facts and Problems* (1930) accepted the statement recorded in the late seventeenth century by Richard Davies, Archdeacon of Coventry, that Shakespeare "died a Papist"

(Schoenbaum 521 and footnote). John Henry de Groot, in *The Shakespeares and "The Old Faith"* (1946, reprinted 1968), concluded:

> There is nothing contrary to the Catholic spirit in Shakespeare's use of the Bible, but rather that there are some indications of his using the Bible as an enlightened Catholic would. . . . The evidence reviewed in this chapter and in the preceding chapters does not warrant the conclusion that Shakespeare was himself a Catholic. But it does supply ground for the opinion that the poet absorbed more of Catholicism in the course of his development than is generally believed and that throughout his mature years he retained a genuine esteem for certain aspects of the Old Faith. (224)

Mutschmann and Wentersdorf are convinced of Shakespeare's Catholicism, and there are few who state their conviction as forthrightly as they do:

> But when we repeatedly come across references to Catholic dogmas, ideas and customs, when we repeatedly meet with evidence of a predilection for Catholic ecclesiastics and their ministrations, at the same time as we notice an aversion to Protestant preachers and teachings, . . . we are in every respect justified in accepting these as irrefutable testimony of the poet's personal views, which are quite clearly pro-Catholic and anti-Protestant. (212)

Peter Milward in *Shakespeare's Religious Background* (1973), has written about many points of intersection between Shakespeare and the Catholic seminary priests and Jesuits, as for example, his observations on *Macbeth* in which he sees:

> [an] . . . attitude that is generally favorable to the Jesuits. . . . What is certain is that Shakespeare was very much alive to everything that was going on around him, not omitting the intense activity of the Jesuits and the even more intense propaganda of their enemies against them. The evidence of the plays tends to show that he sympathized with the former rather than with the latter. . . . (67)

More recently, E. A. J. Honigmann, in *Shakespeare: 'The Lost Years'* (1985), has presented a strong case that Shakespeare was a Catholic in his youth by reviewing the evidence that the William Shakeshafte named in Alexander Hoghton's will in Lancashire in 1581 was actually William Shakespeare. The Hoghton home was a center of Jesuit and seminary priest activity related to the Counter-Reformation, and Shakespeare's presence there would be a strong indication he was a Catholic. Chambers, in *The Elizabethan Stage*

(1923), had mentioned the will and asked if William Shakespeare might be the William Shakeshafte in Lancashire but failed to follow up with an answer. Oliver Baker's *Shakespeare's Warwickshire and the Unknown Years* (1937) picked up on the story to explain part of the "lost years" of Shakespeare, and the inquiry was later more fully pursued again by Chambers in *Shakespearean Gleanings* (1944). Honigmann shows that the Hoghtons and Stanleys were close friends who had private acting groups, a relationship which could help explain Shakespeare's early membership in Lord Stanley's acting troupe at least by 1588. Much of what follows here draws heavily on Honigmann's evidence that Shakeshafte was indeed Shakespeare, and one of my focuses will be to strengthen Honigmann's theory by making additional ties between Stratford, the Lancashire setting, the Catholic priests who congregated there, and the theater world where Shakespeare eventually emerged.

One way to substantiate the theory that Shakespeare spent his late teen years in a Catholic environment from which he then moved into the theater world is to be attuned to possible ambiguities that could be read as criticism of the queen, her government, or religion in the plays. Stephen Greenblatt recognizes a kind of subversive element in Shakespeare's plays and suggests the theater of the sixteenth and seventeenth centuries "constantly violated its interest and transgressed its boundaries" (16). A dramatist who engaged in religious controversies in the Elizabethan theater was forced to send subliminal messages because of government censorship which forbade presentation of religious issues on the stage. Greenblatt notes the analogy of the theater to the Catholic Mass that was recognized in Shakespeare's time:

> Forces both within and without the theater were constantly calling attention to theatrical practices that violated the established conventions of the English playhouse. When Protestant polemicists characterized the Catholic Mass as theater, the attack conjured up a theater in which (1) the playhouse disguised itself as a holy place; (2) the audience did not think of itself as an audience but as a community of believers. (15)

The theater developed from the long tradition of civic miracle and morality plays supported by the Catholic Church, lending the church a sort of ownership of theater; consequently, the theater was frequently criticized by Puritans as a Catholic evil. Burbage's new theater was called "the chapel of Satan" in 1580 (Mutschmann and Wentersdorf 101). As late as 1587, a Puritan correspondent complained to Walsingham: "The daily abuse of stage plays is such an offense to the godly. . . . When the bells toll to the lecturer, the trumpets sound to the stages, whereat the wicked faction of Rome laugheth for joy while the godly weep for sorrow" (101).

The subversive nature noted by Greenblatt was by no means limited to the topic of religion. Louis Montrose, as quoted by Jean Howard, described

41

the public stage in the Elizabethan period as "the site for challenges to traditional orthodoxies" (35). Leah Marcus sees a veiled allusion to Queen Elizabeth in the portrayal of Joan of Arc in *Henry VI*, suggesting "the play's vision of an outwardly immaculate virgin 'ruler' who turns out to be a slut underneath brings common gossip about Elizabeth to pungent dramatic life" (70). Criticism of the queen was often tied to criticism of the official religion. I suggest we at least explore the possibility Shakespeare consciously used the theater both to criticize the queen and her government, as well as to conjure up memories of the Old Faith, and while his plays were unquestionable works of art, they were also a form of subtle persuasion. Catholic sympathy and a Catholic point of view are subtly disguised under an orthodox overlay in such a way that the plays draw analogies between historical past and present reality which subliminally pose subversive questions about contemporary political and religious issues.

An additional way of deducing Shakespeare's own beliefs is to look at his close friends, his business acquaintances, and certainly at his patron, Henry Wriothesley, third Earl of Southampton, to see how they might have influenced him. Donna Hamilton and Ted Hughes regard Southampton as a Puritan, whereas I hope to present convincing evidence that Wriothesley was a Catholic and that religion probably brought them together in the first place. Hamilton does not offer an opinion on Shakespeare's religion but rather limits her interpretation of Shakespeare's work to how it reflects the ideology of his patrons, the Earls of Southampton, Essex, and Pembroke— all of whom she identifies as Puritans. Ted Hughes, on the other hand, suggests some of Shakespeare's Sonnets appear to criticize Southampton for rejecting the Catholic Church (personified as the Great Goddess of Divine Love, in Hughes' theory) and for having succumbed to the Puritan ideology. Hughes has devised a complicated interpretation of the Shakespeare/Southampton relationship which interprets Henry Wriothesley as an Adonis/Christ figure (57).

Hughes envisions Shakespeare's work as an exploration of the relationship between the two dominant religious forces, Catholicism and Puritanism, an evolution moving Shakespeare as a committed Catholic to a mature phase of "being on both sides," to finally facing the reality that the Divine Goddess of Love, which represents the Catholic faith in some ways, would never be restored in England. In his extended metaphor, Hughes outlines the Tragic Equation which he sees in operation in all of Shakespeare's work, an equation composed of two opposing myths—halves of the whole Elizabethan religious problem: the 'myth' of Catholicism ("Venus and Adonis") and the "myth" of Puritanism ("Lucrece") (516). Hughes suggests "Shakespeare's attention seems to have been focused on this theme by some obsessive private experience" which combined with the contemporary religious fanaticism (a claustrophobic crucible) to form "the composite myth of the English Reformation itself" (5). Hughes suggests

Shakespeare was "indeed not merely crypto-Catholic but committed to Catholicism with an instinct that amounted to fanatic heroism . . . his whole oeuvre can be seen as Shakespeare's record of the sufferings of the Goddess, and his heroic, lifelong patient attempt to rescue the Female—in some way or other to salvage the Goddess" (90). However, Hughes suggests Shakespeare's extraordinary vision enabled him to foresee both the Catholic defeat and the Puritan triumph waiting in the wings in the form of the civil war, and so Shakespeare was "on both sides" simultaneously (92). Hughes views Shakespeare as a prophet of the "ascendant, revolutionary, Puritan will (in its Elizabethan and Jacobean phase)," as well as a "visionary, redemptive shaman of the Catholic defeat" (91). His mind could encompass both "the Goddess's suffering and the Puritan that makes her suffer but destroys himself in the process" (92) so that both these "demonic, vatic personalities fight to come to terms inside his head—and inside his heart and throughout his nervous system" (90). Hughes perceives in the last plays a kind of concession to the inevitable Puritan predominance revealed in speeches which are "more alarming, more absolute and savage, and somehow more personal, than in the Tragedies proper . . . doorways, maybe, into the rapidly darkening real world where the weaponry of the Civil War was being cleaned and primed, and where, for a while, all outcomes would be pitiless, all worst fears would be realized" (487). *Othello* and *The Tempest*, in particular, are singled out as doing no more than introducing "the possibility of an unlikely hope—almost certainly a vain hope, nothing more really than a resolution to pray without hope" (488). Hughes envisions Shakespeare as a living being who wrestles with religious contradictions, passionately struggling to resolve them through his poetry and plays. He shows how completely the plays are an extension of a man who devoted his life "to rescue the Female—in some way or other to salvage the Goddess, who personifies Catholicism" (90).

Hughes' approach allows us to appreciate the plays as dramatic art, while it also frees us to bring into play what was happening in Shakespeare's personal life and his participation in the larger world. Surely the plays represent more than the viewpoint of Shakespeare's patron, and surely some of Shakespeare's positions on controversial topics are reflected in his plays. Historicizing Shakespeare and the plays becomes a complicated matter, as illustrated by the fact that the Earls of Southampton and of Essex are assigned opposing religions by respected scholars. If it is not a simple matter to say his patron was a Catholic or a Puritan, how much more difficult is it to decipher Shakespeare's ideology when his plays were subject to government censorship? If he had disagreed with government policy, he would have been obliged to write ambiguously.

It was dangerous to parody important people blatantly, as Shakespeare learned in the case of Oldcastle/Falstaff when he was required to change Falstaff's name because the new patron of the Chamberlain's Men, Lord Cobham, who succeeded Lord Hudson to that office in 1596, and who was descended from Oldcastle, felt the play was an unfavorable allusion to a family ancestor. Dutton points to " . . . the one attentive contemporary reading we know that virtually all plays for the public theater received after 1581, that of the censor and licenser, the **Master** of the Revels." Janet Clare indicates that Revels Master Tilney censored on the strength of a royal patent of December 24, 1581, which, among other provisions, gave him power:

> to warne commaunde and appoint in all places within this our Realme of England [. . .] all and every plaier or plaiers with their playmakers, either belonging to any noble man or otherwise, bearinge the name or names or usinge the facultie of playmakers or plaiers of Comedies, Tragedies, Enterludes or whatever other showes soever, from tyme to tyme and at all tymes to appeare before him with such plaies, Tragedies, Comedies, or showes as they have in readines or meane to sett forth, and them to recite before our said Servant [. . .] whom we ordeyne appointe and aucthorise by these presente of all such showes, plaies, plaiers, and plaie makers, together with their playing places, to order and reform, auctorize and put downe, as shalbe thought meete or unmeete unto himself. (ES iv, 285-87) (13)

Clare also identifies the evidence of the censor's hand in Shakespeare's plays and indicates that "He was also given the power to punish anyone who resisted him in this" (13). Shakespeare also probably realized being truly persuasive meant not alienating the subject he intended to persuade, another reason to avoid blatant criticism. A more effective method would have been to engross the viewer in the situation depicted in the play to persuade the targeted person his or her behavior was unfair, or unwise, or unworthy, that is, to use the stage as a tool to mold thinking. This would reflect the Catholics' realization that the only war they could win was a war waged with the printed word. In a pamphlet war waged against the Protestants, secret printing presses were kept busy printing the Catholic side of the issues. D.C. Peck quotes expatriate, former Secretary Sir Francis Englefield, who wrote to a friend: "In steded therfore of the sword, which we cannot obtayne, we must fight with paper and pennes, which can not be taken from us" (164). Shakespeare's plays could have been a very effective part of the war.

An example of the kind of subliminal subtext I see in many of Shakespeare's plays appears in *Twelfth Night,* on the surface a light-hearted comedy about love, but centered on the conflict between Catholics and Puritans. This serious theme is so well disguised in humor and the play so craftily structured, the viewer is fully engaged in the performance and "absorbs" the more weighty matters almost unconsciously, or as Hamlet might have phrased it, "the banter is the cheese that lures the audiences' conscience into the mousetrap" (3.2. 247-254). In plays of a more serious nature, where the portrayal of the theme is of overriding importance, some-times one character in the play serves as an analog for various contempo-rary figures, as when Richard II seems to represent both Mary, Queen of Scots, and Queen Elizabeth, depending upon which trait of Richard's applies to which queen. The fully self-conscious, pathetic Richard, who sys-tematically divests himself of the outward show of kingship reminds the audience of Mary, Queen of Scots, who was similarly stripped of her regali-ty. The other facet of Richard, the Richard who is accused of mismanaging the country's resources, represents Queen Elizabeth, who was criticized for the very same flaw. On a more personal level, there are moments when Shakespeare seems to acknowledge friends through his plays, perhaps by simply mentioning the friends' names—Bardolphe, Hackett, Walter of the Dale, etc. The sentiment accompanying the brief reference can sometimes provide a clue about how he evaluated that person. Occasionally, the play provides a forum for serious public praise as when he seems to eulogize Edmund Campion in *2 Henry IV*. Shakespeare himself provided keys to understanding his objectives, explaining that playwrights were "the abstracts and brief chronicles of the time" (*Hamlet* 2.2.549), just as he told us through Hamlet the conscience of a king could be caught through a play. It is for us to find moments in the plays when he tried to do that and to deduce why. The more we understand the influences on him—his friends, contem-porary political and religious conflicts, and family matrix—the more clearly the allusions in the plays stand forth and the more thoroughly we can dis-cover his ultimate motivation for selecting, highlighting, shading, and alter-ing the characters and situations in his plays.

When many of the extant pieces of the puzzle of Shakespeare's life are assembled, it is very difficult to deny his Catholicism. Initially, William Shakespeare's religion was probably shaped in a Catholic home with some interaction with the Catholic Counter-Reformation activity, and there is some evidence William Shakespeare himself was somehow connected with Robert Parsons and Edmund Campion, the most renowned missionary priests. Shakespeare's father was very likely a Roman Catholic recusant who subtly demonstrated his protest against the Elizabethan Church. In addition, some of Shakespeare's mother's relatives were staunch and courageous Catholics, who risked their lives in attempts to restore the Catholic faith in England. To what degree would Shakespeare's perception of Queen Elizabeth have been colored if he actually did grow up in a devotedly Catholic family who, as most Catholics, would have regarded the Queen as a bastard and a usurper? It seems likely that because Shakespeare was raised in that kind of environment he would have absorbed some of the biases against Elizabeth and her church. A primary objective here is to add to the evidence that Shakespeare was a Catholic, that he began his work as a dramatist and actor in Lancashire, was patronized by a Catholic, and that he may have used the theater as a means of catching the religious conscience of the queen as well as the religious conscience of the country.

Today we read the information allowed to be entered in the Pipe Rolls, the Calendar of State Papers, and other government records as history, but it was selective and skewed, and there is very little way of retrieving what was omitted. Additionally, the Elizabethan historian was forced to be very circumspect in his recording of events, as John Hayward lamented:

> . . . it may seeme not impertinent to write of the stile of a history . . . what thinges are to be suppressed at large: how credit may be won and suspition avoyded: what is to bee observed in the order of times . . . what liberty a writer may use in framing speeches, and in declaring the causes, counsailes and eventes of thinges done: how farre hee must bend himselfe to profit . . . but this were too large a field to enter into. (John Hayward, Address to the Reader, *The First Part of the Life and Raigne of King, Henry III,* 1599) (Clare 60)

Such a biased recording of history is bound to obscure and, in some cases, obliterate evidence related to Shakespeare's religion. Unfortunately, we are left to glean bits of information from scattered sources, intuit meaning from meager facts, and read between the lines of incomplete or biased historical accounts.

John Shakespeare's Religion

Schoenbaum considers the faith in which William Shakespeare was reared "a matter of no small moment, to ordinary readers as well as to theologians" (53). The family in which he was raised exerted the first, and probably the strongest, religious influence on him, and for that reason it is important to examine the evidence which indicates the man who reared Shakespeare was a Catholic. De Groot concluded that John Shakespeare "was a strong Catholic throughout his life and that his household was infused with the spirit of the Old Faith" (110). Mutschmann and Wentersdorf concur with De Groot's conclusion and add: "Shakespeare received at home a thorough grounding in Catholicism" (75). Peter Milward observed it was likely Shakespeare's parents "adhered to the 'old faith,' [and] they would naturally have been concerned about the religious education of their eldest son" (24). F. W. Brownlow argues that " . . . the conclusion that John Shakespeare was a Catholic is the economical one, requiring no forcing of the evidence. If that is so, then of course it means that William Shakespeare as a boy and young man experienced the curious, underground world of Elizabethan Catholic loyalism" (189). John Shakespeare's religious faith, then, is of no small consequence and calls for close scrutiny of evidence he was a Catholic.

What is the evidence for John Shakespeare's Catholic faith, and how did it influence the religion of Shakespeare? John Shakespeare was active in civic affairs in Stratford for the first nineteen years of Queen Elizabeth's reign, but his behavior altered dramatically in 1577, a date which coincides with the arrival and the first executions of the missionary priests who preceded Campion and Parsons. After that date, much of his behavior paralleled that of a Catholic trying to survive and safeguard his religion in a hostile world, and the measures he took coincided with dates of important activity of the mission. John Shakespeare was one of 220 citizens called to court in 1580 by the government for some mysterious breach of the peace (Mutschmann and Wentersdorf 49). His subsequent behavior, such as his real estate transactions, which were apparent efforts to protect his property from government confiscation, was probably strongly influenced by guidance from the priests. For example, he twice applied to the Heralds for a coat of arms and was successful in procuring it in 1599. This desire for a coat of arms undermines the theory he was a Puritan, for Puritans frowned on heraldry and coats of arms. Further evidence of John Shakespeare's opposition to the government was his persistent refusal to contribute to the musters levied in Stratford, for the troops were being raised to enforce the repressive laws against the Catholics (48). And finally, he was twice listed as a recusant by a government commission.7

John Shakespeare's long civic career began in 1556 when he was elected aletaster for the Corporation of Stratford. Thereafter, his rise was steady to chief burgess in 1557, constable in 1558, affeeror in 1559, chamberlain from 1561 to 1563, bailiff in 1568, and chief alderman in 1571. After having attended the meetings of the borough council faithfully for thirteen years, having been absent only once, he suddenly stopped attending the meetings in January 1577. It has been suggested the reason for this was that he had fallen on hard times, but his real estate transactions and other business affairs give no evidence this was so. Mutschmann and Wentersdorf, moreover, state this refusal to participate in the civic government was in response to the mission's efforts to rouse people to stand up publicly for their religion. The choice a person faced was either to continue in office and sign the Oath of Supremacy or to drop out completely in order to avoid signing the oath (44). John Shakespeare's choice was not to sign the Oath of Supremacy.

The important dates related to his withdrawal from civic affairs and his application for a coat of arms coincide with the founding of Catholic seminaries abroad.8 It is significant that William Allen, founder of the first seminary at Douai in 1568, and John Shakespeare were perhaps acquainted in

---

7   The term,"recusant" referred to any person who refused to conform to Queen Elizabeth's state church, although it is loosely used to refer only to Roman Catholic non-conformists. "The whole of the north-western district, in fact, was full of recusants, some of them of Roman Catholic, and others of Puritan opinions; ... " (Baines 418). In 1577, Cheney, the Bishop of Gloucester, divided recusants into three classes: those who excused their non-attendance at church by the plea of ill health; those who used the plea of debt—both classes "suspected of Popery"; and thirdly, Puritans ("What Was the Religion ...?" 177, 178).

8 "The English College at Douai, the 'mother and nurse' of all the other seminaries, was officially opened ... 29 Sept 1568 (DXXIX). It was forced by political troubles to move to Rheims 22 Mar 78 where it remained till June 93, when it was possible to return to Douai. The buildings at Douai were

Stratford in 1563 when Allen was the Stratford schoolmaster and John Shakespeare was a civic official, for their early acquaintance increases the probability John Shakespeare supported Allen's seminaries (Stopes. *Shakespeare's Contemporaries* 242). I came upon this connection independently and have subsequently been gratified to read Peter Milward's observations on the Stratford/Lancashire connection, especially his conjecture that William Allen appears to be a key link:

> With regard to the second question [What could have brought the young Shakespeare so far afield as to Lancashire?], recent investigations have disclosed a remarkable number of connections between Stratford and the part of Lancashire round Preston. They may ultimately be derived from no less a person than William Allen. . . . (41)

Allen apparently returned to Lancashire in 1562 and "often visited Oxford, which was near, and there soon converted not a few" (Heywood LXX), Heywood suggests that in Oxford Allen "must have endeavored to prevail on his old associates to join the seminaries he intended founding" (LXXI). Since Stratford is only 30 miles from Oxford, it is possible that Allen was in Stratford in 1562.9

John Shakespeare may have felt the need to proclaim his social status publicly as a supporter of the mission work, and that may be the explanation for his attempt to attain a coat of arms. The two early, and unsuccessful, applications he made to the Heralds coincide with important seminary activity. Schoenbaum shows he made a preliminary application after he became bailiff in 1568 (227). The mother seminary at Douai had officially opened on September 29, 1568 (Anstruther x). Within two years of the beginning of the arrival of the priests, John Shakespeare made his second application for a coat of arms. It seems incongruous that a man who had obviously taken pride in his public service should suddenly cease participating in civic affairs and simultaneously seek the status of "gentleman" by acquiring a coat of arms. There was, of course, prestige involved, but more

---

used during this period as a junior seminary. . . . There were also Jesuit colleges at Anchin (1569), at Eu near Dieppe (1582) and at St. Omers (1593) where younger students could study humanities" (Anstruther x). Anstruther lists other seminaries: Rome, Valladolid, and Seville

9 Edgar Fripp and Richard Savage prepared a printed transcript of the handwritten Stratford Chamberlain's accounts (1553-1566) for the Dugdale Society (1921). Footnote 8 on page 128 reads: "The Usher, William Allen, who succeeded William Gilbert. . . ." (Merriam, Thomas. E-mail 14 October 1999).

than that, the acquisition of arms was a kind of statement that he certainly was no Puritan, as "The Elizabethan puritans . . . regarded coat-armour with abhorrence" (De Groot 60). The requisites for procuring the official status of a gentleman were that he was able to live without manual labor; could "bear the port, countenance, and charge of a man of substance;" and his wife could dress well, have servants, and have leisure time for social life (Fripp, *Shakespeare: Man and Artist* 74). John Shakespeare had fulfilled the additional requirement of being "advanced into an office or dignity of public administration." The grant had several stages over the years: 1568, 1576, 1596, 1599. According to Fripp, the coat of arms was granted in 1576, and only the tricking out—the final approval—was done in 1599. Schoenbaum indicates "nothing came of the application" of 1576 except receiving the pattern or sketch of his arms from the College (38). When the arms were finally granted, it appeared the original pattern was intended to include the arms of the Ardens of Park Hall but was scratched out in favor of a different—but still Catholic—branch of the Ardens (Mutschmann and Wentersdorf 66). The fact that the initial tricking showed the Shakespeare arms quartered with a branch of the Catholic Park Hall Ardens indicates the Shakespeares were willing to acknowledge their relationship with Catholic relatives (De Groot 62, 63). Schoenbaum, on the other hand, attributes the denial of the coat of arms to John Shakespeare's financial decline, which he also ties to his withdrawal from the city government (39).

No one has yet proposed his true motivation in seeking to obtain the arms might have been to be listed with "noblemen, gentlemen, and men of any account in all shires in England" (Strype 316). It seems a very secret list of such Catholics had been circulating for some time and was finally published in "a book new printed, and very secretly kept" (316). This was apparently a list of Catholics who were willing to help shelter the missionary priests. The book was published in 1584, but the list had been around for some years. The withdrawal from public office and application for coat of arms are pieces of the overall picture of John Shakespeare's Catholic behavior. The list of Catholics (perhaps with John Shakespeare's name on it) probably found its way into government hands, and when the government got wind of the arrival of Campion and Parsons in England, the people whose names were on the list were called to court for questioning.

As previously noted, in June 1580, the government called 220 persons throughout the kingdom into court for a "breach of the queen's peace." More than 140 were penalized with fines of from £10 to £200 (Schoenbaum 40). Schoenbaum says the reason for the charges is not known; De Groot suggests that perhaps they had refused to swear a new oath or perhaps they had refused to contribute to the musters (49). Because the date of the mysterious conflict between the government and these citizens coincides with the arrival of Campion and Parsons—Campion having arrived on June 26, 1580—it seems more plausible the government was intimidating and fining those who

50

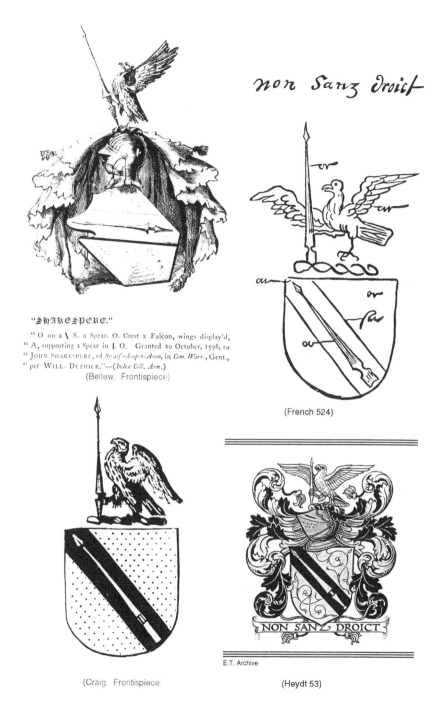

"𝕾𝕳𝕬𝕶𝕰𝕾𝕻𝕰𝕽𝕰."

" O on a \ S. a Spear. O. Crest a Falcon, wings display'd,
" A, supporting a Spear in J. O.   Granted 20 October, 1596, to
" JOHN SHAKESPERE, of *Stratford-upon-Avon*, in *Com. Warr.*, Gent.,
" per WILL. DETHICK."—(*Index Coll. Arm.*)
                    (Bellew. Frontispiece)

(French 524)

E.T. Archive

NON SANZ DROICT

(Craig. Frontispiece)   (Heydt 53)

Various depictions of Shakespeare coat of arms. The sketch from French
is the original tricking by "William Dethike Garter, Principall King of
Armes" (French 524).

51

planned to help with the mission. A complex plan to evade the appearance in court, as well as the fines, was devised by those called in to court, but the government was successful in prosecuting, and "John Shakespeare was fined £20 for non-appearance in Westminster to answer the charges brought against him, and £20 for not bringing in John Audley" (Mutschmann and Wentersdorf 50). It is odd that such a widespread and important court summons has been left unexplained, and I venture to suggest the explanation for the summons was either suppressed by the Elizabethan government, or it has been suppressed subsequently for some reason, perhaps because it tainted families with the suspicion of being Catholic.10

Several key events connected with Campion's visit converge on the Shakespeare/Arden family in a way that almost certainly confirms John Shakespeare (and probably his son) knew of Campion's projected visit to England and were acquainted with early stages of the planning. Campion seems to have had correspondence with a Robert Arden, Campion stopped at the William Catesby's house en route to Lancashire, John Shakespeare was in trouble with the government just as the Campion/Parsons mission arrived in England, and John Shakespeare probably obtained his Catholic will from Campion. After such a meeting with Campion at a relative's home, it is not unrealistic to envision William Shakespeare guiding Campion to Lancashire (and he could have done so whether he was a student recently returned from Catholic studies abroad or was still living in Stratford). Shakespeare's arrival in Lancashire might explain the odd phrasing in Alexander Hoghton's will expressing his concern for the welfare of William Shakeshafte who was "now dwelling" with him (Honigmann 136). The phrase suggests an unusual or temporary arrangement and is not used in regard to any of the other legatees.

Those who sheltered or had any contact with these priests ran the risk of having any and all of the previously outlined penalties imposed. Some of these consequences were that a person could be convicted of treason for sheltering a Catholic priest, as the Arden and Catesby families did, or he or she could be convicted of *praemunire* if he merely possessed Catholic religious items. The latter ruling may explain why John Shakespeare's spiritual will was found hidden under the tile roof of his house by roofers in 1757.

Among several other hypotheses, De Groot suggests "John Shakespeare was among those reached by the Jesuits early in their mission, before the arrival of the printed testaments from Rome" (89). Milward surmises that the will "must have come into the hands of Shakespeare's father when Persons or Campion passed through the Midlands at that time [1580]" (44). Milward is

---

10 Colin Jory, Ph.D. candidate at the Australian National University, has investigated this court case and his findings were to be published in November 1999 by the St. Thomas More Society, Sydney, Australia (Jory E-mail 5 Oct. 1999).

even more specific in attributing the will to Campion: "It may, therefore, be conjectured that John Shakespeare received his copy from Campion at the house of Sir William Catesby...." (21). Mutschmann and Wentersdorf write that Campion and Parsons "spread the idea of the will at the height of their missionary work in England" and "the inference is that it was from or through them that John Shakespeare received the actual form of his spiritual will" (57, 58). Simpson proposes Campion may "have had to enumerate [among his converts] certain aldermen of Stratford, John Wheeler and John Shakespeare, the father of our ever-living poet" (251).

John Henry de Groot provides much of the factual information which follows concerning the Catholic will Campion is believed to have delivered to John Shakespeare. De Groot suggests the will was hidden between the rafters and the thatching of the Henley Street house between 1580 and 1601. It remained there until 1757 when the house was re-roofed. Joseph Mosely, a bricklayer in Stratford, said he found the will and gave it to John Jordan, who tried to publish it, but the article was rejected (72). Jordan then sent the will to Edmond Malone who at first believed it was authentic and published it in 1790, but Malone later repudiated the authenticity of it. The will was missing two of the first original pages, and has since been lost entirely, but the remaining text has been preserved. Credit for proving the authenticity of the will has been attributed to Herbert Thurston, S.J., who published an article on it in May 1882 (79); however, I find an earlier connection (1858) of the will with Cardinal Borromeo:

> ... our prayer-books contain many formulae similar to that used by John Shakespeare, which doubtless comes from some prayer-book of the period, perhaps from Parson's *Directory* itself. There is a similar form attributed to St. Charles Borromeo, who entertained Campion, Parsons, Sherwin, and the other missionaries to England in 1580, at Milan, for a whole week, conferring with them every day. ("What Probably Was the Religion . . . ?" 247)

Regardless of whether Thurston was the first to note this similarity, he studied the problem over a period of thirty years, and in 1923, he found a Spanish version of the same will in the British Museum (De Groot 80). He uncovered additional versions of the will, one in Spanish, one in Romansch, and a third in Italian. An additional French text was found in the *Bibliothèque Nationale* by Clara Longworth (81).

From these documents, scholars have concluded the testaments were formulae of devotion, or confessions of faith, prepared by Cardinal Borromeo, Cardinal Archbishop of Milan, to be distributed by missionary priests to Catholics as a written pronouncement of their faith. Before leaving the continent for England, Campion, Parsons, eight priests, and two laymen in their party had stopped at Milan in May 1580 to confer with Cardinal Borromeo, who provided them with a supply of the testaments to take with them to

England. A detailed account of the visit is given by Simpson in his biography of Edmund Campion.

One of the first stops Campion made after he left London en route to Lancashire was at the home of Sir William Catesby at Lapworth, twelve miles from Stratford (Schoenbaum 51). (See genealogical tables.) It would have been natural for John Shakespeare to be present at the home of a man who was related by marriage to the Park Hall Ardens when Campion stopped there, and this would have been a logical time for Campion to deliver the Borromeo will. It is probable the Stratford Shakespeares were both friendly with and related to the William Catesby family of Lapworth and the Edward Arden family of Park Hall. John and William Shakespeare were directly linked with William and Robert Catesby: "Robert Catesby, Shakespeare's old manorial lord, at one time his neighbour in Stratford, and the uncle of his patron Lord Southampton, was the leader [of the Gunpowder Plot]" ("What Was the Religion . . . ?" 309). Edward Arden, cousin of Shakespeare's mother, was the brother-in-law of Sir William Catesby, the two men having married sisters. Robert Catesby was the son of William Catesby, so it seems the rental of the Arden property at Wilmcote was a family affair.[11] In addition, the Catesbys were a probable connection between Shakespeare and Henry Wriothesley, as the Catesbys were related to Henry Wriothesley's family. Anne, the daughter of William Catesby, was married to Sir Henry Browne, who was the brother of Henry Wriothesley's mother, Mary, Countess of Southampton ("What Was the Religion . . . ?" 170). This distant kinship between William Shakespeare and his patron, the Earl of Southampton, is rarely mentioned: "The poet, therefore, was not only a humble dependent, but also a distant connection, of the earl's relations. May we not attribute the introduction of the two young men to this alliance of their families?" (170).

One circumstantial but interesting conjecture concerning the connection between John Shakespeare and Edmund Campion pertains to the family life going on in spite of the difficulties with which John Shakespeare had to deal. His last son was born May 3, 1580, and was believed by Stopes to have been named "Edmund" after Edmund Lambert, the relative who refused to return Asbies when John Shakespeare wanted it back (Stopes *Shakespeare's Family* 110). There is no documentation Edmund Lambert was the godfather, and it could just as well have been Edmund Campion who

---

11 Wilmcote formed part of the Catesby property, and perhaps was granted to the Ardens on the attainder of William Catesby, (grandfather of William Catesby above) Richard III's minister, by Henry VII. The Catesbys, however, seem to have retained the manorial rights; "for we find in a roll of William Catesby's manors in Warwickshire, in the tenth year of Henry VIII, the name of Welicote. . . . The Ardens, therefore, and afterwards Shakespeare himself, were probably copyholders under Sir William and Robert Catesby" ("What Was the Religion of Shakespeare?" 234).

baptized and named the baby. Campion arrived in London in late June 1580 and had been arrested and dismissed by June 25, 1580. He would have been at the Catesby home shortly after his arrival on his way from London to Lancashire. Admittedly, approximately two months intervened between the birth of the son and Campion's visit, but there is at least a possibility John Shakespeare named his son in honor of Campion. This brother of William Shakespeare, who appears to have lived a dissolute life, became an actor in London and died on December 31, 1607, four months after the death of his own son, "Edward, the base-born son of Edward Shakespeare, Player" (110). Shakespeare honored his brother publicly "with a forenoon knell of the Great Bell of the Church of St. Savior's Southwark" (110).

Beyond the anxiety illegal sheltering of the priests must have instilled in those Catholics courageous enough to take the risk, Catholic recusants were constantly battling the possibility of economic ruin. As I noted earlier, to protect their wealth from confiscation in case of a recusancy conviction, complicated transfers of property were devised. This practice was well developed by the time Campion and Parsons arrived in 1580. A later (1607) excerpt from the *Landsdowne MS* given by de Groot makes it clear the prac- tice was widespread and also well understood by the government:

> Recusants demise their lands to tenants reserving certain rents, and the tenants stuff the grounds with their cattle; and when the commissioners come to seize goods, it is the tenants' goods and the King [in the time of James I] is without remedy. Recusants convey all their lands and goods to friends, and are relieved by those which have the same lands. There are Recusants that labour with their friends to find their lands at small values and get one or other to rent the King's part at that rate, whereby the King is much deceived and the Recusant little hindered. (44)

Some of the real estate transactions of John Shakespeare could fall into this category. His transactions have the earmarks of the behavior of other Catholics who tried to avoid the penalties of heavy fines and loss of prop- erty. On November 12, 1578, he leased eighty-six acres of land in Wilmcote to Thomas Webbe and Humpfrey Hooper. As part of the transaction, George Gibbes was to be the tenant there starting September 29, 1580, until twenty-one years later. Two days later, the Shakespeares mortgaged Asbies in Wilmcote to a brother-in-law, Edmund Lambert. On October 15, 1579, they sold their share in the Snitterfield property to their nephew Robert Webbe. De Groot has investigated John Shakespeare's financial dealings extensively and has concluded the real estate transactions were not under- taken because John was in debt (41).

These arrangements did not always work out satisfactorily, as the Shakespeares were to discover, because they could not redeem Asbies when they decided they wanted it back from Edmund Lambert. When Edmund died in 1587, they tried to get it from his son, supposedly with the help of

C. The Ardens of Park Hall and of Wilmcote

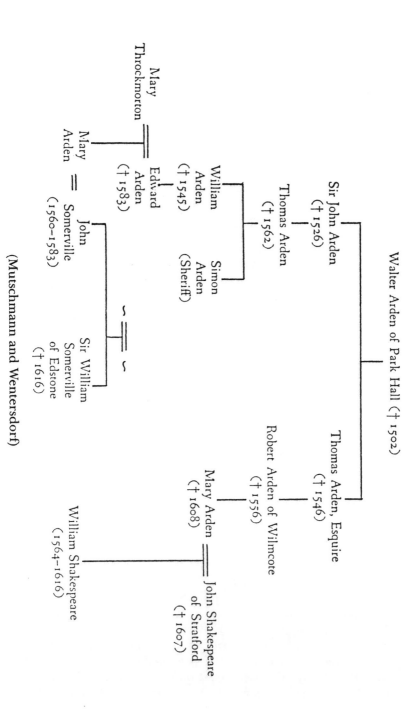

(Muschmann and Wentersdorf)

TABLE IX.

ROBERT ARDEN'S FAMILY.

WALTER ARDEN, of Park-hall, co. Warwick, xvith in descent from the Saxon Sheriff AILWIN, see Tables VI., VII., and VIII., ob. Aug. 5, 1502. Effigy on his tomb at Aston-*juxta*-Birmingham. = ELEANOR, 2nd daughter and co-heir of JOHN HAMPDEN, of Great Hampden, co. Bucks, by his wife Elizabeth, 3rd daughter and co-heir of Sir John Whalesborough, Knight. Buried at Aston-*juxta*-Birmingham. Effigy on tomb.

XVII. THOMAS ARDEN, second son, named in his father's will, 1502, and in that of his brother, Sir John Arden, 1526. Of Aston-Cantlowe from 1501 to 1547. Purchased with his son Robert in 1501, the Sniterfield estate from Mayowe. = N.N.

Agnes Webbe, 2nd wife, = XVIII. ROBERT ARDEN, of Aston-Cantlowe, "filio ejusdem Thomae Arden," in Grant from Mayowe in 1501. Of Wilmecote and Sniterfield from 1501 to 1556. = ... first wife, unknown.

widow of — Hill, no issue by 2nd husband.

| JOHN HEWYNS, 1st husb. ob. S.P. | = | 1. AGNES ARDEN, co-heir. | = | THOMAS STRINGER, of Stockton, 2nd husband. | 2. JOAN ARDEN, co-heir. | = | EDMUND LAMBERT, of Barton-on-the-Heath. | 3. KATHE-RINE ARDEN, of Wilmecote. | = | THOMAS EDKINS, of ARDEN, co-heir. | 4. MAR-GARET ARDEN, co-heir. | = | ALEXANDER WEBBE, of Sniterfield, 1st husband. | 5. JOYCE, co-heir. | 6. ALICE, co-heir, had Asbies. | 7. XIX. MARY ARDEN, co-heir. | = | JOHN SHAKSPEARE, High Bailiff of Stratford-upon-Avon. |

JOHN STRINGER.

ARDEN STRINGER.

JOHN LAMBERT.

THOMAS EDKINS, "the younger."

ROBERT WEBBE. = MARY PERKES.

WILLIAM SHAKSPEARE, xxth in descent from the Sheriff AILWIN.

XX. JOAN SHAKSPEARE. = WILLIAM HART.

See Table V.

(French 467)

their son, William (Stopes, *Shakespeare's Family* 46), but apparently failed, as evidenced by the fact that a commission was appointed to hear both parties in the dispute in 1599. The outcome remains unknown, as the page with the decision is lost (48). The timing of the property mortgages is significant because it occurred within a year of the appointment of the Calvinist Bishop Whitgift to the diocese of Warwickshire with instructions from the queen to seek out recusants. He visited Stratford in September 1577, and the next month he had a message from the queen which instructed him to certify "the names of all persons in his diocese who refused to come to church together with the values of their lands and goods, as he shall think they are, and not as they are given in the Subsidy Book" (Fripp, *Shakespeare: Man and Artist* 151). The Shakespeares were obviously trying to protect their property. They may also have needed ready cash for several other reasons, such as expenses of the mission or to support a son who had gone abroad secretly to study at a Catholic school.

Additional proof of his Catholic recusancy is John Shakespeare's refusal to pay the full levy for the calling up of troops by the government, evidence he was protesting the use of troops to enforce the anti-Catholic laws (Mutschmann and Wentersdorf 46). One month after Whitgift's visit to seek out recusants, a commission for musters visited Stratford, and on the commission was Sir Thomas Lucy, the local Puritan with whom William Shakespeare seems to have been at odds. Lucy's presence on the commission may have fit into the larger picture of animosity between the two. On January 29, 1578, the Stratford levy was made to strengthen the government troops. John Shakespeare was assessed only half of what the other aldermen were assessed, and there is no evidence he ever paid the half levy (46). His name appeared on a predominantly Catholic list among those who had not paid the assessment. This failure to pay has frequently been used as evidence John Shakespeare was in financial difficulty, but De Groot very thoroughly investigated that aspect and concluded:

> When these several indications of John Shakespeare's satisfactory financial condition are considered, the plausibility of the theory of poverty is diminished. It does seem as if some explanation of John Shakespeare's withdrawal from public life other than poverty must be found. The field is left clear for other theories. Important among these theories, from the standpoint of John Shakespeare's religion, is the theory of conscientious protest. (41)

De Groot's final conclusion about John Shakespeare, after reviewing all of the evidence, is that he was a Catholic throughout his life (110). If this is true, his refusal to pay the muster levy appears to be a Catholic's conscientious protest.

Further evidence of John Shakespeare's Catholic response to the growing schism is his name on the recusancy lists. In other words, he stopped attending the state church. There is no way to know if William Shakespeare followed his father's example and absented himself from church as well, but the effect would have been minimal in any case because the Shakespeare family appears to have conformed to some degree to the state religion until Shakespeare was twelve.

Efforts to determine Shakespeare's religion are usually based on his knowledge and use of a particular Bible as evidence that he was a Catholic or a Protestant. This type of evidence must be used with caution, however, because if Shakespeare's parents were Catholic, they would have instructed the children at home in the Catholic faith. De Groot discusses various Catholic books that might have been in the home as instructional material (111). They would not have had a uniquely Catholic Bible, for there was not yet a Catholic translation available (126). So in his formative years, if the Shakespeares attended the state church services, young Shakespeare would have become familiar with one of three Protestant Bibles: the Bishops', the Great Bible, or the Geneva Bible (155, 156). In addition, he would been exposed to the Elizabethan Prayer Book and would have heard or participated in the singing of Psalms (155, 156). If he attended the Stratford Grammar School, he would have had both Catholic and Protestant schoolmasters (142), although Catholic outnumbered Protestant. However, the instructional material was decidedly Protestant, ranging from the Latin Catechism to the Book of Common Prayer and the Psalter.[12] It should not be deduced from Shakespeare's knowledge of these Protestant works that he was therefore a Protestant, for their use was compulsory. More telling is the fact Shakespeare had accurate and extensive knowledge about Catholic practices, which he must have learned in the home.[13] If the Shakespeares

---

12 The Latin Catechism which young William would have had to learn in the lower forms of the Grammar School would most likely have been the Prayer Book Catechism *before* 1572 or Nowell's "Small Catechism" *after* 1572. The Book of Canons of August, 1571, required that "Schoolmasters shall teach no other Latin Catechism than that which was set forth in the year 1570, that is, Nowell's" (De Groot 146).

13 Christopher Devlin notes *Measure for Measure* is a great Christian play that incorporates explicitly Roman Catholic, Papist symbols. He views the end of the play as allegorical and mystical and not sensual, and observes that even though Isabella wins the duke and a marriage is only hinted at (27), Isabella is as pure as a nun at the end of the play.

In addition, I suggest even Hamlet's raving admonition to Ophelia to betake herself to a nunnery is confirmation of the nunnery as a place of refuge and the only place where one can remain pure in such a contaminated world as Elsinore.

attended church services until 1576, William Shakespeare would have been influenced by church liturgy, the reading of the Bible, the singing of Psalms, and various other Protestant literature until the age of twelve. This heavy exposure to Protestant religious literature in Shakespeare's youth would have occurred even if he attended one of the seminary schools abroad because boys were usually not sent overseas until the age of twelve or fourteen.

The fact John Shakespeare's name appeared on two lists of recusants, once in 1591 and again in 1592, has been used as evidence to prove both that he was a Puritan recusant and Catholic recusant. However, the wording of the order to report recusants is so specific in regard to harboring priests and fugitives that it is difficult to see how it can be otherwise interpreted than as a search for Catholics. On November 23, 1591, the Warwickshire commission was to turn in a list of "all persons—women as well as men—of proved or suspected recusancy, including receivers of seminary priests, Jesuits and 'fugitives' (the usual term for priests who had fled from their former cures and gone into hiding)" (Mutschmann and Wentersdorf 60). His name appeared on a second list prepared shortly after September 1592. The 1591 list named seven suspected Catholics and fifteen confessed Catholics. What causes the confusion is the next nine, with whom John Shakespeare is listed, are noted as not coming to church for fear of process for debt. This excuse was commonly used by recusants as a reason for not attending the English Church (Milward 19). This was obviously an excuse, for only one of the men listed, George Bardell, was sued for debt during the year (62). The fact that John Shakespeare had the ready cash of £50 in his effort to redeem Asbies and to pay two fines of £20 each[14] is proof he was not destitute. It seems evident he was a Catholic recusant who was probably following instructions from missionary priests.

As has been shown, John Shakespeare began to behave in a way different from his preceding behavior, just at the time when the mission was in its very early stages in 1577 and in need of moral and financial support. Additionally, 1577 was the year that marked the beginning of the punishment of the priests by hanging, drawing, and quartering. He had been steadily climbing in the Stratford city government and had been in every way an active participant in city life but suddenly stopped with no obvious reason such as financial difficulty. In 1580 he arranged for his property to

---

14 Colin Jory confirmed that John Shakespeare did pay the fines totaling £40: ". . . my investigations indicate that John Shakespeare did indeed surrender that forty pounds. . . ."

   Jory checked the recently catalogued King's Bench writs for 1580 Trinity Term and found "two returned writs of *scire facias*, previously unknown to scholars, naming John Shakespeare" (Address to the St. Thomas More Society. Sidney, Australia, 22 June 1999). (Jory. E-mail 6 Oct. 1999)

be safeguarded by transferring the titles to friends and relatives, and for some egregious breach of the peace he was summoned by the government and fined a substantial sum. All of these apparent aberrations are evidence John Shakespeare was making a conscientious protest, was safeguarding his family's wealth, and was probably involved in the sheltering of some of the priests. If the father exerted any influence on his son in the area of religion, it was definitely a Catholic influence.

The Ardens

The relationship of Shakespeare's mother to the Park Hall Ardens is frustratingly difficult to pin down despite many efforts to do so. Proving an active and frequent interaction between Shakespeare's family and the Ardens at Park Hall, about twenty miles to the north near Birmingham, would be a major breakthrough in linking Shakespeare with the Hoghtons in Lancashire, principally because both families were heavily involved in mission activity. S. Schoenbaum alludes to a possible, but vague connection: "The precise branch to which Robert Arden belonged remains obscure, despite intense genealogical zeal; perhaps he was descended from some younger son of the Ardens of Park Hall, which is in Castle Bromwich in the parish of Arden, not far from Birmingham" (19-20). Eric Sams reports "The Ardens of Wilmcote near Stratford are not known to have attained any such distinction [referring to the distinguished genealogy of the Park Hall Ardens]" (xvii). Ian Wilson leans a bit more in the direction of attributing kinship to the Park Hall Ardens and Mary Arden: "The family's main branch, the very Catholic Ardens of Park Hall, were based at Castle Bromwich, near Birmingham, and although Mary's father's exact relationship to these has never been established with certainty, his will as made out in November 1556 shows him to have been a gentleman. . . ." (31). Well before these recent biographies, Charlotte Stopes in 1901 left the matter unresolved, indicating she could trace only two Thomas Ardens of the appropriate age (in her search for Shakespeare's great-grandfather, Thomas), one of whom lived in London, and the other was the Thomas Arden whose son Robert was Mary Arden's father. In 1869, John French meticulously traced the genealogical record in an attempt to establish the Arden/Shakespeare relationship. He asserted he had conclusively established "the father of Mary Shakespeare,

Robert Arden, was the son of Thomas Arden, who was the second son of Walter Arden of Park-hall, the recognized descendant of Ailwin, the Saxon Vicecomes, or Sheriff of Warwickshire, in the time of Edward the Confessor . . ." (430). If French's conclusion is correct, that means Edward Arden, the head of the Park Hall Ardens, who was attainted and executed when Shakespeare was nineteen years old, was the great-grandson of Sir John Arden, who was the brother of Shakespeare's great-grandfather. French's research is exhaustive and convincing enough for me to accept the connections he established as valid.

The Ardens of Park Hall, as has been indicated, boasted a lineage traceable even beyond the time of William the Conqueror—a branching family that settled in various parts of the country over the centuries. The propensity of Park Hall Ardens and the Cheshire Ardens to display their ancient lineage is in itself a manifestation of their Catholic faith, akin to the importance Catholics placed on qualifying for a family coat of arms. The old and the new were at odds in the middle years of Queen Elizabeth's reign as the new Protestant religion clashed with the old Catholic ways. Just as Puritans abhorred the coat of arms, so would they have belittled a family's aristocratic lineage the arms depicted. Many Catholics, on the other hand, valued antiquity and lineage which harkened back to the days when "Christian" and "Catholic" were synonymous. The Puritan mentality was largely a phenomenon of the widened scope of general education, raising the common man to professional levels that rivaled and threatened the privileged, long-established aristocracy. Few Puritans could legitimately have traced their lineage from William the Conqueror, for "Puritan" was somewhat synonymous with "upstart."

Both the Arden and the Hoghton families prided themselves on their ancient lineage. Honigmann introduces his chapter on the Hoghton family with an excerpt from the *Guide to Hoghton Tower*: "The Hoghtons are descended directly from Walter, one of the companions of William the Conqueror, and through the female line from the Lady Godiva of Coventry, wife of Leofric, Earl of Mercia. After the third generation from the Norman Conquest, Adam de Hoghton first assumed the family name, holding land in Hoghton in 1203" (8). A similar account of the Arden family history is presented by Charlotte Stopes in Chapter 1 on the Park Hall Ardens and also by John French in his chapter entitled "The Family of Arden of Warwickshire."15 A shared religious affinity would have allied the Hoghton

---

15 Stopes traces a complicated lineage succeeding to the Earldom of Warwick to focus on Turchill, son of Alwine who was the direct ancestor of all the Arden branches. Part of Turchill's claim to fame was that he was the last purely Saxon Earl (as opposed to Norman) and was Earl of Warwick even before the arrival of William the Conqueror. According to Stopes, "He [Turchill] fought with William

and the Arden families, both wealthy, respected Catholic families which traced their ancestry to before the time of William the Conqueror. The Catholicism of the two families which engendered ancestral pride was grounds for friendship and a feeling of kinship.

During Shakespeare's lifetime, the Park Hall branch was headed by Edward Arden from 1562 until December 20, 1583, when he was hanged, drawn, and quartered for his supposed complicity in the Somerville attempt to kill the queen. The involvement of Shakespeare's mother's family in the Somerville incident is not often told, perhaps because it might tarnish Shakespeare's image; moreover, the full story of the plot may never be known. Most accounts indicate Robert Dudley, earl of Leicester, was behind it somehow and that the disastrous consequences—the deaths of Edward Arden and his son-in-law, John Somerville—were retribution by Leicester because Edward Arden openly criticized Leicester's intimacy with the countess of Essex while she was still married to Essex. Some accounts hint the gardener, Father Hugh Hall, was a double agent with a double disguise as a Catholic priest and as a gardener, planted in the Arden household to stir up trouble. In the Mutschmann and Wentersdorf account, he is regarded as performing the role of an authentic priest, however. His punishment was light in comparison with Edward Arden's and John Somerville's, although "he suffered a long term of imprisonment before he was released; at the time of the Gunpowder Plot, he was arrested with Father Garnet and again thrown into the Tower, where he apparently died" (Mutschmann and Wentersdorf 53).

---

against Harold, and was ostensibly left in full possession of all his lands. . . He is called Turchil of Warwick by the Normans, but Turchil of Eardene, or of the Woodland, by himself, . . . (*Shakespeare's Family* 165). French adds interesting information about Leofric's Countess Godiva, draped only in her own long hair, who "freed from toll through her famous ride on horseback, . . . " (434). In 33 Edward III, Henry de Arderne (twelfth-generation descendant from Turchill) established the family seat at Park Hall in Warwickshire. Turchill's grandfather was the brother-in-law of Leofric, and the family, as well as much of the kingdom of Mercia, were allied against King Harold (French 436). The point of including this complicated history is to show that there was an ancient family relationship between Ardens and Hoghtons through Leofric and to show that both families fought with William the Conqueror against the English King Harold. The Arden family traced its lineage to Leofric's sister; the Hoghtons traced theirs to Leofric's wife, Lady Godiva.

The Ardens of Park Hall

xv. ROBERT ARDEN, Sheriff, co. Leic. and Warw. = ELIZABETH, dau. and sole-heir of RICHARD CLODSHALE, Sheriff co. Leicester, 16 Hen. VI., ob. 1452, "relinquens 7 prole." Visit. 4 Hen. VI. Brought the Manors of Salley, Water-Orton and Pedimore.

xvi. WALTER ARDEN, of Park-hall, restored = ELEANOR, daughter and co-heir of JOHN HAMPDEN, of Great Hampden, restored by Edw. IV., ob. 1502. by his wife ELIZABETH, daughter of Sir JOHN WHALESBOROUGH, Knt.

2. THOMAS.
4. ROBERT.
5. HENRY.
6. WILLIAM.

MARTIN ARDEN, 3rd son, of Euston. = MARGERY, daughter of HENRY EAST, of Yardley.

XVII. SIR JOHN ARDEN, Knt., Esquire of the body to Hen. VII., ob. 1526. Eld. son and heir. = ALICE, daughter of RICHARD BRACEBRIDGE, of Kingsbury.

JOYCE ARDEN, mar. JOHN CHARNELLS, of Snarston.

ELIZABETH ARDEN, mar. WALTER LEVESON.

MARGARET, ALICE. (Dugdale.)

THOS. GIBBONS, = ELIZABETH = WILLIAM RUGELEY,
2nd husb. | ARDEN, | of Park-hall, eldest
THOMAS GIBBONS. | 1st husb., ob. S. P. | son, ob. 1584, attainted.
and heir, ob. 1567.

XVIII. THOMAS ARDEN, = MARY, THOMAS ARDEN = MARY, dau. of Sir Robert
of Park-hall, eldest son ANDREWS, of Cherwelton, Knt.

SIMON ARDEN, of Longcroft, 2nd son, see Table X. = JOYCE ARDEN, mar. RICHARD CADE, of London.

ELIZABETH ARDEN, married Beaupré.

XIX. WILLIAM ARDEN, of Park-hall, eldest son, ob. vita patris, 1545.

XX. EDWARD ARDEN, of Park-hall, eldest son, ob. 1584, attainted.

XXI. ROBERT ARDEN, of Park-hall, eld. est son, ob. 1635. = ELIZABETH, daughter of REGINALD CORBET, Ju. Com. Pl. by his wife Alice Gratewood, niece and co-heir of Sir Row-land Hill, Knt.

FRANCIS ARDEN, 2nd son, of Pedimore.

KATHERINE = Sir EDWARD DEVEREUX, Knt., Bart.
and heir of EDMUND FOX.

2. THOMAS.
3. GEORGE.
4. FRANCIS.
5. JOHN.
Sir Edw. Devereux, Knt., 3rd son, à quo the present Visc. Hereford, 1807.

BRIDGET ARDEN, mar. HUGH MASSEY.

Alice, ux. — Arden.

Elizabeth. ux. Tho. Warwick.

ELIZABETH, daughter of Edw. CONWAY, of Ragley, by his w. Anne, d.&h. of Richard Burdett.

ANNE ARDEN, m. John Bar-mesley.

CICELY ARDEN, mar. HENRY STIRLEY.

MARY ARDEN, mar. THOMAS WAFERER.

MARGARET = JOHN SOMER-VILLE. Park-hall.

2. GODIVA = Sir HERBERT ARDEN, à PRICE, Knt., had Park-hall, which was sold by their representa-tives to Sir John Bridg-man, Knt., 1637.

XXII. Sir HENRY ARDEN, of Park hall, knighted by James 1, ob. vita patris, 1625.

XXIII. ROBERT ARDEN, last of the male line of Park-hall, ob. Cœlebs, 1643.

= DOROTHY, daughter of BASIL FIELDING, of Nuneham Park.

3. DOROTHY = Col. ARDEN. HERVEY ARDEN, had Saltley.

MARGARET = WALTER FERRERS.

ROBERT THROCKMORTON, m. John Bar-mesley.

BARBARA ARDEN, m. RICH. NEVILL, son of John, Ld. Latimer.

JOYCE ARDEN, m. JOHN LODBROKE.

JOHN ARDEN, 2nd son, ob. 17 Hen. VIII. S.P.M.

ELIZABETH = SIR WILLIAM POLEY, Knt. ARDEN. of Boxtead.
SUSAN POLEY, mar. 1st Anthony Massey, 2nd Richard Savage.

ELIZABETH, daughter of MURIEL = WILLIAM ARDEN, CHARNELLS, of Snarston. = SIMON SHUCK-burgh, of Shuckburgh.

4. ANNE = Sir CHARLES ADDERLEY, Knt.

XXIV. CHARLES CHRISTIAN = THOMAS ARDEN. ADDERLEY, BASIL. à quo Drummond.

ARDEN.

XXIV. ARDEN BAGOT, à quo the Rev. RALPH BAGOT, of Pipe Hayes.

XXIV. ARDEN ADDERLEY, à quo CHARLES BOWYER ADDERLEY, M. P. 1868.

(French 449)

65

Arden's son-in-law, John Somerville, is described as having been a little deranged by inflammatory discussions with the priest about the queen. The result was that on October 25, 1583, Somerville, father of two small children, set out for London from his home six miles north of Stratford (Fripp, *Shakespeare: Man and Artist* 194) with his "dagge" (a small pistol), threatening to kill the queen. The ever-alert Puritan, Sir Thomas Lucy, was instrumental in the fifteen-day search for evidence and in making the arrests. On October 31, a warrant was issued for the arrest of "such as shall be in any way akin to all touched, and to search their houses" (52). As indicated earlier, Father Hugh Hall, chaplain of the Park Hall Ardens, fled to Clopton House in Stratford to avoid being arrested with Edward Arden and John Somerville.

The entire Park Hall household was tried, and Arden and Somerville were condemned. Because John Shakespeare's family was "akin to all touched," his family was probably investigated in connection with the episode, and this would have been a logical time for John Shakespeare to hide his Borromeo testament in the roof of his house. The role Sir Thomas Lucy played in arresting members of Shakespeare's family probably provided the motivation for Shakespeare's satire on Lucy as Justice Shallow, rather than the somewhat questionable story about his having poached deer in Lucy's park.

The arrests of Edward Arden and John Somerville became a notorious case internationally, and the outcome of the charges against the entire Arden family was a topic of great interest. We can only guess at the effect all of this had on the nineteen-year-old relative, William. His mother's "cousin" was hanged, drawn, and quartered; his friend's uncle (or father) was strangled or committed suicide in prison the night before the hanging The heads of both men were subsequently placed on poles on London Bridge. The Mistress of Park Hall was threatened with being burned alive but instead was put in prison along with her daughter, the wife of the purported regicide. Shakespeare's own family would surely have sympathized with the fate of the two men, and they must have trembled with fear because of their kinship.

Beyond French's theory that Shakespeare's great grandfather was born at Park Hall, additional evidence regarding a direct connection between Park Hall and Shakespeare is his friendship with William Somerville, who was either a son or a nephew of John Somerville, the would-be assassin. William Somerville had the Hilliard portrait of Shakespeare painted, and the portrait has remained in the Somerville family as shown by the tradition recorded by a member of the Somerville family in a letter to James Boswell in 1818: "Mr. [William] Somerville of Edstone, near Stratford-upon-Avon . . . lived in habits of intimacy with Shakespeare, particularly after his retirement from the stage, and had this portrait painted, which, as you will perceive, was richly set and carefully preserved by his descendants"

(Mutschmann and Wentersdorf 168).16 The friendship substantiates the acquaintance of Shakespeare with one member of the Park Hall enclave, as well as indicating that Shakespeare was not alienated from William Somerville because of the scandal of the supposed plot.

On the basis of Shakespeare's friendship with William Somerville I would like to proceed on the assumption there was at least an acknowledged acquaintance between Shakespeare's family and their more illustrious Arden relatives who might have provided a route by which Shakespeare migrated to Lancashire. Another logical route to pursue is to look at other branches of the Arden family, who are known to have been living in Cheshire, the shire to the south of Lancashire, since the time of Henry II (Stopes, *Shakespeare's Family* 196).

Again, there is uncertainty about how or if they were related to the Ardens of Warwickshire. French states: "It is by no means certain that the Ardens of *Cheshire* had any right to claim an alliance with the Warwickshire house" (495). However, the possibility they regarded themselves as relatives is suggested by Stopes, who shows Sir Peter, who succeeded to the family estates in 1268, bore arms based on the Warwickshire family (Stopes *Shakespeare's Family* 197). A hint the Shakespeares knew the Cheshire Arderns is the fact that the Cheshire coat of arms was considered for use when John Shakespeare's coat of arms was being devised (French 496). The Cheshire branch of Arderns is brought in at this point because of a will written by a Robert Ardern in 1540, proving he, at least, was closely associated with the Hoghtons of Hoghton Tower. I have not succeeded in linking this Robert Ardern with William Shakespeare, however. Although the erratic spelling of names during the years is a very unreliable tool for identification, the Park Hall Ardens spelled their name "Arden" rather consistently, whereas the Cheshire Arderns more often included the final "r." The spelling as "Ardern" in the will is perhaps a fragile identifying marker.

---

16 Whitfield has an interesting article about what must be the next generation off-spring of Shakespeare's friends, Somerville, Combe, and Green. He shows a William Somerville entered Middle Temple on February 13, 1608, and was friends with Thomas Greene and William Combes there. This would seem to be a younger William Somerville of Edstone, as young men were usually entered at the university in their late teens, and therefore this William would not yet have been born in 1583. This Thomas Greene would not be the cousin who lived in Shakespeare's New Place by 1609 because he began studying law in London in 1595 (170) and surely would have finished before William Somerville entered the Middle Temple in 1608. The relationship of the Greens to William Shakespeare has not been satisfactorily explained. Might they have come from Cheshire? Stopes shows that a Thomas Green (d 1614?) left Melton Farm in Cheshire to his "sister," Ann Ardern, who was also an executor of the will.

In an effort to identify Robert Ardern of the will, I pursued the possibility that he was originally from Park Hall and was a great-uncle of Mary Arden Shakespeare, mother of William Shakespeare. My subsequent conclusion, which is of necessity based on a very frail record, is the Park Hall Robert is not the Robert of the will. Nevertheless, the two different Robert Arden/Ardern(s) share the distinction of being possible entrées through whom Shakespeare could have been introduced to the Hoghton family sometime before 1580 either as a schoolmaster, a scribe, a page, or as a young actor—a position which could have led him to Ferdinando Stanley's acting group at nearby Knowsley and on to the theater in London.

I would first like to explain why the Park Hall Robert appeared to be a good candidate for the writer of the will. I will proceed here on the basis of French's conclusion that Walter Arden of Park Hall (d 1506) was the great-great-grandfather of Edward Arden and the great-grandfather of Mary Arden Shakespeare. Of Walter's ten children, we will be concerned with only John, Thomas, and Robert. Sir John Arden (d 1525) inherited Park Hall; his brother Thomas (2nd son, d 1563) became the great-grandfather of Mary Arden; and Robert Arden (4th son) became page, or groom of the chamber, and was granted Altcar, Co. Lancashire, by King Henry VII (See genealogical table). French corroborates the identity of Robert, for he also records that the page, or groom of the chamber to King Henry VII, was Robert, the son of Walter Arden of Park Hall and "King Henry VII bestowed upon his groom of the chamber his first gift, 'the Keepership of the royal park at Aldecar,' Altcar, co. Lancaster, on February 22, 1502" (425). This Robert Arden was the great-uncle of Mary Arden Shakespeare and the great-great-uncle of Edward Arden of Park Hall. (See map, p. 95.)

If Robert Arden moved to Altcar when it was granted to him, he would have been very near the Hoghtons and the Heskeths. Altcar is located about ten miles southwest of Rufford Hall where Thomas Hesketh lived; about ten miles northwest of Knowsley and west of Lathom, where Ferdinando Stanley lived, and about eighteen miles from Hoghton Tower and Lea Hall. (Altcar is spelled "Alker" on the 1588 Saxton map and is known today as "Great Altcar.") Written inquiries to the Manchester Department of Libraries and Theatres and to the Lancashire Record Office have yielded no information about Ardens living in or near Altcar in Shakespeare's time, but a thorough search would require an onsite check of parish records. The possibility Shakespeare had relatives so near these places, if verified, would be valuable information to supplement E. A. J. Honigmann's theory that William Shakespeare was introduced to the Hoghton family by the Stratford schoolmaster, John Cottam, whose father was one of Hoghtons' tenants.[17]

---

17 Honigmann credits Peter Milward, S.J., with having pointed out the connection between Cottam and Lancashire in *Shakespeare's Religious Background* (5).

My initial interest in identifying Robert Arden was the discovery of a Robert Ardern's will, dated 22 October 1540, ("Lancashire and Cheshire Wills" 138). To judge from acquaintances named in his will, he moved in the same social circle with the Hoghtons and the Leighs of Lyme (See Appendix I). In response to my inquiry to the Cheshire Records Office, I came upon the name of a different Robert Ardern who seems to me more likely to be the author of the will. Again, there is not much evidence to work with. The Robert Ardern (one of several of Robert Arderns of Cheshire) which fits with the chronology, is named in the account provided to me by the Cheshire Record Office:

XII. Ralph Arderne, who succeeded, is fixed as son of John Arderne and—Heaton by the Visitation, and as son of John by the Inquisition taken after his own son's death (6 Edward VI), and must therefore be the Ralph, whose betrothed wife, Margaret Davenport, occurs (as above) in 13 Henry VII, and who was trustee of his brother Thomas, 22 Henry VII, as above. By this wife Margaret, daughter of Thomas Davenport of Henbury, Esp., and of his wife Catherine, daughter of Sir Alexander Radclyffe of Ordsall, he had issue John, *Robert*, [my italics] and Elizabeth, and as by Inquisition p.m. 30 Henry VIII, died seized of lands in Alvanley, the manor of Harden, and lands in Bredbury, Werneth, Romilegh, Offerton, and Stockport. John Arderne, son and heir of; (Omerod. "Arderne, or Arden, or Alvanley" 92)

There is too little evidence available to positively assign the will in question to this Robert Ardern, whom I deduce to be of Alvanley. However, the date of the will as 1540 and the fact that this Robert was alive in Henry VIII's time make it possible. Also, the places named in the will correspond with the places named in the above extract. The will is of interest, in any case, in connection with the theory that Shakespeare was in Lancashire in his youth, because it brings into direct contact the Hoghton family with at least one person with the surname of Ardern. The key element missing here, unfortunately, is a direct link between the Warwickshire Ardens and the Cheshire Arderns. The nearest I have come to establishing one is tenuous, but interesting, and is concerned with a possible tie through a family named Green.

Stopes mentions an Alice Green, who had first married an Arden (Stopes surmised that it was John Arden) and who later married Sir John Holgrave (205). (All of the material presented here is based on *Shakespeare's Family* by *Charlotte Stopes*, pages 205 - 206). This Alice Green, who is mentioned in several Cheshire wills, had a son, Thomas Green. It will be recalled Shakespeare had a "cousin" Thomas Green who lived in New Place for several years. Of course, these are not the same Thomas Greenes, because the will in which Alice Green is named was proved in September 1487, but there was a strong tendency to repeat given names within families at that time, so Alice's son could have been Shakespeare's cousin's father or uncle. Curiously, a Master Walter Arden is named as an executor of the will, and as Walter Arden of Park Hall died in 1501, at least the dates are right to make it possible that "Master Walter Arden" is the Park Hall Arden. Stopes suggests, but offers no proof, Alice Green had been married previously to John Arden and had children by him. It is at least a possibility this is the same John Arderne, named as the heir and head of the family by Ralph Arderne and who would have been the brother of Robert. Stopes further suggests this John Arden, former husband of Alice Green, was a son-in-law of a Walter Green who had another son-in-law named John Catesby. The connection between the name Catesby and Arden is of interest because John Shakespeare had business dealings with the Stratford Catesbys, Mary Arden was related by marriage to William Catesby of Lapworth, and members of the Arden family were associated with Robert Catesby in the Gunpowder Plot in 1605 (See my "Religion of John Shakespeare"). This possible connection between the Cheshire Arderns and Shakespeare is another one that should be pursued, but such a search would require time and money. This type of close fit of names and relationships gets one tantalizingly close to a direct tie between Shakespeare and Lancashire, but there are often too many unknowns to say for certain there was communication between the branches of the family.

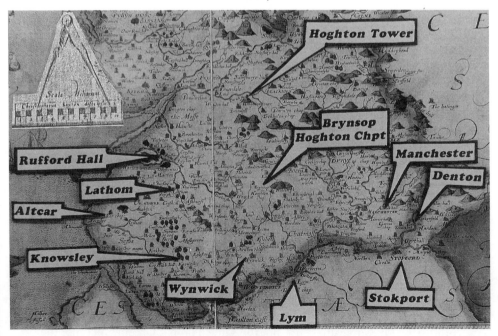

Based on Lancashire Map (Saxton 78/79)

Robert Ardern wills his "body to be buryed in the pische churche," but neither the location of the church nor his place of residence is named. His bequests help to establish his approximate location. He leaves money to the poor of Manchester and Stokport as well as money to several churches: the chapel of Saint Stephen of Alvandley, Wynwhyck, Denton, and Norton, and he mentions the city of Lyme. From these geographic points, his residence might be deduced to be near the southwest border of Lancashire and the northern border of Cheshire, probably no further than twenty miles from Hoghton Chapter. (See map.) Also, he would have been within fifteen miles of the Wynwhyck mentioned in his will. Robert Ardern is linked with the Leigh (Legh and Lea) family of Lyme. A footnote adds that Sir Peter Legh of Lyme (d August 1527) appointed Robert "Ardern" one of the executors of his will ("Lancashire and Cheshire Wills" 139). A younger Sir Peter Leigh of Lyme (d 1590) was the grandfather of a brother-in-law (also called Peter Leigh of Lyme) of Richard Hoghton of Hoghton Tower. It would seem safe to deduce from the close relationship of the older Peter Leigh and Robert Ardern that there had been a long-standing relationship between the Ardern and the Leigh families, and by association, with the Hoghton family.[18]

Unfortunately, from the material available to me at the present, no definite tie between Shakespeare and either Robert Arden can be established with certainty. The most that can be said about Shakespeare's acquaintance with the Ardens of Park Hall is he was at least friendly with William Somerville, Edward Arden's grandson, a friendship which indicates Shakespeare was at least aware of his Park Hall relatives. I assume his family therefore would also have been aware of any Arden descendants of great-uncle Robert Arden in Altcar if he had offspring who settled there. The proximity of Altcar to the Lancashire area where Shakespeare may have been in his teen years makes a very tenuous connection at least a very intriguing one. In regard to the identification of the Robert Ardern who wrote the will, no proof has been offered here that he and the Robert named as the son of Ralph Arden (above) are one and the same, but the convergence of the names Arden, Green, and Catesby with the Hoghton family and Shakespeare's possible connection with all of these, is, to say the least, interesting. In view of the scant records which exist, it may not be possible to get closer than these near misses in tying Shakespeare to the

---

18 Further evidence Arderns were acquainted with some of the Hoghton family is shown in a will of the wife of John Arderne of Alvanley, county of Chester. She was born Margaret Hawarden, the daughter of Sir John Stanley, knight. Her will was proved 17 January 1520. In her will she named Sir Otnell Hoghton ("Lancashire and Cheshire Wills" 7), Thomas Hoghton (11), and Sir Richard Hoghton (27). Margaret Hoghton was her goddaughter (10).

Lancashire setting in his "lost years." However, the fact that the Cheshire Arderns were acquainted with Peter Leigh of Lyme, who was related to Richard Hoghton of Hoghton Tower, is significant. The Cheshire Ardens should be studied as a possible route through whom Shakespeare could have been introduced to the Hoghtons.

Shakespeare and the Hoghton Will

The naming of William Shakeshafte in the 1581 will of Alexander Hoghton in Lancashire has led to speculation that Shakespeare was in Lancashire in his youth. If Shakespeare spent his late teen years in a Catholic home in Lancashire, as has been suggested by Chambers, Baker, and Honigmann, he would have been in an area that remained firmly committed to Catholiscism and for that reason was regarded by the government as posing a threat to Queen Elizabeth. He would have lived near families such as the Percies and Stanleys who themselves drew parallels between their present wrongs inflicted by Queen Elizabeth and those suffered by their ancestors under Henry IV.

Shakespeare would have been within sixty miles of the battlefields of the Percy Rebellion against Henry IV, dramatized by Shakespeare, and the later, and somewhat parallel, Rising of North of 1569, against Queen Elizabeth, two rebellions in which the Percy family played leading roles. Although the original Percy family seat was in Northumbria, in 1568 the earl of Northumberland, Thomas Percy, owned the manors of Tadcaster and Spofforth and was steward of the Liberty of Ripon in the West Riding of Yorkshire (Aveling 206). It can be seen these three places are within sixty miles of Houghton Tower and Rufford Hall, and they are situated at the heart of the area where the two rebellions centered in the West Riding. (See map.) Shakespeare's interest in the complaint of the Percy and Neville families in both rebellions might be attributable to the fact that in his late teens he lived near the scenes of action and was surrounded by people who had a stake in the causes. The *Henry* plays can be read as a justification for the Percy rebellion as retribution for the king's ingratitude toward the Percies, who helped Henry attain the throne. They simultaneously convey the contemporary message that the queen had behaved with similar ingratitude toward the Northern lords.

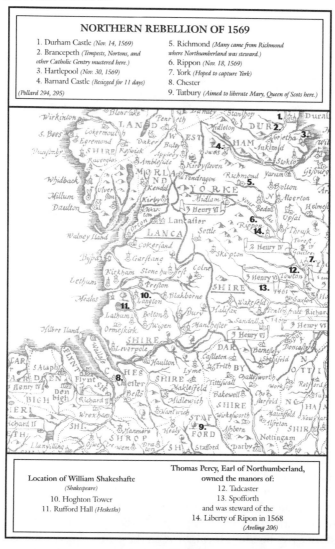

NORTHERN REBELLION OF 1569

1. Durham Castle *(Nov. 14, 1569)*
2. Brancepeth *(Tempests, Nortons, and other Catholic Gentry mustered here.)*
3. Hartlepool *(Nov. 30, 1569)*
4. Barnard Castle *(Besieged for 11 days)*
(Pollard 294, 295)

5. Richmond *(Many came from Richmond where Northumberland was steward.)*
6. Rippon *(Nov. 18, 1569)*
7. York *(Hoped to capture York)*
8. Chester
9. Tutbury *(Aimed to liberate Mary, Queen of Scots here.)*

Location of William Shakeshafte
(Shakespeare)
10. Hoghton Tower
11. Rufford Hall *(Heskeths)*

Thomas Percy, Earl of Northumberland, owned the manors of:
12. Tadcaster
13. Spofforth
and was steward of the
14. Liberty of Ripon in 1568
(Aveling 206)

Proximity of proposed Shakespeare Lancashire setting to Percy holdings in Yorkshire, the Wars of the Roses setting, and the area of the Northern Rebellion of 1569.
(Adapted from *"Shakespeare's Britain." National Geographic*, May 1964.)

In addition to proximity to these historical settings, Shakespeare's family was allied to the Percy and Neville families through the Park Hall Ardens. Edward Arden's sister, Barbara, married Richard Neville, descended from the first earl of Westmoreland (Stopes, *Shakespeare's Warwickshire Contemporaries* 123). Richard Neville's niece, Catherine, married Henry Percy, earl of Northumberland (125). Shakespeare's Catesby relatives were friends with another Percy, Thomas, who was a conspirator with the Catesbys in the Gunpowder Plot. He was a younger son of Edward Percy and second cousin of the ninth earl of Northumberland (refer to Gillow's "Thomas Percy"). Charles and Jocelyn Percy, close friends of the earl of Essex, are an additional Shakespeare/Percy connection. The Percy brothers, the third and sixth sons of Henry Percy, eighth earl of Northumberland, participated in the Essex conspiracy and were instrumental in persuading the Globe players to perform Shakespeare's *Richard II* before the insurrection (Barroll 446). The family ties between the Shakespeare family, combined with the possibility Shakespeare was in the midst of adherents and followers of the Percy and Neville families, would have been strong motivation for Shakespeare to focus on the deposition of Richard II as a precursor to the Wars of the Roses in order to make a contemporary statement regarding the relationship between the Northern Catholic lords with their Protestant queen. Envisioning a mature Shakespeare airing the parallel grievances of Northern families in his plays makes logical sense as an interest that stemmed from his acquaintance with those who were involved in disputes with their monarchs.

Similarly, other evidence—names and events long associated with Shakespeare—seem to fall into place naturally with the Lancashire setting. This can be seen if we investigate reports by three contemporaries: John Speed, William Beeston, and Richard Davies. John Speed's pairing of the names of Shakespeare and Robert Parsons places Shakespeare's name beside probably the most outspoken Catholic of the time. If Shakespeare really presented the ideas of Parsons on the stage, Shakespeare, too, was participating in the Counter-Reformation—exactly the kind of activity that was heavily supported by the Hoghton and Hesketh families. A Catholic dramatist echoing Robert Parsons' ideas on the stage could have had an early start as a schoolmaster in a Catholic home in his teen years. Perhaps William Beeston was right about Shakespeare when he said he was a schoolmaster in the country in his youth.

The third contemporary report comes from a man who may have been acquainted with Shakespeare. Richard Davies, chaplain of Corpus Christi College, Oxford, a little more than fifty years after Shakespeare's death stated with no equivocation, "Shakespeare died a Papist" (Schoenbaum 55). Upon what authority did Davies make this statement about the most private moment in Shakespeare's life? It is likely Richard Davies was related to two other Davies from Hereford who probably knew Shakespeare personally:

another Richard Davies (2) and the poet and writing master, John Davies, who praised Shakespeare in his own work. John Davies has intrigued Shakespeare scholars for years with his suggestion in his epigram no. 159, "To our English Terence, Mr. Will. Shakespeare" in *Scourge of Folly* (1610) that Shakespeare somehow could have been a companion for a king (200, 201). John Davies moved in the same circle Shakespeare moved in as evidenced by Davies' dedication to the earls of Pembroke and Montgomery, the two dedicatees of the first folio of Shakespeare's plays. Davies also dedicated a religious poem to the countess of Derby and her three daughters, and as it is generally accepted Shakespeare was a member of Ferdinando Stanley's acting group at the Derby household, it appears both Shakespeare and John Davies knew the countess of Derby. John Davies was commonly referred to as "of Hereford." The other Davies from Hereford, Richard Davies (2), was a Catholic priest who had been ordained in Rheims and then sent to England on the Catholic mission in 1577. John and Richard Davies priest of Hereford were either brothers or cousins. One of several aliases Richard used was "Hill," of interest in relation to Shakespeare because Shakespeare's step-grandmother was Agnes Hill, second wife of William Shakespeare's grandfather, Robert Arden. As priests often incorporated some part of the names of their sponsors or the mother's maiden surname, in their aliases, there is the possibility of a kinship between Richard Davies (2) and the wife of Robert Arden, Shakespeare's maternal grandmother.

It may even be that William Shakespeare, returning from his education abroad, was with the priest, Richard Davies (2) in 1580. A 1586 court deposition reported Davies "passed as a layman and was the principal person that received Campion, Parsons, and Edmunds and conducted them through England, and the corrupter of William Fitton's mother-in-law and all their family, with divers others" (DNB). The possibility Shakespeare guided Campion to Lancashire has already been suggested. In addition to leading Campion to the home of Richard Hoghton at Charnock Richard and to the Hoghton House in 1580—which was raided in 1581 because of Campion's visit (Honigmann 22)—they might have led Campion to the house of William Fitton, where Campion is known to have been. William Fitton was a brother of Mary Fitton's father, Sir Edward Fitton of Gawsworth, Cheshire.

Mary Fitton has often been associated with Shakespeare as a candidate for the Dark Lady of the sonnets. She must have been an alluring young lady to many besides Shakespeare. She became the mistress of William Herbert, the earl of Pembroke (mentioned in relation to the First Folio) and had an illegitimate child by him. In addition, the DNB indicates she had two illegitimate daughters by Sir Richard Leveson, knight. Honigmann shows Richard Leveson was a cousin of William Leveson, who was a trustee for the building of the Globe Theater in 1599 and was therefore someone Shakespeare knew.

Was there perhaps an even closer connection between the Levesons and Shakespeare? French notes Elizabeth Arden was the wife of Walter Leveson of Wolverhampton (French 453). He further shows Elizabeth Arden Leveson was probably a daughter of Walter Arden of Park Hall and therefore a sister of Thomas Arden, Shakespeare's maternal great-grandfather, which would make her Shakespeare's great-aunt. The Levesons were related to both the Ardens and the Fittons, and, interestingly, the Fittons were related by marriage to the Heskeths. Mary Fitton's mother was Alice Holcroft, who later married Sir Thomas Hesketh, the brother-in-law of Alexander Hoghton. This is the Thomas Hesketh who was to inherit Alexander Hoghton's players if his brother Thomas Hoghton decided he did not want them.

Many threads in these relationships seem to lead back to Shakespeare from the two Richard Davies, John Davies, Campion and Parsons, the Heskeths and the Hoghtons of Lancashire, Mary Fitton, the Levesons, the household of the earl of Derby, and the earl of Pembroke and the earl of Montgomery. Four of these connections to Shakespeare have been accepted by some scholars: Mary Fitton as a candidate for the Dark Lady, the earls of Pembroke and Montgomery in connection with the First Folio, William Leveson as a trustee for the Globe Theater, and the Derby family as patrons of the early acting group with which Shakespeare was associated. When these relationships are added to the fact Shakespeare may have had relatives who were descendants of his great-uncle Robert Arden/Ardern living near the earl of Derby and the Hoghtons, or relatives in Cheshire he knew who were friendly with the Hoghtons, the probability of equating William Shakespeare with William Shakeshafte of the will is increased.

A contemporary report adding fuel to the Shakespeare/Lancashire/ Catholic theory came from John Aubrey, who, in 1681, recorded in his biography of Shakespeare that he "understood Latin pretty well, for he had been in his younger years a schoolmaster in the country" (Honigmann 2). Aubrey was a collector of biographical stories about Shakespeare, and this particular one comes from an important source. As Honigmann shows, Aubrey went to Hoglane in Shoreditch to interview William Beeston personally because he had been told Beeston knew the most about Shakespeare. William Beeston (1606-1682) was the son of Christopher Beeston (d 1638), a minor actor with Lord Strange's Men and later an actor with the Chamberlain's Men (Honigmann 59), who progressed to being the manager of various theaters and eventually built the Phoenix Theater in 1616 (Schoenbaum 110). He was the most important figure in the London theater world from 1616 until his death in 1638 (110). It is certain Christopher Beeston and William Shakespeare knew each other personally.

For years, the idea Shakespeare was a schoolmaster in the country was not considered of much importance, but the discovery of Alexander Hoghton's 1581 will has stirred new interest in Beeston's story. Mutschmann and Wentersdorf show Christopher Beeston, long associated with Shakespeare in the Chamberlain's Men, was apparently a Catholic who was singled out by William Prynne when he observed "most of our present English *actors* [are] professed *Papists*" (103). No one has yet connected Christopher or William Beeston with Hugh Beeston, Esq., who was a visitor on several occasions in the Derby home (*Derby Household Books* 19, 50, 176). If Christopher Beeston was related to Hugh Beeston, Christopher's assertion that Shakespeare was a schoolmaster in the country becomes much more significant in tying Shakespeare to the Hoghtons and Heskeths, who were frequent visitors at the Derby home. If both Christopher Beeston and William Shakespeare were in the area, and both were apparently interested in acting, it would have been logical for them to join Lord Strange's theatrical group.

The theory Shakespeare was in Lancashire largely rests on the will of Alexander Hoghton of Lea, Esq., which was written 3 August 1581 and proved 12 September 1581. The passage of particular interest expresses Alexander Hoghton's concern that "William Shakeshafte" be placed with a suitable master after Hoghton's death:

> Yt ys my wyll that Thomas Houghton of Brynescoules my brother shall haue all my istruments (sic) belonginge to mewsycks and all manner of playe clothes yf he be mynded to keppe and doe keppe players And yf he wyll not keppe and manteyne players then yt ys my wyll that Sr Thomas Heskethe knyght shall haue the same instruments and playe clothes And I most herelye requyre the said Sr Thomas to be ffrendlye unto ffuke Gyllome and Willm Shakshafte now dwellynge with me and ether to take theym unto his servyce or els to helpe theym to some good Mr [master] . . . [He then names grants to a long list of "his servants," among whom are:] . . . ffoke Gyllom Willm Shakeshafte Thomas Gyllom . . . ("Lancashire and Cheshire Wills," 51: 238)

The Sir Thomas Heskethe named here has been noted earlier as the husband of Mary Fitton's mother, Alice Holcroft, and the association of Mary Fitton's name with Shakespeare is longstanding. Fulke Gyllom[19] apparently did move to the Hesketh home rather than going to Brynescoules because Honigmann notes he appears as a witness on a document for Thomas Hesketh's son ten years later (21). Honigmann also notes that the two names, Gyllom and Shakshafte, seemed to be paired twice as if they belonged together for some reason. He further shows that "Foulk Gillam" was the son of Thomas Gillam of Chester, who was a Broderer [embroiderer], and cites Keen as interpreting this to mean both father and son were guild-players (32).

---

19 The spelling of the name has many variations depending upon the source. The various forms used here are generally regarded as referring to the same person.

Honigmann presents a convincing account of "a folk tradition of long standing at Rufford which links Shakespeare with the Hall" (34). It was first recorded by Mr. Philip Ashcroft who said his grandfather, Lawrence Alty, told the tale to Ashcroft's mother (34). The story predates any other suggested connection between Shakespeare and the Heskeths at Rufford Hall. The Rufford "tradition" did not specify Shakespeare's role in the home. The later discovery of the Houghton will indicates that William Shakeshafte (Shakespeare?) was a player. William Beeston's observation (c. 1681) that Shakespeare was a schoolmaster in the country is another possible role. Such employment would, of course, have been secret and perhaps performed under an alias, so it is therefore difficult to identify such tutors. Many families retained private Catholic tutors in the same capacity Shakespeare is thought to have filled in the homes of Alexander Hoghton and Thomas Hesketh. Other branches of these families are known to have employed unlicensed tutors as shown by Honigmann:

An apostate priest informed Lord Burghley in 1592 that Richard Hoghton of Park Hall 'hath kept a recusant schoolmaster I think this twenty years. He hath had one after another; the name of one was Scholes, of the other Fawcett, as I remember, but I stand in doubt of the names.' The same informer claimed that Mrs. Anne Hoghton, the widow of Thomas II, kept at her house in Lea Richard Blundell, brother to William Blundell, of Crosbie, gent., 'an obstinate papist,' to teach her children to sing and play on the virginals; and that Mr. Bartholomew Hesketh (the brother of Alexander Hoghton's widow) 'had kept for sundry years a certain Gabriel Shaw to be his schoolmaster;' and that William Hulton of Hulton, Esq., a close friend of the Hoghtons, had kept a recusant school-master 'many years.' (20)

Whatever his role in the Hesketh household, his presence there could have been a stepping stone toward joining Ferdinando Stanley's acting group, and it is with Stanley's group of actors that we begin to get the first reliable information of Shakespeare's whereabouts and activities.

The Derby Household Book of 1588 records numerous visits by many members of the Hoghton and Hesketh families to the Derby home of Henry Stanley, father of Ferdinando, Lord Strange. Chambers and Honigmann suggest Shakespeare moved into Lord Strange's acting group after his association with the Hoghtons and Heskeths, a natural transition considering the frequent contact between the families. Plays were performed in the Derby home frequently, as shown by the entries, indicating Leicester's and the queen's players performed as well as other unnamed groups. There is considerable speculation as to whether Shakespeare might have been a member of what appears to be a group of players belonging to Sir Thomas Hesketh who played at the Derby household in 1587: " . . . on

Saturday Sr Tho. Hesketh, Players went awaie, . . . " (46). If Shakeshafte moved to the Thomas Hesketh household, he well could have moved there to join Hesketh's theater group.

These additional, and sometimes circumstantial, ties between Shakespeare and the Lancashire area corroborate the acknowledged fact Shakespeare began his acting career in Lord Strange's acting group.

Hathaway/Guillim Connection

Honigmann did not show a possible relationship between the Hathaways and the Gylloms (variants: Gyllom, Gwillim, Guillim, Gillam, and probably more). The following genealogy indicates the Gylloms were related to Anne Hathaway's family, and if this is true, the relationship would be important in verifying the association of Shakespeare with Fulke Gyllom in the Hoghton home. French outlines the relationship between the Gylloms and Hathaways:

> The quaint old heraldic writer, Guillim, was allied to a family of the name of Hatheway, . . . Without insisting that the Shottery family must be allied to the ancient house of Hatheway in Gloucestershire, we may bear in mind Mr. Hunter's argument for a common origin, where the name is peculiar, as is that of Anne Shakespeare's family; and it is evident that her father was a person of respectability and good means, and his grandson, Richard Hathaway, who is styled "Gentleman," became High bailiff of Stratford in 1626. (375, 376)

French therefore concludes (without insisting) the family of Shakespeare's wife, the Hathaways of Shottery, were related to the ancient Hatheway family who were related to the Herald, John Guillim, born at Hereford in 1565. Following French's strategy, the name, "Guillim," (in all its various spellings) is peculiar enough to suggest that the Herald Guillim is related to the broderer/actor Gylloms.

Because John Guillim became famous by publishing *A Display of Heraldrie* in 1610, his biography is better documented than the sketchy bits recorded about Thomas and Fulke. John Guillim was born at Hereford in 1565 and attended grammar school at Oxford, matriculating at Brasenose College, Oxford, in 1581. John Davies and Richard Davies were also from Hereford, and not surprisingly, John Davies and John Guillim were acquainted, for John Davies prefixed complimentary poems to Guillim's book on heraldry (DNB). The Guillims and the Davies were acquainted with each other, John Davies dedicated epigrams to Shakespeare, and Fulke Gyllom knew William Shakeshafte. Might this algebraic-type relationship, if solved, show that Shakespeare equals Shakeshafte?

The Gyllom actors' relatives, the Hathaway family, also had at least one member who was involved in the theater: Richard Hathaway (fl 1602). He is noted by the DNB as being a native of Warwickshire and "possibly related to the Shottery family." Richard Hathaway, Fulke Gyllom, and William Shakespeare all have in common the fact they were actors or playwrights. The names Hathaway, Guillim, and Davies have intriguing ties with both William Shakespeare and William Shakeshafte.

The Hathaways may be an even more direct link between Shakespeare and Lancashire, for they were related by marriage to the Ardens, the Cottams, and John Weever, antiquarian and poet who wrote about the Hoghtons and also dedicated poems to Shakespeare. (A connection between Weevers and the Cheshire Arderns is that the *Arderne Quarterings* shown in the record provided by the Cheshire Record Office indicates that the Weever family is quartered on the Arderne arms and that "Wever being [is] heir general of the Alderley branch of Arderne" (Omerod 97). It will be recalled a major thesis of Honigmann's is that Shakespeare was introduced to the Hoghton family by the Stratford schoolmaster, John Cottam.[20] John

---

20 John's brother, Father Thomas Cottam (spelled variously as Cottam, Cotham, and perhaps Catan), returned to England in 1580 with the Parsons/Campion contingent and was executed two years later. The Cottam brothers were from Tarnacre, eleven miles from Hoghton Tower, where Shakespeare may have been. Honigmann's theory is that John Cottam, Stratford schoolmaster from 1579 to 1581 (40), who later served as a witness to a Hoghton document of April 11, 1606 (46), perhaps introduced Shakespeare to the Hoghtons as a bright young schoolmaster around 1579/80. Honigmann earlier had shown the priest, Thomas Cottam, was a good friend of Robert Debdale, someone Shakespeare surely knew. Cottam entered the Society of Jesus in Rome before returning to England because of ill health (Allen 84). Thomas Cottam may have been named in the Hoghton will in which William Shakeshafte is named. Honigmann identifies "John Cotham," designated as a legatee in Alexander Hoghton's will of August 3, 1581, as John Cottam the Stratford schoolmaster (6), but he does not suggest "Thomas Coston," another legatee, might be Thomas Cottam, brother of John. Elizabethan spelling was variable, and names were often spelled differently within a single text, as the name "Cottam" may have been here. Additionally, Elizabethan script is difficult to decipher and has frequently been misconstrued by modern paleographers. Such a misreading may have produced "Coston" for "Cotham" or "Cottam." William Allen's account of the executions of the twelve priests associated with Campion's capture gives an account of Thomas Cottam's whereabouts. He left Rheims on June 5, 1580, was apprehended and committed to the Marshalsea June 27, 1580, was moved to the Tower December 4, 1580, and was executed on May 30, 1582. In August of 1581, Alexander Hoghton could not have known that Thomas Cottam was going to be executed within nine months, but he would have known that he was in the Tower and had living expenses, so it is possible that the grant to Thomas Coston (Cottam) in the will was made to meet those expenses. The Cottams are a clear tie between Stratford, Shakespeare, and the Hoghton family in Lancashire, as Honigmann has clearly outlined.

Weever seems to have been related to both the Arden and the Cottom families, and his sister probably married a Hathaway. Whether or not Weever was personally acquainted with Shakespeare, he was at least an admirer of Shakespeare's work and wrote verses "Ad Gulielmum Shakespeare" in his *Epigrammes* (1599). Weever was somehow connected with the Hoghton family, for he wrote a long poem about various members of the family. He seems to have been related to the Arden family as suggested in a note by Stopes which says that John Arden, a younger brother of the Cheshire Ardens, "settled at Alderley (Edward III), and ended in a few descents in a female heir, who married into the Weever family, whose heiress married the ancestor of Sir J. Stanley" (Stopes, *Shakespeare's Family* 233). This is a tenuous, but certainly interesting, connection. However, it becomes more significant with the added information that John Weever's sister (whom he identifies with the surname of "Caton") seems to have married a Hathaway. John Weever's will is printed in Honigmann (145), in which he names his sister, Anne Caton. This is probably Anne Catan of Loxley who married George Hathaway on October 22, 1570 (Bellew 379). There is nothing to indicate whether Anne Caton was a stepsister or perhaps a sister-in-law of Weever or if she became Widow Catan and then married George Hathaway. It does appear, however, John Weever, who was in some way related to the Ardens and the Stanleys, probably had a sister who was married to a Hathaway, was acquainted with the Hoghtons, and probably knew William Shakespeare.

The Stanley Connection

Honigmann offers additional links to support the theory Shakespeare was in Lancashire. One has to do with epitaphs, attributed to Shakespeare, for Sir Thomas (d 1576) and his son, Sir Edward, Stanley, in the chancel of Tong Church in Shropshire. Honigmann indicates Chambers dismissed the identification of the epitaphs as written by Shakespeare because of the discrepancy in the dates. Sir Edward, who owned Tong,[21] died in 1632, and Shakespeare died in 1616 (78). Honigmann believes, however, that because of financial problems, Sir Thomas was not able to afford the monuments himself and that his son probably commissioned them long before his own death (80). Sir Edward was a cousin of Lord Strange, and since Shakespeare was an actor with Strange's group, it was natural for Sir Edward to employ Shakespeare to write the epitaphs. Tong Castle is within fifty miles of Rufford Hall, Hoghton Tower, Lathom, and most of the other Lancashire settings which play important roles in the theory Shakespeare was in Lancashire in his youth.

---

21 Honigmann notes that Sir Edward was "of Winwick and Tong" (80). "Wynwhyck," was a beneficiary named in the will of Robert Arden, as noted earlier. Tong (in Shropshire) is within fifty miles of Winwick (in Lancashire).

The ties enumerated here between Shakespeare and the Lancashire setting are consonant with information we have about Shakespeare in later settings documented with greater precision. The early connections with Lord Strange's acting group and Shakespeare's later associates in the London theater world can be traced to Lancashire. The Hathaway, Davies, Fitton information relating to Shakespeare falls into line with facts and traditions about Shakespeare in later life. Nothing in any of the connections negates Beeston's report that Shakespeare was a schoolmaster in the country. The conclusion drawn from the present state of the evidence is there is a strong probability William Shakeshafte named in the will and William Shakespeare, playwright from Stratford, were the same person.

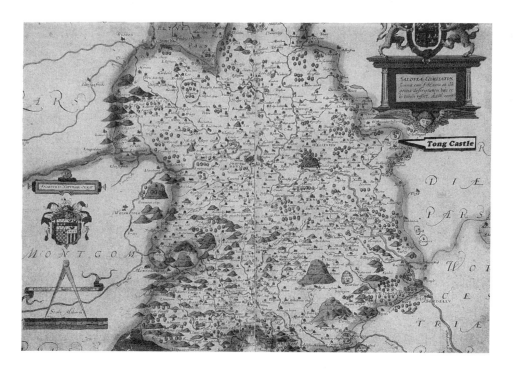

Shropshire (Adapted from Saxton map, 66/67.)

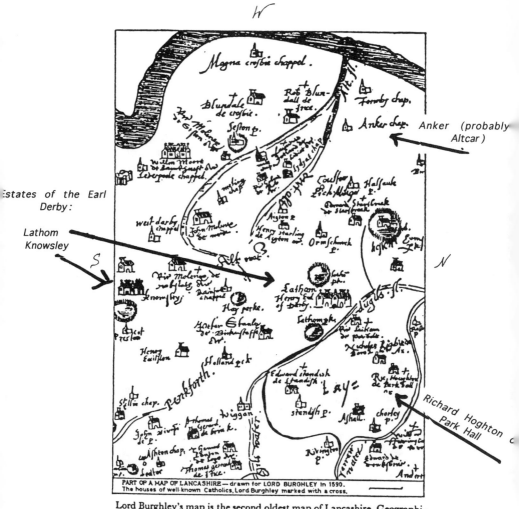

W

Estates of the Earl Derby:

Lathom
Knowsley

Anker (probably Altcar)

N

Richard Hoghton of Park Hall

PART OF A MAP OF LANCASHIRE — drawn for LORD BURGHLEY in 1590.
The houses of well-known Catholics, Lord Burghley marked with a cross.

Lord Burghley's map is the second oldest map of Lancashire. Geographically it has little use, but it was only intended to show the relative position of the houses of gentlemen, so that Burghley could the more easily take precautionary measures against hostility from Lancashire Catholics. The map is drawn with the west at the top, and the top of this section shows the coastline between the Ribble and the Mersey. The original map is in the British Museum, but it has been published by the Catholic Record Society under the title *Lord Burghley's Map of Lancashire, 1590.*

Part of a map of Lancashire—Drawn for Lord Burghley in 1590

The Shakespeares, the Ardens, and the Catholic Mission

William Allen recognized that if the Catholic faith were to survive, a means had to be devised to educate children in the Catholic faith, as well as to train Catholic priests to replace the few aging priests remaining in England. The man who envisioned solving this problem was a nexus linking Stratford with the Hoghton family. He may also have been the link between William Shakespeare, the seminaries, the Hoghton family, and especially with Edmund Campion, for the seminaries William Allen and Robert Parsons established in Douai/Rheims and Rome, along with other Catholic seminaries and schools that followed, became aligned with the Jesuits in the English mission in 1580. Allen was related to the Hesketh family, and it has been noted Allen may also have known John Shakespeare.

The Hoghtons and the Heskeths, in addition to being Catholics who would naturally have supported the Catholic schools, were relatives and friends of William Allen. William Allen and Thomas Hoghton I worked together on founding the seminary school at Douai, as shown by Honigmann: "Thomas I greatly assisted his friend, the later Cardinal Allen, in founding Douay College" (24). Thomas Hesketh, son of the Rufford

Thomas Hesketh and William Allen's sister, followed his uncle to Europe and remained with Allen (Heywood lxxiv) in his various posts at Rome, Douai, and Rheims. The first English College was at Douai from September 29, 1568, until it was forced by political difficulties to move to Rheims on March 22, 1578. During this ten-year period, the Douai buildings were used as a junior seminary "where students who were too young to bear arms and their professors were allowed to live" (Anstruther x). In addition, there were Jesuit colleges at Anchin (1569), at Eu near Dieppe (1582) and at St. Omer (1593) "where younger students could study humanities" (x). Another seminary developed at Rome in 1579. In Spain, a seminary was opened at Valladolid September 1, 1589, and another was founded at Seville in November 1592 (xi). Not every student who attended one of these Catholic schools had to declare for the priesthood. It simply was a way, albeit a dangerous way, for Catholic parents to assure that their children had a Catholic education.

It seems an odd omission in Shakespeare scholarship that no one has yet suggested Shakespeare attended one of these schools. The records for the Stratford grammar school are not extant for the time when he was of an age to have been a student there, but it is assumed that Shakespeare did attend the Stratford school. If he attended a Catholic school abroad after leaving grammar school, the most probable one would have been Douai or Rheims, staffed by Jesuit scholars, regarded even then as superior. An education in a Jesuit school would have provided Shakespeare with the excellent education he seems to have had. Some of his classmates would have been young men training for the priesthood who would have returned to England to save the Catholic religion there. If Shakespeare was a student in one of the Catholic schools abroad, it would help explain why it seems Shakespeare knew some of the priests personally.

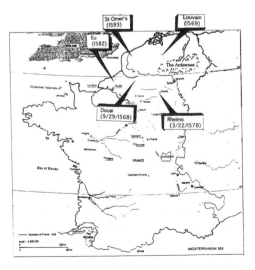

Catholic Seminaries in France and Belgium

86

As was shown earlier, the seminary priests who began filtering into England after 1575 were distinguished by the government from those priests who had been ordained in Mary Tudor's reign. These distinctions between the priests were to result in internal friction in the 1580s, which the Elizabethan government was only too happy to help fuel. "The latter [Marian priests] could be fined and imprisoned for recusancy and even hanged for being 'reconciled,' but they were not affected by this particular Act [Act of 27 Eliz. c. 2 (1585)] which stamped the seminary priests as traitors" (Anstruther ix). After 1585, the young priests trained at Allen's and the Jesuit seminaries entered the country at great risk because, by the new laws, they were traitors even though they were instructed to deal only with spiritual matters and not to deal in politics. Unfortunately, the pope, backed by Spain, unwisely planned an invasion of England by way of Ireland, making it appear the Irish invasion and the priests' arrival were linked.

The first official act in what was to be a systematic persecution of the Catholic priests occurred June 1, 1571, when Dr. Storey was kidnapped from exile in Spain and brought to England to be hanged, drawn, and quartered for having abetted a fellow exile at Antwerp (Simpson 62). Dr. Storey's martyrdom was a strong influence on Edmund Campion's decision to become a Jesuit. Although the Jesuits had not yet joined the mission, they were beginning to be recognized as a threat to the religious health of England.

The execution of Father Storey was followed by several more in the 1570s, and by the 1580s, the gallows and the butchers were kept busy. In 1573 Thomas Woodhouse who was first a Marian priest and is believed to have become a Jesuit in the Fleet Prison, was hanged for his refusal to subscribe to the religious changes (Bassett 17). In 1577 the first casualty of the treason act of 1571 fell when Cuthbert Mayne was executed for suspected Spanish intrigue in Cornwall. In 1578 two more priests were hanged, and then began the Catholic mission's intensive invasion of England. Spanish Ambassador Mendoza noted on December 28, 1579, that 100 priests in the seminaries were trained within twelve months and were in England secretly converting members to the Catholic faith (Pollard 372). By 1603, 450 priests had been smuggled into England (Leys 27). As noted earlier, John Shakespeare's retirement from public office and his seeming financial difficulties also occurring in 1577 coincide with the arrival of the priests and the increasing number of executions.

In 1579, Father William Allen and the Jesuit Robert Parsons had conferred at the English College at Rome, and after lengthy consideration, Father Mercurian agreed to send Jesuits to the English mission (Bassett 136). Father Parsons was appointed as the superior on the mission, and Father Edmund Campion was selected to go with him. These two men complemented each other; Parsons was a fiery, politically minded activist whereas Father Campion was devoted solely to spiritual matters. Campion's brilliance had attracted the queen's attention early in his career, and at her suggestion,

Leicester had patronized Campion at Oxford, anticipating that Campion's glorious renown would reflect well on the English Church. Because of the personal favor the queen and Leicester had shown Campion, Campion realized he would be hounded with particular alacrity and would eventually be martyred for having gone over to the enemy. Even after his conviction in 1581, Campion was repeatedly tempted to yield his Catholic faith and thereby save his life. If he yielded, McCoog states " . . . he was promised not only his life and liberty, but great preferment within the Anglican Church" (906).

The eleven members of Campion and Parsons' initial group left for England, traveling separately or in twos for safety, some leaving from Boulogne, some from Dunkirk, and some from Dieppe. Some dressed as returning prisoners of war, some as merchants, others as returning soldiers. Parsons was dressed in a captain's uniform "trimmed with gold lace with a hat and a feather to match" (Simpson 171). Although Campion accepted the orders of his general with the full knowledge he was probably going to his martyrdom, he could nevertheless appreciate the humor in their preparations, which he revealed in his description of Parsons as "such a peacock, such a swaggerer, that a man needs must have very sharp eyes to catch a glimpse of any holiness and modesty shrouded beneath such a garb, such a look, such a strut" (175). Campion himself was disguised as a merchant. Thomas Cottam, brother of the Stratford schoolmaster, John Cottam, joined the group to return to England in the hope his native air would cure a lingering illness. Parsons went immediately to the Marshalsea prison to get information from Thomas Pound, the Catholic relative of the Earl of Southampton. Pound had been imprisoned since 1574 but had somehow managed to help George Gilbert plan his association to finance and shelter the priests.

Perhaps part of the enormous amount of money needed to finance the mission came from recusant Catholics, raised through peculiar business deals such as those John Shakespeare transacted in the 1580s. All of the priests needed clothes, an identity cover, travel money, and money for other expenses such as books and religious items used in the mass. Some of the money must have been contributed by individuals who sponsored specific priests, the sponsor's name sometimes incorporated in the alias the priest used. Much of the expense was borne by George Gilbert, a young man who had inherited a fortune and used it to support the priests. He devoted the rest of his life to the mission, even at the expense of having to cancel his impending marriage. Gilbert made friends with Thomas Pound, who was in prison for religious reasons, and the two men founded the association of young men of good birth who would devote their lives and fortunes to assisting the priests on the mission. The members' duties were to prepare Protestants for conversion to the Catholic religion, to conduct the priests around the country, and to procure alms for the support of the priests. Gillow lists some of the members: Vaux, Throckmortons, Tichbornes, Abingtons, Fitzherberts, Stoners, Lord Oxford, Lord Henry Howard, Lord

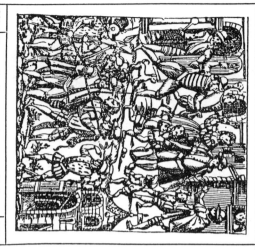

En quos Presbyteros pretio corruptus Judas
Prodidit, aut poenis legum conterritus hospes:
Funibus implicitos, claudendos carcere, custos
Accipit, in limbos et tetra ergastula trudens.

A SPY or False Brother will sometimes cry upon the Martyr in the street, as Tregonwell did on Sherwood. The Rabble, armed with the first weapons to hand, runs out upon him, and even the boys throw stones.

At last, surrounded by pike-men, tied with a rope, mocked by onlookers, he is led to prison, where the Keeper has ready the dungeon and the gyves.

Captos dum celebrant, in sacro lictor amictu
Raptat per medias populo insultante plateas.
Capti rure alii, manibus pedibusque ligati
Imponuntur equis, primusque voluntur ad urbes.

IF the Priest be captured at Mass, or with his Vestments, he is led to gaol clothed in them. Even the ladies may be dragged along with him.

F. Campion was carried to the Tower, pinioned and his feet tied beneath the horse's belly; an inscription on his hat, Torchmen in front and the Sheriff behind. The Keeper re-

Woodcuts from Pollen, *A True Report of the Death and Martyrdom of Jesuit and Priest*. Pages not given. (See Appendix II.)

III. EXAMINATION WITH TORMENT

Devincti ad carros, perque urbis compita ducti,
Libera servili lacerantur terga flagello.
Supplicio hoc functis, mox tanquam erronibus aures
Perfossae, igniti terebrantur acumine ferri.

SOME Catholics are flogged at the Cart's tail. Some are branded with irons, which are heated close by. But examination to find matter of death against oneself and others is worse still, and the Ministers are ever near to dispute.

IV. THE RACK

Ut quibus excepti domibus mysteria Christi
Egerunt, quosque a funesto schismate sanctae
Funxere Ecclesiae prodant, et talia multa,
Distendunt miseros diris cruciatibus artus.

THOSE who resist the lesser torments are racked. Their hands and feet are extended by ropes and windlasses while the questioning continues. Other prisoners are kept near enough to hear the cries and moans of the sufferer, and are warned to avoid his fate.

V. TO TYBURNE

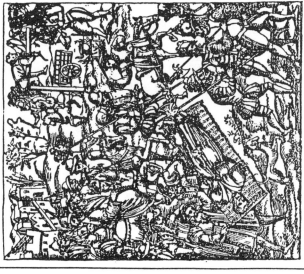

🙪🙪 🙪🙪
🙪🙪 🙪🙪
🙪🙪 🙪🙪
🙪🙪 🙪🙪

In crate viminea positi, lorisque ligati,
Per saxa ad furcas et per loca fœda trahuntur.
Carnifices laqueos, cultrosque, ignesque parati
Expediunt, primæque attendunt tempora mortis.

PINIONED to the wicker hurdle, which is dragged by a sorry nag, the Martyr is drawn from the Tower to Tyburne. Ministers worry him with arguments and quotation, but he turns away. In the distance the fire is crackling. One executioner prepares the noose, while another sharpens the knife. The cart is waiting.

VI. EXECUTION

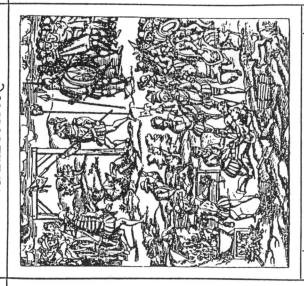

🙪🙪 🙪🙪
🙪🙪 🙪🙪
🙪🙪 🙪🙪
🙪🙪 🙪🙪

Ad breve suspensi tempus, cum morte secunda
Configunt, ferroque armatus viscera tortor
Eruit et flammis mandat: sed membra, capuique
Dissecat, et contis summa ad pinnacula figit.

CUT down ere fully dead, the Martyr sits up after the fall. The executioner cuts out his heart, which is shown to the people, then cast into the fire. The body is quartered, and the head and quarters are carried back on poles to be set over the city gates.

Paget, and Thomas Pound (Gillow "George Gilbert"), Thomas Salisbury (Gillow "Salisbury"), Henry Orton, Edward Brooksby, and Thomas Jay. Many of these were later executed in the Babington Plot of 1586. Pollen indicates there is no authentic roll of the conspirators who were involved in the Babington Plot and gives the list compiled by the government:

1. John Ballard, late of London, clerk.
2. Edward Wyndsore, late of Brandenham, Buck., Esquire.
3. Anthony Babyngton, late of Dethycke, in the county of Derby, Esquire.
4. John Savage, late of London, Gentleman.
5. Thomas Salysburye, late of Llewenny, Denbigh, Esquire.
6. Edward Abyngton, late of Henlyppe, Worcester, Esquire.
7. Chidiock Tychborne, late of Porchester, county Southampton, Gentleman.
8. Charles Tylney, late of London, Esquire.
9. Robert Barnewell, late of London, Gentleman.
10. Edward Jones, late of Cadogan, Denbigh, Esquire.
11. John Traves, late of Prescott, Lancashire, Gentleman.
12. Henry Dunne, late of London, Gentleman.
13. Gilbert Gifford, late of London, Gentleman. On the 27th of July two more joined:
14. Sir Thomas Gerrard, late of Wynwicke, Lancs., Knight. John Charnock, late of London, Gentleman. On the twelfth of August: Elizabeth (sic) Bellamy, late of Harrow on the Hyll, widow. A second indictment follows calling her 'Katherine'. Jerome Bellamy, of Harrow on the Hyll, Gentleman.
18. Robert Gage, late of London, Gentleman.

(cxvi, cxvii)

Looking in these lists for connections to William Shakespeare is a bit like bumping into a hornets' nest with so many connections flying about one cannot decide which to swat first. Some have been discussed elsewhere. In addition to those, a few of the more significant connections should be considered here in the order they appear in the lists.

John Savage. John Savage, conspirator in the Babington Plot of 1586, as described in the DNB, "probably belonged to the family of Derbyshire." John Savage, the conspirator, can be identified more precisely, however. He is shown to be of the "Rock Savage family" (*The Derby Household Books* lx). He is very likely related to Sir John Savage, who was a frequent visitor at the Derby home of Knowsley in Lancashire, as shown by several notations in the *Household Books* of his visits: "Saterday my L. Strandge retorned from London, & Sr John Savadge dep'ted" (52). Rock Savage was in the vicinity of the Derby home as it appears that Derby rode there easily: "On Sondaye Mr Rec'. dep'ted home; on Mondaye my L. Bushoppe of Chester & his wiffe & also Sr Edmonde Traifforth did all d'te awae; on Tvesday my L. rode to Rock Savadge; . . . " (34).

A relationship between John Savage, the conspirator, and Thomas Savage, the goldsmith who was a trustee for the financing of the Globe Theater in 1599, is not clearly defined in any of the sources used here, yet circumstantial evidence indicates they are from the same family. In addition, the Savages were connected with the Hesketh family, important if Shakespeare served in the Hesketh family. There are apparent connections between John Hemmings of London, as well as with Hemmings and the Savages who were acquaintances of John Shakespeare in Stratford. Leslie Hotson was the first to note the connection between Thomas Savage and the Hesketh family, a Lancashire tie Honigmann considers significant:

> When we find the player William Shakespeare in 1599 in London choosing as a trustee a man not only from Sir Thomas Hesketh's Lancashire village of Rufford . . . but also related to the Rufford Heskeths by marriage it clearly does not make [Chamber's] conjectural identification look less interesting. To be sure, we may have here an astonishing coincidence and nothing more. (Honigmann 34)

Thomas Savage's mother was probably Janet Hesketh, a sister or niece of Sir Thomas Hesketh to whom William Shakeshafte and the playclothes were willed in 1581 (Honigmann 85). After Thomas became a goldsmith in London, he seems to have maintained his ties and friendships with Rufford Hall (86). His relationship with the Heskeths is corroborated by the fact that Thomas Savage left to his cousin Hesketh, "widow, late wife of Thomas Hesketh of Rufforth, the sum of twenty shillings" (144). She was not the wife of the Thomas Hesketh to whose care William Shakeshafte was willed in 1581 but was probably the wife of one of his sons (84). Thomas Savage's eldest son was Richard Savage, who became an apprentice goldsmith in London in 1601 (85, 143). De Groot mentions a Richard Savage of Stratford, but no relationship is shown between the Stratford Richard and Thomas Savage's son. It is an odd coincidence, however, that there was a beadle in Stratford named John Hemmings, and the Savages and John Hemmings of the London theater were associated in London. Thomas Savage's youngest son was John Savage, to whom, according to his will, he left: " . . . the house in Addle St, parish of St Mary in Aldermanbury, 'wherin Mr John Heminges, grocer, now dwelleth.' (This is John Heminges, the actor, a member of Shakespeare's company, who belonged to the Grocers' Company)" (143).

There is no proof Thomas Savage of the Globe fame was related to the priest, a Babington conspirator, but the probability they were of the same family is increased because Thomas knew and was related to the Hesketh family and because John's family was friendly with the earl of Derby.

Thomas Savage obviously knew William Shakespeare and had business dealings with him. John Savage would have known the Hoghtons through the Derby connection and would have therefore at least been aware of William Shakeshafte. The likelihood John Savage, conspirator, is related to John Savage, the son of the Globe trustee and acquainted with John Hemmings and probably acquainted with Shakespeare, is increased because Savage and Shakespeare appear to overlap in the Lancashire environment, in the theater environment, and perhaps in Stratford. These types of relationships are probably impossible to prove because key records are no longer extant. However, the association of the names Savage, Hemmings, and Hesketh with both William Shakeshafte and William Shakespeare should not be totally discounted. These relationships could link Catholic priests; theater; Shakespeare; the Hoghton/Hesketh world; and obliquely, the Babington Plot.

Thomas Salisbury. Shakespeare must have been acquainted with the Salisbury family because he dedicated his untitled poem, now known as "The Phoenix and the Turtle," to "the love and merit of the true-noble knight, Sir John Salusbury [sic]" (Honigmann 91). The poem was first published in Robert Chester's "Love's Martyr" in 1601. John Salisbury married Ursula Stanley, illegitimate but recognized daughter of Henry Stanley, fourth earl of Derby. Thomas, who took part in the Babington Conspiracy, was the older brother of John Salisbury (Honigmann 91).

Abingtons. Shakespeare would no doubt have been aware of Sir Thomas Lucy's pursuit of Edward and Thomas Habington (Abington), accused of complicity in the Babington Plot. The fugitives took refuge at Hindlip Hall near Worcester (about fifteen miles from Stratford) in a hiding place so well concealed it took Lucy and his men eight days to discover it (Mutschmann and Wentersdorf 68). Lucy, a conscientious recusant hunter, was instrumental in the conviction and execution of Edward Arden. As has been noted, William Shakespeare was engaged in some type of controversy with Sir Thomas which may have caused Shakespeare to leave Stratford.

Charles Tilney. Charles Tilney was related to Edmund Tilney, master of the revels, although the DNB does not make the relationship clear. Both were from Shelley, Suffolk, and both were cousins of Emery Tilney. Shakespeare would have been aware Edmund Tilney was related to the theater at least by 1592 and probably earlier. This in no way proves Shakespeare knew Charles Tilney, but it is another example of the link between his name and Catholics.

A few additional and interesting links between participants in Catholic plots and Shakespeare's acquaintances and relatives include:

Thomas Pound. The Catesbys, the Earl of Southampton, and Thomas Pound were related. Thomas Pound was the uncle of the Earl of Southampton, Shakespeare's patron. The Earl of Southampton's cousin, Sir Henry Browne, married William Catesby's daughter. Shakespeare could have been acquainted with Thomas Pound through his Catesby relatives or through his patron, Henry Wriothesley, Earl of Southampton.

The Throckmortons. Of the many branches of the Throckmortons, the most likely to have been referred to by Gillow were members of the Catholic family of Sir George Throckmorton, Kt., of Coughton. Edward Arden of Park Hall had been in wardship to Sir George and married his daughter, Mary Throckmorton. Edward and Mary were the parents of Catherine, who married Sir Edward Devereux, and Margaret, who married John Somerville. Shakespeare could have known Edward Devereux in conjunction with the Essex Conspiracy, which Morey points out attracted Catholic followers and which the government labeled as a popish plot engineered by Spain. It has been shown Shakespeare was friendly with William Somerville of Park Hall. Robert Catesby and Francis Tresham, alleged ringleaders of the Gunpowder Plot, in 1605 were nephews of Edward and Mary Arden (Mutschmann and Wentersdorf 67). Thomas, Robert, and John Winter, also "ringleaders," were the grandsons of Mary Arden's aunt, Katherine Throckmorton (67).

The apparent reluctance of scholars to acknowledge the relationship of the Shakespeare family with the Park Hall Arden relatives probably stems from the Park Hall association with people like the Throckmortons and because of both families' involvement in several plots against Queen Elizabeth and James I. Shakespeare's great-grandfather, Richard Shakespeare, rented a farm from the Ardens at least by 1543, and Stopes suggests the Shakespeare family must have known the Park Hall Ardens because they knew of Robert Throckmorton in 1501. In a 1501 document, Robert Throckmorton was associated with Robert Arden of Wilmcote in Mayowe's transfer of the Snitterfield lands to Thomas Arden (Stopes, *Shakespeare's Warwickshire Contemporaries* 134). The association of Robert Arden and Robert Throckmorton, owner of Coughton, "in a manner which witnesses to great intimacy, . . . goes far to prove the relationship of Thomas Arden of Wilmcote to the Ardens of Park Hall, for this same Robert Throckmorton was also a trustee" (134). Thomas Arden was Mary Arden's grandfather. John Shakespeare's father rented the property from Robert Arden, who was to become Shakespeare's grandfather when John married Robert's daughter, Mary Arden. If Shakespeare knew the Park Hall Ardens, he undoubtedly also knew the Throckmorton family.

In tracing these acquaintances of Shakespeare, I repeatedly found threads that almost, but not quite, connect William Shakespeare with Edmund Campion. If Shakespeare had gone abroad to study after grammar school, he probably would have been at Rheims or Douai with some of the priests he already knew from Stratford. By 1580, he would have finished his study there, for he would have been sixteen and would have been ready to return to England. It is not hard to imagine, but very difficult to prove, Shakespeare met Campion and Parsons in Flanders and then offered, or was asked, to lead the priests to Stratford and on up to Lancashire after they

D. The Arden-Winter-Tresham-Catesby Connections

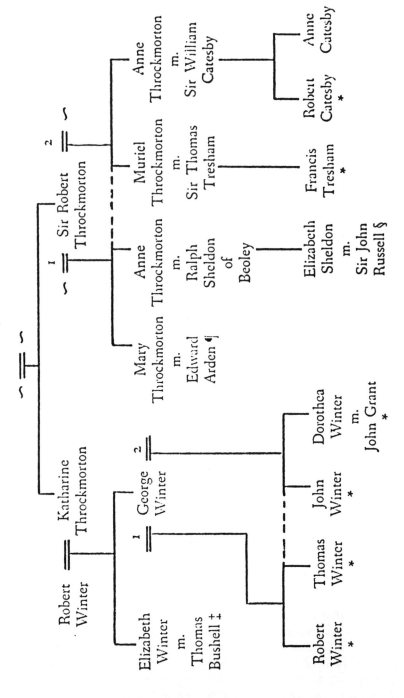

(Mutschmann and Wentersdorf)

stopped at Edward Arden's and William Catesby's in Stratford. Such a scenario could explain the presence of William Shakeshafte (William Shakespeare?) at the Hoghton house at that crucial time when Campion stayed with the Hoghtons in 1580. For "In 1580, according to *The de Hoghton Estate*, the Jesuit Campion had visited and preached in 'the house' (at Lea?), and the following year it was raided on that account" (Honigmann 22, 23). As noted earlier, Campion had stayed with Richard Hoghton, for " . . . when Edmund Campion was captured by the authorities in 1581, it was reported the Jesuit had stayed with leading Catholics in Lancashire, whose houses were searched by order of the Privy Council— and especially the house of Richard Hoghton, where it is said the said Campion left his books" (11).

One of the original ten priests who were in Campion's group was named Will Kemp, described by De Groot as a an "ancient, grave priest" (85). Unfortunately, there is no Will Kemp, priest, listed in Gillow or in Anstruther to provide biographical material for comparison with Will Kemp, the actor. How interesting a connection if this priest Will Kemp were related to the actor Will Kemp who knew Shakespeare so well. The actor Will Kemp's father may have been W. Kempe, "servant with William Holliday (15 April 1589)" (DNB). Shakespeare's actor friend knew "Mistris" Anne Fitton well enough to dedicate "Kemps Nine Daies Wonder" to her, and since she was the sister of Mary Fitton (Dyce 3), Will Kemp, the actor, had ties with Lancashire also. Father Will Kemp is not mentioned as having been martyred with the original group William Allen wrote about in his account of the executions of Campion and eleven other priests. All we can say at this point is Campion and Shakespeare each knew a man named Will Kemp.

The special association John Shakespeare and the Arden family had with Edmund Campion provides the most convincing evidence that Shakespeare knew Campion. Edmund Campion apparently was acquainted with a Robert Arden (of Warwickshire) at Oxford and remained in contact with him as late as 1577. Before Campion left Prague, on August 6, 1577, he wrote to a Robert Arden of Warwickshire: "If you are the Arden I fancy, this is not our first acquaintance; for we were members of neighbouring colleges in Oxford, I of St. John's, you of Trinity" (Simpson 121). Arden seems to have written concerning plans for "restoring and tilling that vineyard [England]" (121) and promised to produce a most abundant harvest. Might Campion have been corresponding with Robert Arden, eldest son and heir of Edward Arden of Park Hall, the son of Mary Arden's cousin Edward? French tells the story of Edward Arden's execution and then indicates the heir, Robert Arden, eventually retrieved his father's confiscated property after all the trees had been cut down. Robert refused to wear the Earl of Leicester's colors because Leicester had hounded and done away with Robert's father. If this is an early tie with Robert Arden, it strengthens my theory that Campion and Shakespeare were personally acquainted.

Shakespeare probably knew Robert Arden and his two brothers. French indicates the brothers, John and Thomas, accompanied the Earl of Leicester's contingent from Warwickshire in his expedition to the Netherlands in 1585 "in whose train it has been supposed that Shakespeare went, thither, . . ." (460). Shakespeare probably would not have gone as a soldier but was more likely a member of an acting group that accompanied the Earl of Leicester. Although a group of "musiconers" is listed as Leicester's servants, no actors are named, even though Will Kemp is known to have been with Leicester in the Low Countries (Thoms 120, 121). The facts that Shakespeare and Kemp were fellow actors later, and that Shakespeare can possibly be traced as a member of Leicester's company in 1589 (121) increase the probability Shakespeare would have accompanied his Arden cousins on the 1585 expedition to the Low Countries. This would have been a logical progression from schoolmaster—and probably budding actor and playwright in a private home—to being selected as an actor to accompany Leicester abroad.

Shakespeare could have become acquainted with some of Campion's writings during the time the two would have overlapped in Lancashire. Shortly before Campion's capture, on July 11, 1581, Campion was supposed to return to Lancashire "where he had left the greater part of his books and papers in the care of Mr. Houghton" (Simpson 309). Campion did not return to Richard Hoghton's Park Hall to retrieve his books, however, having been persuaded to stay at Lyford to preach to a group of nuns gathered specifically to hear him. There he was betrayed by the spy, George "Judas" Eliot. Ralph Emerson was sent to Lancashire to retrieve the papers, but the papers never caught up with Campion.

Campion had written a *History of Ireland* which had been confiscated by the authorities when he fled in disguise from Ireland in 1571, and he still did not know what had become of it when he died. Simpson shows that it was published in vol II of Holinshed's *Chronicles* in 1586 (59). A part of Shakespeare's *Henry VIII* is so close to Campion's wording as to be almost a paraphrase of it. It is generally known Shakespeare got his information from Holinshed, but it is not generally known Holinshed used Campion's *History* verbatim. If Shakespeare and Campion were in contact in 1581, earlier than when Holinshed published his *Chronicles*, Shakespeare could have acquired his information from the original source. In 1877 G. Wilkes noted the similarity between Griffith's vindication of Cardinal Wolsey and a passage in Campion's *History*:

From Shakespeare's *Henry VIII*:	From Campion's *History:*
This cardinal,	
Though from an humble stock undoubtedly,	They all hated the Cardinall. A man undoubtedly born to honour, exceeding wise, faire spoken, high-minded, full of revenge, vicious of
Was fashioned to much honour from his cradle.	
He was a scholar, and a ripe and good one:	

Exceeding wise, fair-spoken and persuading:
Lofty and sour to them that loved him not,
But to those men that sought him sweet as summer.
And though he were unsatisfied in getting,
(Which was a sin), yet in bestowing, madam,
He was most princely: ever witness for him
Those twins of learning that he raised in yon
Ipswich and Oxford! one of which fell with him,
Unwilling to outlive the good that did it;
The other, though unfinished, yet so famous,
So excellent in art, and still so rising,
That Christendom shall ever speak his virtue.
His overthrow heaped happiness upon him;
For then, and not till then, he felt himself,
And found the blessedness of being little:
And to add greater honour to his age
Than man could give him, he died fearing God. (4.2.48-68)

his body, lofty to his enemies, were they never so bigge, to those that accepted and sought his friendship wonderful, courteous, rype schooleman, thrall to affections, brought a bed with flattery, in-satiable to get and more prince-like in bestowing; as appeareth by his two Colledges at Ipswich and at Oxenford, th'other unfinished and yet as it lieth a house of students incomparable through Christen-dome. . . . A great preferrer of his servants, advancer of learning, stoute in every quarrel, never happy, till his overthrow. Therein he showed such moderation and ended so patiently that the houre of his death did him more honour than all the pompe of life passed.

Mutschmann and Wentersdorf also note the similarity in the characterization of Wolsey by Shakespeare and Campion. They point out scholars disagree on the extent to which the play can be attributed to Shakespeare, but they have determined it should be assumed the portrait of Wolsey is by Shakespeare (302). They further show the criticism of Cardinal Wolsey is in line with Catherine of Aragon's assessment of him as ambitious, without pity, and duplicitous. The light Wolsey saw at the end of his life in the two excerpts above, they observe, was in accordance with contemporary Catholic accounts of Wolsey (302). It could be a young scholar

(Shakespeare?) at the Hoghton house served as a scribe for Campion, who was dictating the history which was later lost. This is speculation, of course, but it is speculation based on some very peculiar coincidences.

Campion probably left his books at Park Hall, the home of Richard Houghton, illegitimate son of Sir Richard de Hoghton (d 1559) and brother of Thomas Hoghton I who took refuge in Belgium because of his Catholic faith. Simpson's quote above in regard to the books specifies it was at the home of "Mr." Hoghton and not "Sir" Hoghton, which would have been the title of Alexander Hoghton and Richard Hoghton, Alexander's nephew. If Shakespeare was a schoolmaster or member of an acting group at Lea Hall or Hoghton Tower, it is probable he, too, would have at least visited Richard Hoghton.

A friendship between Campion and Shakespeare might explain why the mulberry tree seems to have a special meaning in their lives. Shakespeare planted a mulberry tree at his Stratford home, New Place, that was subsequently cut down by a later owner of the property because he was plagued by souvenir hunters who wanted a piece of the tree. It is entirely possible the tree is not related to Campion, and yet there is a story about Campion and a mulberry tree that could explain how it took on a special meaning for a Catholic. Simpson tells the story of Campion's vision in a mulberry tree which foretold his martyrdom:

> Schmidl, however, tells us that Campion's presentiment of martyrdom was grounded upon a vision he saw in the garden at Brunn, where the Blessed Virgin, in likeness as she is painted in the picture at Santa Maria Maggiore at Rome, attributed to St. Luke . . . appeared to him in an old Mulberry-tree, and exhibited to him a purple cloth, which he understood to be a sign that he was to shed his blood for religion. (104)

Shakespeare's tree could have been a memorial to Campion, the martyr, as well as to Campion, the friend.

There are situations in Shakespeare's plays which seem to be subtle allusions to the martyred hero for the theater audience, or sometimes a turn of phrase echoes an idea or phrasing of Campion's. Shakespeare may have adopted some of Campion's thinking out of sheer admiration for Campion's intellect, or perhaps as a way of memorializing Campion or perpetuating his impact. This special tie between Shakespeare and Campion is deeper than the fact they seem to have had the same acquaintances in Stratford and Lancashire. The subtle allusions to Campion in the plays reveal a deep admiration for a remarkable man, a man who may have served as a role model for the scholar Shakespeare became.

Shakespeare perhaps adopted Campion's idol, Sir Thomas More, for such a reason. Campion's life sometimes paralleled More's life, and

Campion was known to have emulated More. G. Marc'hadour noted Campion's admiration of More: " . . . Campion voit en lui moins l'écrivain que le martyr. Le précédent de More l'inspire quand lui-même confesse sa foi par la plume, puis au prix de sa liberté et de sa vie" (203). Marc'hadour further notes that when Campion was teaching in Prague before being called to the English Mission, he wrote an account of Henry VIII's divorce in which a long passage evokes the resistance of More (203). Thomas Merriam suggests that Shakespeare was influenced by Sir Thomas More, and the influence "is not difficult to detect, providing we make allowance for the fact that an obvious influence would have been likely to attract adverse attention from the Master of the Revels" (91). It seems probable Shakespeare admired both More and Campion and was influenced by Campion's attachment to More.

It may be Shakespeare followed Campion's lead in adopting Catholic heroes from the history of Henry VIII's time, which Shakespeare used as examples and models of his current mode of thinking or belief. Heroes from history could safely be used for a subversive purpose. Shakespeare's revision of several pages of Anthony Munday's *Sir Thomas More* links it with the rebellion of the Earl of Essex, as Schoenbaum infers: "If 'Sir Thomas More' was written then [1600 or 1601]—and this is only speculation—its theme of rebellion and execution would assume an ominous topical significance" (217). Anthony Munday was the spy whose testimony against Edmund Campion was instrumental in Campion's conviction and execution. Shakespeare may have derived particular pleasure in revising Munday's play to suit his own ends in a manner meeting with Campion's approval.22 Munday's role in Campion's trial might also have been an influence in the battle over the character of Falstaff in Shakespeare's *Henry IV* plays. The rivalry between the Admiral's Men and the Chamberlain's Men, which involved the characterization of Falstaff from two opposing religious points of view, could very well have grown out of Munday's role as a spy against the Catholics and the witness directly responsible for the death of Edmund Campion. When Shakespeare satirized Oldcastle as a comic Protestant martyr and was forced to alter the character to a less objectionable "Falstaff," Munday joined in the vindication of the Cobham ancestor as part-author of *The Life of Sir John Oldcastle*. There is an interesting overlap between these heroes, Sir Thomas More, Edmund Campion, and the Earl of Essex (see "Essex, Southampton, and Shakespeare" below) with Shakespeare.

---

22 Greg identifies "Hand S" as that of Anthony Munday and further defines the hand as "responsible for the whole of the original fair draft" and it "took no part in the revision." Greg suggests "Hand D" "may be Shakespeare's" and "D" completes the insertion begun by two other writers, "B" and "C" (45).

If Shakespeare obtained his remarkable education in a Jesuit school abroad, some of the puzzlement about the exceptionally high quality of his knowledge and training would be resolved. I visited St. Omer, Douai, and Louvain in January 1996 in the hope of tracking down some tie between Shakespeare and one of the schools, but none of the original seminary buildings presently exists, and the records for the crucial years are difficult to obtain or lost. Sadly there is little local memory of the English Counter-Reformation schools. In Douai, a William Allen Association has been established to foster interest in the subject, but there was little evidence in St. Omer or Louvain that the history of the English schools has elicited much interest. The registration records available should be carefully searched to see if Shakespeare's name, or a logical pseudonym, is listed there from 1576 through 1581. Anstruther indicates the book of matriculations at Louvain University was printed by A. Schillings in 1961 and covers the sixteenth century. The records for Douai and Rheims are housed in the Westminster Library in London (Anstruther xi). It is unlikely the name, "William Shakespeare," would have been recorded in the register because it was common for the students to use an alias for protection but if one came across, for example, a "William Hoghton," whose family cannot be identified, such a name would warrant further investigation.

There are fewer possible ties between Parsons and Shakespeare than between Campion and Shakespeare. The only direct association of the two comes from the contemporary Puritan historian, John Speed. Speed suggested, in his *History of Great Britaine* (1611, first published in 1587), there was a relationship between the two: "And his (Person's) [sic] authority, taken from the stage-players, is more befitting the pen of his slanderous report than the credit of the judicious, being only grounded from this Papist and his poet, of like conscience for lies, the one ever feigning and the other ever falsifying the truth . . ." (Devlin 25). A more complete quotation from Speed's *History of Great Britain* by Titherley adds: "That N.D. [Nicholas Doleman was believed to be the pseudonym for Parsons], author of the three conversions, hath made Ouldcastle a Ruffien, a Robber, and a Rebell, and his authoritie taken from the Stage-players . . . " (42). Speed does not name either Parsons or Shakespeare directly in either quotation cited here, but his allusion to both of them as being connected in the depiction of Oldcastle is clear. Devlin's conclusion is John Speed "was not a fanatic; he was intelligent and aimed at being judicious" (25) and there "must have been some ground for his accusation; and the only possible ground is that Shakespeare's plays in his lifetime were believed to be guardedly but consistently pro-Catholic" (25, 26). Devlin sees a relationship between Speed's pairing of Shakespeare with Parsons as a kind of rebuttal to both Shakespeare's *King John* and *Henry IV* plays and Parson's diatribes against the Protestant religion. It seems Speed regarded the plays as vehicles for a Catholic interpretation of actual history, afoul of his own Puritan ideas.

Linking Shakespeare with the Jesuit Parsons by an intelligent contemporary is a primary source, unfiltered by 400 years of scholarship.

To summarize, Shakespeare's family connections with the mission were routes by which Shakespeare would have been in close proximity to the priests and their activity. It is also a realistic possibility he attended one of the Catholic schools abroad after leaving the Stratford grammar school, where he would have had many future priests as classmates. He surely was acquainted with some of the priests who had ties with Stratford such as Robert Debdale and Thomas Cottam, both of whom were executed for treason in the prescribed Elizabethan manner. In addition we have John Speed's report that Shakespeare and Parsons were connected in some way. It also appears Campion may have corresponded with Shakespeare's distant cousin, Robert Arden. Shakespeare's near-paraphrase of a part of Campion's book in the play, *Henry VIII*, suggests the possibility he knew Edmund Campion personally. The close association of the Shakespeare and Arden families with the priests and Edmund Campion, in particular, are direct links to the Hoghton and Hesketh setting where Campion went immediately upon leaving Stratford in 1580.

Essex, Southampton, and Shakespeare

Shakespeare's role in the Essex Rebellion has stimulated much speculation, usually resulting in the complete exoneration of Shakespeare as a confederate of Robert Devereux, earl of Essex. This is a peculiar conclusion, even if one does no more than set up an equation of the relationship between earl of Southampton, Shakespeare, and Essex. Southampton was the bosom friend of Essex, and Southampton was also extremely close to Shakespeare. It seems unrealistic to conclude Shakespeare did not know Essex well. This relationship and the fact Shakespeare's play was used to rouse the Essex followers to victory make it difficult to envision Shakespeare as an aloof playwright unaware of the intrigue about him. A more general view of Shakespeare as a participant in historical controversy can be used in corroboration with what I see as Shakespeare's relationship to Essex:

> Shakespeare's historical plays are not just *reflections* of a cultural debate: they are *interventions* in that debate, *contributions* to the historiographical effort to reconstruct the past and discover the methods and principles of that reconstruction. They are as much locations of historical controversy as the history books: they are, in themselves and not derivatively, historiography. (Pugliatti 239)

Even before the fatal rebellion of the earl, Shakespeare appeared to have supported Essex through a favorable parallel he drew in the *Henriad* between Essex and Henry IV. At least that was a common contemporary explanation of Shakespeare's *Henry IV* plays. As we observed with the figure of Richard II, the character of Henry IV in the plays might also have had the capacity to assume a chameleon-like coloration, depending upon Shakespeare's immediate purpose. There are definite parallels between the return of Essex from Ireland and Henry IV's return to England. Just as she had done with the Richard II play, however, it would have been to Queen Elizabeth's advantage to deflect any allusion to her as Henry IV, and therefore to her advantage to foster the impression that Shakespeare was alluding to Essex. This apparent praise of Essex could have served as a rationale for the government's suspicion of the motives that led to the special presentation of Shakespeare's *Richard II* the day before the uprising.

The government questioned the motives of the players, for Shakespeares's colleague in the Chamberlain's Players, Augustine Philips, was called to depose before the court during the Essex trial. On February 18, 1601, Philips explained the staging of the play:

> On Thursday or Friday sevennight, Sir Chas, Percy, Sir Josceline Percy, Lord Monteagle, and several others spoke to some of the players to play the deposing and killing of King Richard II, and promised to give them 40s. more than their ordinary, to do so. Examinate and his fellows had determined to play some other play, holding that of King Richard as being so old and so long out of use that they should have a small company at it, but at this request they were content to play it. (Albright, "Shakespeare's *Richard II* . . . ." 690)

This explanation seemed to suffice to clear the Lord Chamberlain's Players, for there is no evidence that they were punished (690).

Behind this one presentation at the time of the Essex uprising, however, was a long history of unauthorized presentations of the play which delighted Essex and perturbed Queen Elizabeth. There is some evidence Robert Cecil initiated the idea of using the play in connection with Essex in 1595 when it was a new play. Even in those early days Raleigh, Robert Cecil, and Essex viewed the play as having a special connection with Essex's claim to the throne. It appears the use of the play in relation to Essex was part of Robert Cecil's plan either to set him up for a fall or to uncover any designs Essex had for succeeding to the throne on Elizabeth's death—all the while, of course, pretending to be a friend of Essex. Cecil's design may explain why on December 7, 1595, Sir Edmund Hoby invited Robert Cecil to his home for a private viewing of the play (697). Later, on July 6, 1597, Raleigh wrote to Robert Cecil about the play and its connection with Essex:

> I acquainted my Lord Genrall [Essex, then in command over Raleigh on the expedition] with your letter to mee, and your kind acceptance of your entertaynment. He was also wonderfull merry at your consayt of Richard II. I hope it shall never alter, and whereof I shalbe most gladd if it is the trew way to all our good, quiet, and advancement, and most of all for her sake whose affairs shall truely fynd better progression I will ever be yours. (698)

This could be evidence that at one time Robert Cecil backed Essex as the successor, and then again it could be Raleigh and Cecil were plotting to eliminate Essex to clear the path for James I. The play obviously had a significance beyond its theatrical appeal. It did for Essex as well, for he took great delight in attending the performances, as was stated at the trial:

Essex's own actions confirm the intent of this treason. His permitting underhand that treasonable book of *Henry IV* to be printed and published; it being plainly deciphered, not only by the matter, and by the epistle itself, for what end and for whose behalf it was made, but also the Earl himself being so often present at the playing thereof, and with great applause giving countenance to it. (Albright, "Shakespeare's *Richard II* . . . " 701)

The book referred to here was Sir John Haywood's *First Part of the Life and Raigne of King Henrie the Fourth*, published in 1599, although it had been contemplated and was in the process of being written for some time. Albright suggests Shakespeare's play and Haywood's book were connected in some way, and the above quotation shows the play was regarded as a staging of the book. The queen complained that unauthorized presentations of it had been played in the streets forty times. Whether the forbidden deposition scene, an original addition to the actual history by Shakespeare, was played in these unauthorized versions is not revealed. If read as criticism of the contemporary scene, both contained very dangerous material. The queen's life had been threatened repeatedly, so an analogy between her possible fate and Richard II's would naturally have displeased her. Probably more important in Elizabeth's estimation was the fear that criticism of Henry IV for having executed his cousins could have been criticism of her for having executed her cousins; the duke of Norfolk; and Mary, Queen of Scots. The play provided an opportunity to refer to contemporary England, and specifically to faults in the Elizabethan management of government. Evelyn Albright identified the following parallels: the reign of favorites, exaction of benevolences, and excessive taxation (693).

An argument developed between Essex and Robert Cecil that eventually became an open one, in which each side accused the other of collusion with Catholics. Essex claimed Cecil was dealing with Philip of Spain in favor of the Infanta as successor, a claim that may have had some validity. Cecil, on the other hand, charged Essex with being engaged in a popish plot, and Essex was indeed involved with a number of Catholics. The government knew all about Essex's designs on the throne and about the support he was receiving from Catholics. In fact, Robert Cecil's sharpest accusation against Essex at the trial was for being a Catholic: "God be thanked, we now know you; for indeed your religion appears by Blount, Davis and Tresham, your chief counselors, and by your promising liberty of conscience hereafter" (Mutschmann and Wentersdorf 123). As has been noted, at the trial,

Attorney General Coke described Essex and his followers as "a Catiline, popish, dissolute and desperate company" (123). Some evidence suggests James VI of Scotland favored the Catholic religion at this time, and communication between Essex and James VI suggests Essex at some point was backing James as a successor. (See my discussion of *Hamlet*.) Once Essex was eliminated, Robert Cecil skillfully moved over to James's side and continued in office as the king's principal advisor.

The extent to which Shakespeare was expressing his own opinions in the play about the state of the union and the extent to which he wrote to please Southampton probably can never be determined. However, he had reason to have more than just a dramatist's interest in all that surrounded Essex and the selection of *Richard II* as the particular play to be shown in conjunction with the rebellion. Shakespeare must have been well acquainted with several of Essex's followers, who were citizens of Stratford, and in some cases, were relatives of Shakespeare's own family. Stopes shows the names of John Arden and Sir Henry Neville appear on a list of twenty-eight followers of Essex (Stopes. *Shakespeare and the Third Earl of Southampton* 197, 202). Henry Neville was probably related to Edmund Neville, a relative of Edward Arden of Park Hall.[23] Neighbors of Shakespeare from Stratford who participated were Robert Catesby, William Green, John Wheeler, John Arden ("What Was the Religion . . . ?" 305). Thomas Greene (d 1590) and the sons Thomas, John, and Richard, all cousins of Shakespeare (Fripp, *Shakespeare, Man and Artist* 245) were possibly related to Willliam Green.

The most important connection between the Ardens, Essex, and possibly Shakespeare is that Robert Devereux, the earl of Essex, was the halfbrother of Sir Edward Devereux, Baronet, who married Catherine, daughter of Edward Arden. This relationship has never been recognized to my knowledge. Although French delineates the marriage between Catherine and Edward Devereux, he does not show the relationship between Edward and Robert Devereux (French 458, 459). The grandfather of Essex, Walter Devereux, viscount Hereford, outlived his firstborn son. Richard died in Walter Devereux's lifetime and left a young family—Walter, George, Elizabeth, and Anne. This young son, Walter, became Lord Ferrers of Chartley and Viscount Hereford. Walter married Lettice Knolleys in 1561-62, and their son was Robert Devereux (Stopes, *Third Earl of Southampton* 39).

---

23 An older Sir Edward Neville was executed 1538. His grandfather was the uncle of Richard Neville, the king-maker. His eldest daughter married Clement Throckmorton, son of George Throckmorton, of Coughton, Co. Warwick (DNB). Edward Arden's wife was Mary Throckmorton, daughter of George Throckmorton (French 458). Edmund Neville, a conspirator in the Gunpowder Plot, was a nephew of of Edward Arden on the mother's side and was connected with the earl of Westmorland on the father's. In the Parry Plot of 1584, he turned Queen's evidence and condemned his accomplice and cousin, Parry (Pollard 388).

Edward Devereux was his youngest son by Margaret, his second wife. The tomb of Sir Edward Devereux (d 1622) and of his wife, Katharine Arden (d 1627), are preserved in the Church of Aston, near Birmingham, beside those of her ancestors, Walter and Eleanor [the grandmother?] (Stopes, *Shakespeare's Family* 231).24 It seems more than coincidence that Shakespeare's play just happened to be the play that suited the rebellion, and Shakespeare just happened to be distantly related by marriage to the brother of the earl of Essex. This is a much closer connection between Shakespeare and the Earl of Essex and his cause than has been recognized to this point.

A key supporter of Essex before and throughout the rebellion was Henry Wriothesley, earl of Southampton and Shakespeare's patron. In spite of the queen's effort to mold Henry Wriothesley into a good Protestant after his father died, placing him in wardship to Lord Burghley and later to the earl of Pembroke, he seems to have remained loyal to his family's Catholic faith. Henry Wriothesley's father was a Catholic noted for sheltering a Portuguese Jesuit along with other Catholics he was protecting in 1573, and he had earlier been sent to the Tower for his part in the Catholic Northern Rebellion. He appears to have played a role in the Catholic mission, as there was direct contact between Campion, Thomas Pound, and the earl when the mission first arrived in 1580, a year before the earl died. According to Rowse: "We find his cousin Pound—later sent to Wisbech Castle as a noted Recusant in time of danger—aiding Father Campion and giving him a token to direct to Dymoke in order to gain access to Southampton" (40). Mutschmann and Wentersdorf also indicate the elder Southampton and his wife, the countess, were in contact with Campion in 1580-81 (109). Through the Catesby connection, there was a family tie with Mary, countess of Southampton, Shakespeare's patron's mother. William Catesby's daughter, Anne, married Sir Henry Browne, son of the first Lord Montague, and Sir Henry was the brother of the countess of Southampton ("What Was the Religion . . . ?" 170).25 This relationship has been referred to earlier, but it seems important to highlight the family connection between Shakespeare and Southampton here.

---

24 This Katharine Arden was the daughter of Edward Arden, who inherited Park Hall on the death of his grandfather in 1563 (French 458). Edward Arden's grandfather was a cousin of Mary Arden Shakespeare's father. This relationship may seem distant by modern practice, but Whitfield shows that the Shakespeares and Park Hall Ardens were friendly and acknowledged the family relationship.

25 A later reference to the Catesby/Southampton relationship calls Robert Catesby the uncle of Southampton ("What was the Religion of Shakespeare?" 309).

The young earl of Southampton may have been a connection between Shakespeare and the mission activity because of Southampton's relationship to Thomas Pound, one of the founders of the mission who seemed to be perpetually impounded. Pound's mother was Anne Wriothesley, sister of Thomas, earl of Southampton (Gillow, "Thomas Pound"). Evidence the young earl remained a Catholic is the inclusion of his name on a 1604-05 list of recusants, and the fact Southampton's house was searched in January 1605 for papist literature that was confiscated and burned (Mutschmann and Wentersdorf 112). It is clear Shakespeare's patron was raised Catholic in his very young years, and in spite of his having been placed in wardship, "he seems to have grown up in the care of his mother, and she brought him up a Catholic" (28).

The offer and the acceptance of patronage was a mutual agreement that denoted an affinity of ideas beyond any reward of money or prestige. The friendship between Southampton and Shakespeare is strong evidence Shakespeare was a Catholic, for if the two disagreed on the profound question of religion, how could they agree at all? To return to the opening discussion, the evidence simply does not support the argument that Shakespeare represented Protestant views because his patron, the earl of Southampton, was a Protestant. The interconnection of the Ardens, Catesbys, Southamptons, Essex, Campion, and Shakespeare should be taken into account if one is to solve the problem of Shakespeare's religious beliefs. Their relationship is positive support for Shakespeare's Catholicism.

Un-Whole-Some Hamlets

Very few would argue against the idea that Shakespeare was pondering religious issues as he wrote *Hamlet*. However, beyond that point of agreement, interpretations diverge. The ghost has been interpreted as a Catholic ghost returned from purgatory, a "post-Christian" pagan ghost (Reed 130), the spirit of old England, a Protestant devil, etc. It is clear to most critics the ghost has a religious significance, but there is not much agreement about the meaning or about the significance of the religious overtones pervading the play. A recent religious controversy over *Hamlet* suggests Shakespeare was covertly depicting the argument between Henry VIII and Martin Luther, and Hamlet represents Martin Luther (Remnick, *The New Yorker* 66-81). If that theory is correct, all of the circumstantial evidence presented here indicating Shakespeare was a Catholic is overturned. It is indeed difficult to picture Shakespeare as having rejected all of the Catholic influences presented above to become a proponent of Martin Luther, and until more convincing evidence is forthcoming, I will continue to interpret Shakespeare's works as those of a Catholic.

Reading *Hamlet* in the light of its contemporary setting perhaps can illumine at least a part of Shakespeare's own struggle to resolve some personal conflicts, for Hamlet reveals much about Shakespeare himself. Understanding the political backdrop Shakespeare had in mind when he wrote *Hamlet* is a good beginning point. With that in mind, I propose to take a pragmatic route to recreate part of the political scene of the years 1598-1600 to uncover any possible cause the play might support. I have chosen 1598 as the earliest possible date because it seems likely that Lord Burghley was still alive when the pointed characterization of Polonius was written. The play is not mentioned by Meres in 1598 (Craig, 899), which indicates it was not written before that year. The original Q1 may date from 1598-1601 (900), suggesting 1601 is the latest limit.

By 1598 the question of the succession to Queen Elizabeth had become a critical issue that could hardly be discussed openly. The fact she was aging could not be disguised by the inch-thick paint on her face and neck, yet she refused to name a successor.26 The idea of masking one's age in such a manner seems odious to Hamlet: "I have heard of your paintings too, well enough; God had given you one face, and you make yourselves another" (3.2.148-50). He sneers at the futility of hiding from death when he instructs Yorick's skull: "Now get you to my lady's chamber, and tell her, let her paint an inch thick, to this favour she must come; make her laugh at that" (5.1.112- 15). Anthony Rivers, a Jesuit priest, reported that at Christmas celebrations in 1600 Elizabeth was painted "in some places near half an inch thick" (Mullaney 148). Stories were rife that a major reason the question of succession was left hanging was Queen Elizabeth could not abide being reminded of her mortality. Janet Clare has noted the insecurity and unrest characterizing the end of the century:

. . . the proscriptive measures [of theater censorship] of the early 1590s were intensified as a result of the *fin-de-siècle* political tensions generated by anticipation of the Queen's death and the factionalism which accompanied   the uncertain succession.

The Queen's physical decline was causing more pronounced fissures in the body politic than had yet appeared. The earl of Essex was in secret correspondence with James VI of Scotland and was engaged in creating a faction in support of James's claim to the throne. In opposition to the young earl were the sons of the elder statesmen, Lords Burghley and Cobham, Robert Cecil and Henry Brooke. (61)

Henry V, which was written approximately one year before *Hamlet*, dealt with the same political crisis. Paola Pugliatti noted, "Indeed, Henry's condition as foreign pretender and heir to the throne of France is as awkward as was the Scottish James Stewart's condition as foreign pretender to the throne of England. When Shakespeare wrote *Henry V*, the debate about Elizabeth's succession and the controversy between Stuart and Suffolk supporters was very hot" (245, footnote 17).

The Tudor line was in imminent danger of dying with the queen, and according to her father's will, the Suffolk line should follow. After a series of revised wills, Henry VIII's last one had stipulated if Edward VI, Mary, or Elizabeth had no heirs, the throne would go to the Suffolks. However,

---

26 In 1599, when she was sixty-six , it was observed the queen painted not only her face but her neck and bosom also, in some places near half an inch thick. She also put fine cloths in her mouth to hide the falling in of her cheeks" (Hosking 139).

a question did arise about the validity of the will because Henry was believed to have signed it with the stamp of his signature, not with his own hand. Questions regarding the validity of the will opened succession to James VI of Scotland, the nearest descendant of Henry VII. The problem with the will was one of many concerning succession. It was complicated by factions and schemers who escalated the total number of candidates to at least fourteen (Bruce xi). There seemed to be general accord in the country, however, that James VI had the strongest claim, and in 1598 the earl of Essex may have supported James.

Essex had just reached the pinnacle of his career, having performed brilliantly in the Cadiz raid in 1596, subsequently being appointed Earl Marshal and master of the Ordnance in 1597 (Bindoff 300). His grandest assignment came in 1597 when he was assigned the task of subjugating Ireland (Bindoff 300). In the course of 1598, which Essex spent rather fruitlessly in Ireland, the conflict between Robert Cecil and Essex over court appointments became intermeshed with the succession question. Each charged the other with the worst possible crime: collusion with the Catholics. In truth, each was secretly carrying on negotiations with Catholics. One of Essex's charges was that Cecil supported the Infanta, the candidate known to be the favorite of the Jesuit, Robert Parsons. Could it have been that both Cecil and Essex were dealing with Parsons simultaneously? James and Essex had been corresponding secretly for some time, beginning in 1598 (Bruce xxi). Even though Essex was generally believed to be a Protestant, it is probable "Essex coquetted with puritans and catholics alike" (Pollard 471). We have already seen that Cecil charged in court after the Essex rebellion that Essex himself was thought to be dealing with the Catholics, which indeed he was. James, too, was flexible on the question of religion, so long as he got the throne in the end. Catholics in England generally rated his claim higher than that of the Jesuit/Spanish candidate, the Infanta, and many Catholics supported him, in part out of a kind of loyalty to his mother, Mary, Queen of Scots.

Because Shakespeare's *Hamlet* to some degree revolves on the succession question, and because Robert Parsons was deeply embroiled in the Appellants' quarrel raging among the Catholic clergy that also centered around the question of succession, it is not unthinkable that Shakespeare could have used Parsons' work in his play. Considering the fact that John Speed referred to Shakespeare as Parsons' poet, the play is perhaps an example of what Speed meant. Was the play written to parallel the plan of Essex's followers, and might Robert Parsons have been interested in such a plan if James were going to reinstate the Catholic religion in England? From several perspectives, *Hamlet* is connected with Essex and his political maneuverings. If Shakespeare's play reflects these maneuverings, Christopher Devlin's hesitant reference to some evidence that Hamlet's spiritual struggles seem to derive from Parson's *Christian Directory* might apply here. He notes, "Hamlet's tendency to preach points to the use of some book of divinity. I propose to take Robert Person's *Christian Directory* as a typical devotional work of the period" (36). After presenting a lengthy comparison of passages from the play with passages from Parson's book, Devlin's final conclusion is that he is "not anxious to show that the *Christian Directory* was actually used by Shakespeare" and then proceeds to show parallels between *Lear* and the *Directory* (41). Peter Milward, too, sees interesting parallels between Parsons' book and passages in the play that are too similar and too frequent to attribute to chance. Milward notes that "Time and again one comes across words and sentences that seem to be taken up in the plays, especially in *Hamlet*" (45). The following are a few selections from Parsons' *Christian Directory* taken from Milward (45-46). The correlations with the play are my own:

Parsons	*Hamlet*
that body, which was before so delicately entertained . . . whereupon the wind might not be suffered to blow, nor the sun to shine . . . is left for a prey to be devoured of worms.	. . . so loving to my mother That he might not beteem the winds of heaven Visit her face too roughly. (1.2.140-42)
how this earth is enriched with inestimable and endless treasures, and yet itself standing, or hanging rather, with all this weight and poise, in the midst of the air, as a little ball without prop or pillar.	. . . that this goodly frame, the earth, seems to be a sterile promontory, this most excellent canopy, the air, look you, this brave o'er hanging firmament, this majestical roof fretted with golden fire, why, it appears no other thing than a foul and pestilent congregation of vapours. (2.2.309-114)
death . . . layeth truly before us, what a man is, how frail and miserable a creature, how fond and vain in the haughtiness of his cogitations while he is in health and prosperity. It is the true glass that representeth a man as he is indeed: other glasses are false and counterfeit.	What a piece of work is a man! How noble in reason! How infinite in faculty! In form and moving how express and admirable! In action how like an angel! In apprehension how like a god! The beauty of the world! The the paragon of ani-

113

Where will all your delights,
recreations and vanities be?
all your pleasant pastimes?
all your pride and bravery in
apparel? your glistering in
gold? your wanton dalliances
and pleasant entertainments?
(45-46)

Where be his quiddities now, his
quillets, his cases, his tenures, and
his tricks?
(5.1.107-8)

A point Milward makes is that many of the parallels have to do with the day of our death. A prominent theme in the play is that we all return to dust, queens and peasants alike, probably a way of reminding the queen she, too, was mortal and someone was going to replace her. This theme, of course, could have been used by any of the various factions, because everyone was concerned about the fact the queen refused to confront the succession issue. Yet it is odd Shakespeare patterned some of his phraseology on Parsons' *Directory*—phrases recognizable to others, for many were reading Parsons' book and being influenced by it, even though it was only available in a pirated edition (45). A man as conscious of the use of words as Shakespeare surely would have seen the parallels between his syntax and import and that of Parsons. If Essex and Parsons had temporarily joined forces, an outgrowth might have been for Shakespeare to represent some of Parsons' ideas in the play. Parsons' principal battle cry against Elizabeth was an echo of the major themes of the play: regicide and usurpation. It was possible to draw an analogy between Elizabeth, who was directly responsible for the suffering of English Catholics, with Claudius, who was responsible for the suffering of old King Hamlet.

In the short interim between the beginning of the fall of Essex and his final condemnation, how were the principals aligned? Between the sudden return of Essex from Ireland and his final fate, although he was banished from court and his movements restricted, he and his supporters probably did not yet realize he was doomed. Mountjoy, Essex's successor in Ireland, " . . . anxious for his safety, wrote to King James soliciting his interference. James replied by a messenger, that he 'would think of it, and put himself in a readiness to take any good occasion'" (Bruce xxi). This little-known plan which Mountjoy proposed to James was:

James should prepare an army, should march at the head of it to the Borders, should thence fulminate a demand to the English government, of an open declaration of his right to the succession, should support the demand by sending an ambassador into England, and of course, although not so state, if his demand were refused, should cross the Borders as an invader (xxi).

Mountjoy had further plans. He would go to Ireland as Lord Deputy and return with one half of the queen's army to support the demand of James. Essex was to raise his friends within the kingdom (xxii). The earl of Southampton wrote to James that he offered his services in this invasion, and Southampton said James accepted his offer (xxii). In view of the fact *Richard II* had been used once to drum up support for Essex's rebellion, might it be *Hamlet* was used in a similar way for this invasion? But the hero, Hamlet, was sung to his death by flights of angels before the plan could be put into action.

There is some evidence Hamlet represented Essex, in part based upon the final prayer Essex offered as he put his head on the block: "Send thy blessed angels which may receive my soul and convey it to thy joys in heaven" (Milward 28). This prayer seems to be echoed by Horatio at the moment of Hamlet's death when he says, "And flights of angel sing thee to thy rest!" (5.2.371). Milward suggests Horatio's blessing echoes the antiphon regularly chanted at the Catholic burial service: "In paradisum deducant te angeli: in tuo adventu suscipiant te Martyres, et perducant te in civitatem sanctam Jerusalem. Chorus angelorum te suscipiat, et cum Lasaro quondam paupere aeternam habeas requiem" (28). However, Milward does not speculate on the religion of Essex, or Horatio's prayer and its possible meaning as a kind of final pronouncement in the play. At the least, it makes Hamlet appear to die a papist, and if Hamlet stood for Essex, it may be a clue that Essex was a secret Catholic. The throne of England would probably have been worth a mass to James Stuart, and it may be that had this plan succeeded, it would have resulted in a Catholic England under King James. In the original plan, which seemed to call for Essex to hand England over to James, James would have had a role similar to that of Fortinbras, (a pairing of Fortinbras and James Christopher Devlin has also identified [43]), and all would live happily ever after except Robert Cecil. If the plan had succeeded, Essex would have secured his future by winning the favor of James. He no longer had a future with Queen Elizabeth. In the end, it became clear Essex would be eliminated, so Robert Cecil eventually maneuvered his position to support James, convincing James there was no need to be aggressive: he would slip naturally into Queen Elizabeth's throne upon her death.

The more obvious parallel between James and the play is the sordid story of his mother's suspected complicity in the death of his father, Darnley, and the all-too-hasty marriage of his mother to Bothwell. However, this might not have been the key appeal of the play for James. The crime driving the entire play is the killing of a monarch by his cousin monarch. The analogy to real life, in James's case, was the execution of his own mother by her cousin Elizabeth. The staging of the murder of a Catholic monarch by his brother would surely have evoked memories in the audience of the execution of Mary, Queen of Scots, which had occurred only ten years earlier. A viewer who understood this analogy would similarly have understood the counterpart to Polonius was Burghley. After a prolonged campaign, Burghley had finally persuaded Elizabeth to make the fatal decision to execute Mary. While there is no direct evidence in the play that Polonius was complicit in the death of Claudius, he willingly transferred his allegiance to the new king. Numerous parallels have been drawn between Burghley and Polonius from the fact that each had a fragile, vulnerable, marriageable daughter to the fatherly admonitions each gave his son. Burghley and Polonius were alike, also, in contributing to the blight which was infecting both nations. Both Denmark and England were riddled with conspiracy, duplicity, and eavesdropping, which were normal modes of operation for Burghley and Polonius. Catholics in an Elizabethan audience, and James Stuart, would probably have seen the parallel between the two Machiavellian counselors who served usurping regicides.

Hamlet may originally have been designed as a "mousetrap" to catch the conscience of the queen, in a religious sense, by attempting to persuade her to name a Catholic James to succeed her. In part, the play may also have presented a justification for Essex's move against the government in an effort to rally support for his rebellion. The extreme frustration and resentment Essex harbored against the queen in the last months before his fall have some parallels with the bitterness of Hamlet's feelings toward Claudius. If Parsons was involved with Essex, the play can be seen as revealing a touch of the vindictiveness with which Parsons attacked the queen in some of his diatribes against her. Their acidic bitterness toward Elizabeth would have been cause enough for Essex and Parsons to work together against her and to favor James and the Catholic religion.

Hamlet's hesitation to suffer his outrageous fortune or take arms against a sea of troubles parallels the quandary of Essex in taking arms against the queen. The Protestant approach to meeting adversity was that it was "nobler to suffer the slings and arrows," as explained by Bishop Bilson in his *True Difference* (1585), which specified "any taking of arms to change 'the law's delay,' the insolence of office: and all the other abuses, real or imagined, would merely lead to other and far worse ills, both in this world and in the hereafter" (Frye 189). Essex may have chosen to engage in "violent action when necessary to achieve virtuous ends," a charge often leveled against the Jesuits. Robert Parsons may have unwittingly abetted Essex's "violent action" of revolt to achieve the "good end" of placing James on the English throne. Parsons, along with many Catholics, hoped James would restore, or at least tolerate, Catholicism in England. For Essex, it would have assured his ascendancy over Robert Cecil through an alliance between Essex and James. A requisite for this scenario would have been that, at least temporarily, James appeared to favor the establishment of the Catholic religion in England over Elizabeth's English Church.

Hamlet's quandary over the nature of the ghost parallels this Protestant/Catholic dilemma with which James and Essex seemed to struggle. In his opposition to Elizabeth, was Essex being impelled to rebel by a Protestant devil who was leading him to his own destruction? Or was the spirit and power of the Catholic Church commanding him to redeem the religion and thereby leading him to glory? The ghost in the play is a Catholic suffering a prolonged agony that conforms in every detail with the Catholic conception of Purgatory, yet the ultimate effect of the ghost is perhaps that of a Protestant devil which leads Hamlet (and Essex) to their final destruction. Hamlet's revenge is accomplished almost by accident and at the cost of his own life. Essex, it appears, may have been lured to his destruction by a Protestant devil in the form of Robert Cecil who misled and then manipulated Essex for political reasons. Cecil at one time pretended to be his friend, while in reality he was only sounding him out to charge him with treasonous behavior.

The chameleon-like quality of James's religious convictions was reflected in his position concerning the existence of ghosts. Publicly, James was aligned with the Protestants, who insisted that "dead men doe neither walke, nor appeare in bodie and soule after death" (Reed, quoted from William Perkins 131). In his book, *Daemonologie* (1597), James added: "Neither can the spirite of the defunct returne to his friend [there being no purgatory], or yet an Angell use such formes" (131). However, his uncertainty seems to be reflected in his explanation of the reasons simple folk claim to "see" ghosts, for it reveals that to some extent they were still real phenomena for him. Reed has summarized James' explanation: "King James of Scotland contends in *Daemonologie* that a devil often assumed a lately 'deade bodie' and thus communicated with country persons; the intent was to make them [being ignorant of formal Protestant dogma] beleeve that it was some good spirite [a ghost] appeared to them . . . to discover unto them the will of the defunct, or what was the way of his slauchter" (131). His uncertainty about the existence of ghosts is revealed in these two contradictory statements which could reflect his uncertainty about the larger question of the Catholic versus the Protestant religion.

The ghost of Mary, Queen of Scots, hovers over the play, reminding the audience and Queen Elizabeth of Mary's execution. Who should have been most moved at the death of Mary, Queen of Scots? James VI, the son, under normal circumstances, and *Hamlet* can be read as playing on James's resentment over Elizbeth's treatment of his mother. Many English Catholics transferred their feelings for Mary to her son, so that he and Catholicism became fused in their minds. *Hamlet* could have played on those sentiments to rally support for James in his play for the English crown *before* he came under the influence of Robert Cecil following the fall of Essex. After the disastrous failure of the Essex "coup," Shakespeare's "mousetrap" shrank to an effort to save Essex's life by persuading the queen to reconsider her rejection of Essex. Elizabeth had put to death two cousins: the duke of Norfolk and Mary, Queen of Scots. Perhaps one role of the play was to make her realize she was about to commit another such crime in regard to Essex. If Queen Elizabeth had procrastinated in the decision to execute Essex, as she had with Norfolk and Mary, the plan to invade England might have saved the life of Essex, given James the English throne, and re-established Catholicism and Robert Parsons in England. The final scene in Shakespeare's play would then have ended very differently.

Of Deposition and Usurpation

Suspend for a moment any preconceptions about Shakespeare's religious inclinations and imagine he was a Catholic when he wrote *Richard II* (variously dated between 1595 and 1597), and let us on your imaginary forces work. Suspend the popular notion that the criticism of misused kingship through the figure of Richard was meant not only to represent Elizabeth but was also an emotional revival of the hope that had elated those who supported Mary, Queen of Scots, as the rightful heir to the English throne. Imagine the reference to Mary was intended to support the cause of the earl of Essex, first in 1595, and later in 1601.

Essex is traditionally associated with Bolingbroke because in 1595, like Bolingbroke, Essex had temporarily fallen from favor, culminating in the loss of his inheritance in Lancaster through which he claimed descent from Bolingbroke. The Lancaster inheritance went instead to Robert Cecil (Clark 126-7). Essex's protest about his mistreatment coincided with the appearance of *A Conference about Succession to the Crown* which was dedicated to Essex, thereby implicating him as approving the contents (124). A threat of a second Armada's being sent against England in 1595 raised the religious question again, placing Essex at the head of a Catholic faction in a manner somewhat analogous to the position Mary, Queen of Scots, held as a figurehead for the Catholics before the 1588 Armada.

The play is believed by some to have been written in 1595, several years after the execution of Mary, Queen of Scots, in 1587 and the defeat of the 1588 Armada—two catastrophes that had dashed the hopes of English Catholics for the re-establishment of Catholicism. The claims of Essex and Isabella were new efforts to accomplish Mary's objective. Deposition and usurpation were not approved topics for discussion, especially since

Elizabeth's position had parallels with Bolingbroke's position in the play. Considering the queen's touchiness about any reference to her death, the succession, and plots to depose her, it seems a daring move for a playwright to stage all of these forbidden topics (veiled in the context of Richard's time) as Shakespeare did with *Richard II*. Whether or not Shakespeare intended the play as a forum for addressing those issues, it operated as such.

Evelyn Albright has vigorously defended the argument that Shakespeare's play was indeed the one used by Essex and his supporters in his rebellion of February 7, 1601. In Shakespeare's time, it had become popular to draw comparisons between Elizabeth and Richard and Essex and Bolingbroke, and the play, *Richard II*, has generally been interpreted from this point of view to the present. Albright does not offer an opinion on the origin of the political comment in Shakespeare's play, i.e., whether it originated with Shakespeare or with his patron, Southampton, who was a principal conspirator with Essex. The point of view taken in this present consideration will be that Shakespeare himself was committed to Essex as a Catholic supporter and that the parallels drawn in the play were, for the most part, between Richard and Mary. At the same time, Richard's weaknesses served as a vehicle for commenting on weaknesses in Queen Elizabeth's governance.

If Shakespeare wrote the play at a time when Essex was a figurehead for Catholicism, the idea of Shakespeare as his supporter fits well with the clues of Shakespeare's Catholicism that have been presented to this point. We have already seen that some relatives, and the John Arden who participated was perhaps also a relative, and friends of Shakespeare were followers of Essex, but the most direct link between Shakespeare and Essex is that Essex's brother, Edward, had married into the Arden family. It is difficult to imagine Shakespeare aloof in an ivory tower creating a play that, just by chance, was acutely applicable to the times when his friends, relatives, and patrons were at the center of the maelstrom.

For some years before the staging of the play, analogies had been drawn between Richard II and Queen Elizabeth by the queen's ministers to point up mismanagement of the government (Albright 695). Perhaps Shakespeare was aware that Mary, too, saw parallels between herself and Richard II. Fraser describes Mary as responding to her adversity with "a spirited defense of her station, in which her studies in English history prompted her to compare herself to King Richard II in the hands of his enemies" (612). That Richard in the play elicits sympathy from the spectator is obvious. Catholicism and sympathy with Mary were unpopular with Elizabeth and would have necessitated a subtle and skillful touch.

If one approaches *Richard II* from the unorthodox point of view that Shakespeare was calling up the memory of Mary as a rallying cry to support Essex and one that was intended to inspire those disappointed Catholics who had pinned their hopes on Mary to restore Catholicism, depose

Elizabeth, and herself become queen, it is clear why he focused so sharply on the two key questions: the consequences of the deposition of an anointed monarch and the usurpation of the throne through illegitimate means. This approach offers an explanation as to why Shakespeare invented the deposition scene portraying Richard as a pathetic human with whom the spectator sympathizes. In the play, the figure of Richard becomes something of a religious symbol, a picture which agrees with the older chronicles of the 1399 rebellion before it was rewritten to please the Lancastrians:

> Moreover, the most remarkable fact about the four original pro-Richard chronicles is that they already, as we shall see later, give utterance to that mystical conception of the martyred king which we find in Shakespeare, and compare his betrayal with that of Christ and his enemies with Pilate and Judas, much as the play itself does. Nor is it certain that they are not in this nearer the truth than the orthodox modern historian who has on the whole accepted the Lancastrian version of the revolution of 1399. (Child xviii)

One sympathizes with Richard, but one does not respect him. The contrast between Richard's somewhat abject renunciation and the courageous defense put forward by Mary, left ill, alone, and unaided in the face of a formidable battery of nobles and lawyers (many of whom were former supporters of hers) must have been an obvious contrast in the minds of many of Shakespeare's Catholic contemporaries.

If Shakespeare used Richard's situation to provide a forum for discussing what, to many, was the great crime of Elizabeth's reign, the obvious parallel with Bolingbroke, the usurper, was Elizabeth herself, but such an inference in a play would have required a delicate touch. Her Roman Catholic opponents, especially Cardinal William Allen, charged Elizabeth with the worst crimes imaginable: bastardy and usurpation. Elizabeth, like Bolingbroke, was keenly aware the Catholic challenge to her right to the throne could be substantiated. Elizabeth could not have proved to Catholics she ruled by divine right; she could only substantiate her claim to the throne through her descent from Henry VIII, but Henry's marriage had been pronounced null by the pope, making Elizabeth illegitimate. Therefore, to Catholics, Elizabeth's claim was invalid, and the next in line to the English throne was Mary Stuart, granddaughter of Henry's sister.

Unfortunately for those Catholics who had anticipated the restoration of Catholicism with Mary, her personal character had been as weak as Richard's. Death had bored through Mary's castle wall when Elizabeth, after twenty years of vacillation and procrastination, finally signed Mary's death warrant. Personally, Mary's life was a disaster. She had antagonized the Protestants beyond a point of conciliation; she had flouted Elizabeth's admonition not to marry Darnley; she had cheated on Darnley; betrayed him; probably colluded with Darnley's murderer, Bothwell; and then married Bothwell. She was ineffective in dealing with the opposition in Scotland and finally was forced to flee for her life, taking "refuge" in England, expecting Elizabeth to uphold the sanctity of a fellow queen's position. When Elizabeth violated this royal code, her behavior was analogous to Gaunt's refusal to avenge the death of his brother Gloucester, for which he was roundly admonished by the Duchess of Gloucester. Gaunt, in "suffering this [his] brother to be slaughtered" (1.2.30) was complicit and did "consent in some measure to this father's death [and his own]" (1.2.26-7). Elizabeth, consenting to her cousin Mary's execution, had paved the way for her own destruction. At least that would have been the hope of Roman Catholics, who expected a Spanish invasion to restore Catholicism in England. Mary's reputation, on the other hand, began to glow with the glory of martyrdom.

One of the efforts to destroy Elizabeth and the plot which led directly to Mary's downfall, the Babington Plot, was reminiscent of the plot against Henry Bolingbroke that Aumerle was about to join to the outrage of his feudally minded father, York, and the distracted terror of his mother. The scene in the play becomes almost comic, but to contemporaries of Shakespeare, the real-life tragedy of Babington and his fellow conspirators would surely have been evoked. York's condemnation of the conspiracy in which his own son was involved must have been a poignant reminder of the dozen Babington victims: "Thou fond mad woman, / Wilt thou conceal this dark conspiracy? / A dozen of them here have ta'en the sacrament, / To kill the king at Oxford" (5.2.95-98). In 1595, the mention of a conspiracy involving "a dozen" would have elicited from a part of the audience, at least, sympathy for the young men who died such atrocious deaths and resentment toward those responsible. As has been shown, Shakespeare probably knew some of the young men who suffered the traitors' death, along with Babington, as a result of their idealistic dreams and plotting. The scene in which Aumerle and his mother plead for his life would have had a totally different impact on an Elizabethan audience acquainted with the fate of the offspring of well-known contemporaries from its impact on present-day audiences. Fraser quotes Camden on the savageness of the punishment: "They were all cut down, their privities were cut off, bowelled alive and seeing, and quartered" (585).

A parallel can be seen in Mary and Richard as pawns and ultimate victims of the religious power struggles driving the diplomacy of their times. Many in the audience would have known the history of the confrontation of the precursor of the Yorkist, Richard, with Lancastrian Bolingbroke, and many would have identified with the characters who represented his or her particular allegiance. Many would have understood that in Richard's time, Gloucester rose to power on the crest of the Lords Appellant in the struggles between the factions clustered around the two popes, Clement VII, at

Avignon and the Italian pope, Urban VI, at Rome. England sided with the Italian pope largely because anything French was automatically the enemy. In 1386, when France threatened to invade England via the Low Countries, Uncle Gloucester (Thomas of Woodstock) and his faction posed as defenders of the realm to wrest power from Richard. The important government positions were parceled out to Gloucester's friends, and Richard was virtually forced to hand over all power, including the Exchequer and the Great Privy Seal (Hutchinson 107). In a similar way, Mary had been edged off the Scottish throne through the machinations of her half-brother, James Stuart, earl of Moray, and his Protestant supporters. Mary and Richard were reduced to being mere figureheads—powerless and yet the anointed monarchs. After their forced abdications, both Mary and Richard II were left with only two things that could not be eradicated by human hands: their royal blood and their religion.

While there are some apt parallels between Richard with both Queen Elizabeth and Mary, Queen of Scots, it is a mistake to attempt an exact overlay of a contemporary situation to conform to the play in every detail. Scattered throughout the play are condemnatory pronouncements concerning guilt and punishment for regicide. Any one of these statements, if spoken to or about Queen Elizabeth would have spelled doom for Shakespeare, yet these statements could be made publicly in a non-contemporary setting with impunity. Mowbray was, of course, a figure in the actual history, but for Shakespeare, Mowbray may have been important as the vehicle for a public statement revealing Bolingbroke's designs on Richard, which was also intended to reveal something about Queen Elizabeth: "But what thou art, God, thou, and I do know; And all too soon, I fear, the king shall rue" (1.3. 204, 205). York could boast of his father, Edward III, that "his hands were guilty of no kindred blood" (2.1. 182), leaving the audience to ponder Elizabeth's treatment of her cousin, Mary. The Bishop of Carlisle and the Abbot of Westminster could safely assess Richard's imprisonment as "a woeful pageant" and predict that more evil would descend on future generations and that they "Shall feel this day as sharp to them as thorn" (4.1.321-322), a reminder of the dire consequences which were applicable to current events. Carlisle's reprimand of the lords assembled in the Parliament could have effectively been delivered to those former friends of Mary, Queen of Scots, who sat in judgment on her: "What subject can give sentence on his king? . . . shall the figure of God's majesty, / His captain, steward, deputy-elect, / Anointed, crowned, planted many years, / Be judged by subject and inferior breath, / And he himself not present?" (4.1.121-129). Throughout the play there is a strong emphasis on the kinship of Richard and Bolingbroke, and the usually endearing term of "cousin" is magnified when Richard physically hands Bolingbroke the crown and says: "Give me the crown. Here, cousin, seize the crown; / Here, cousin; On this side my hand, and on that side yours" (4.1.181-182). How many in the audience would have contemplated the execution of Mary by her cousin, Elizabeth?

Stories were no doubt in circulation about Mary's last days before her execution, stories such as her reaction to the particularly grueling first day of her final trial, which ended with all of the counselors shouting at her that she was guilty. Mary told her servants that the scene reminded her of the passion of Christ. The judges had treated her as the Jews treated Jesus, shouting "Tolle, Tolle, Crucifige" (Fraser 605). Some in the audience would surely have heard an echo of Mary's allusion when Richard cried out poignantly to those who should have defended him, pricking the consciences of guilty onlookers:

> Nay, all of you that stand and look upon
> Whilst that my wretchedness dothe bait myself,
> Though some of you with Pilate wash your hands,
> Showing an outward pity, yet you Pilates
> Here have delivered me to my sad cross,
> And water cannot wash away your sin. (4.1.237-43)

Later, Mary's feelings must have been quite similar as she looked at her judges just before her execution, noting many former friends sitting in judgment of her at her trial. There sat her old friend, Sir Christopher Hatton, and the earl of Shrewsbury, her jailer-turned-friend, who had been admonished by Lord Chancellor Bromley: "I would advise you not to be absent [from the trial]" (Fraser 593). At the actual execution, Shrewsbury's face was wet with tears and he could not speak (635). Mary had told her servant earlier that she had noticed expressions of emotions among the crowd (608). Mary, like Richard, could have said, "Yet I well remember/ The favors of these men. Were they not mine? Did they not sometime cry 'All hail!' to me?" (4.1.167-9).

Striking similarities in the tenacious insistence that a monarch is appointed by God and man cannot alter that appointment can be seen in both Mary's and Richard's statements:

Richard: Not all the water in the rough rude sea
                Can wash the balm off from an anointed king.
                The breath of worldly men cannot deposed
                The deputy elected by the Lord. (3.2.54-7)

Mary: As a sinner, I am truly conscious of having often
                offended my Creator, and I beg him to forgive
                me, but as Queen and Sovereign, I am aware of
                no offence for which I have to render account to
                any one here below (Fraser 592).

Mary was grossly insulted by the demeanor of her jailer, Amyas Paulet, who in the last few weeks of her life went out of his way to insult her by removing the royal cloth of state above her chair and refusing to cover his head in her presence because she would soon be dead and no longer a queen. Richard's treatment in the play is quite parallel to the point at which Richard warns that God will send armies of pestilence to right this wrong. It was expected that Spain would aid Essex to accomplish the objective Mary had set for herself, and Richard's speech possibly alludes to the contemporary war on the horizon while at the same time predicting the ensuing Wars of the Roses:

> We are amazed, and thus long have we stood
> To watch the fearful bending of thy knee
> Because we thought ourself thy lawful King.
> And if we be, how dare thy joints forget
> To pay their awful duty to our presence? . . .
> Yet know my master, God Omnipotent,
> Is mustering in His clouds on our behalf
> Armies of pestilence; and they shall strike
> Your children yet unborn and unbegot,
> That lift your vassal hands against my head
> And threat the glory of my precious crown.
> (3.3.72-90)

And Carlisle affirms "disorder," "horror," "fear," and "mutiny" are the expected consequences of regicide (4.1.125-148). Perhaps the play predicted this sort of disorder which could be expected to follow Mary's execution.

Because both Mary and Richard refused to sign confessions of guilt which would have negated their royalty, their respective jailers, Northumberland and Paulet, felt uneasy about proceeding against them. Paulet informed Mary that her "misdeeds were to be punished by the interrogation of certain lords, and advised her in her own interests to beg pardon and confess her faults . . . ," to which she replied: "I do not wish for pardon; I do not seek, nor would I accept it from anyone living" (Fraser 592). Paulet's request, to which Mary never acceded, is very like Northumberland's to Richard:

> . . . read
> These accusations and these grievous crimes
> Committed by your person and your followers
> Against the state and profit of this land,
> That, by confessing them, the souls of men
> May deem that you are worthily deposed.
> (4.1.224-7)

Both Mary and Richard saw themselves as beggars and sinners. Richard said: " . . . Sometimes am I King, / Then treasons make me wish myself a beggar, / And so I am" (5.5.32-4). To a group of beggars in Staffordshire, Mary said sadly: "Alas, good people, I have now nothing to give you. For I am as much a beggar as you are yourselves" (Fraser 584). The evening before her death, Mary asked her serving woman to read about some great sinner, commenting, "In truth, he was a great sinner, but not so great as I have been" (628). She, like Richard had "wasted time" and now time wasted her.

Catholic religious imagery envelops Richard II, who somewhat wistfully recognizes he must trade his subjects for a pair of carved saints (*Richard II* 3.3. 148, 52). Queen Mary's realization was very similar to Richard's when she finally saw, because she would never regain the throne, she must capitalize upon her death as a Catholic martyr. Mary, herself, saw the parallel between her downward trajectory and that of Richard II. In the final days before her execution, she and her jailer, Paulet, held their own private disputations, and during one of them he consoled her over her approaching death with: "You are now only a dead woman without the dignity or honours of a Queen" (Fraser 612). It was in response to Paulet that Mary compared herself with Richard II (612). Queen Elizabeth herself probably recognized the similarity and the potential the role had for eliciting sympathy, for Mary Stuart's predicament was a closer parallel to Richard's than Elizabeth's was. Elizabeth could say of herself, "I am Richard II, know ye not that?" (692), to parry the epithet of "usurper," a parallel that Catholics would readily have seen between Elizabeth and Henry IV. To Catholics, "Elizabeth, child of an unlawful union, could not be a legitimate sovereign, and her throne ought to pass without delay to the person next in line whose legitimacy was beyond dispute. Such at least was the letter of the canon law" (Bindoff 185), and for Catholics, that rightful queen was Mary, Queen of Scotland.

Neither Bolingbroke (in the play) nor Elizabeth would accept responsibility for the final death sentences. Exton only thought Henry wished Richard dead; Elizabeth was more explicit. Francis Walsingham and William Davison conveyed the queen's wishes in a letter to Mary's last jailer, Sir Amyas Paulet, on February 1, 1586:

After our hearty commendations, we find by speech lately uttered by her majesty that she doth note in you both a lack of that care and zeal of her service that she looketh for at your hands, in that you have not in all this time of yourselves (without provocation) found out some way to shorten the life of that Queen, considering the great peril she is subject unto hourly so long as the said Queen shall live. (Paulet 359)

Paulet, unlike Exton, however, did not take matters into his own hands. An elaborate ruse had to be staged to trick Elizabeth into signing the execution warrant (622). The scapegoat, William Davison, one of the authors of the directions to Paulet, was the counterpart to Exton, who, surmising he had been assigned the task of eliminating Richard and expecting thanks for the deed, found he was condemned. A spectator departs with the last few lines of a play reverberating in his mind. The play is structured so that the interchange between Bolingbroke and Exton comes at the very end, thereby stimulating the transfer to the present in some people's minds. Davison might have been told by Queen Elizabeth:

> Exton [Davison], I thank thee not; for thou hast wrought
> A deed of slander with thy fatal hand
> Upon my head and all this famous land.

And Davison might have protested:

"From your own mouth, my lord [lady], did I this deed." (5.6.35-39)

A possible contemporary echoing of the word "convey" might indicate an awareness of the parallels between Bolingbroke and Queen Elizabeth. Richard focuses on the word "convey" immediately before his death when Bolingbroke directs that Richard be conveyed to the Tower. Richard replies, "Oh, good! Convey? Conveyers are you all/ That rise thus nimbly by a true king's fall" (4.1.316-18). The clerk of the Council, Beale, who was directed to deliver the death warrant to Mary at Fotheringhay, used the very word: "Afterward Beale believed that this mission had fatally blighted his career: in 1599 he attributed his failure to find advancement 'for that my name was made odious to the whole world for conveying down the Commission for the execution of the Scottish Queen'" (Paulet 623). Shakespeare perhaps intended to condemn all of those who had had a part in sentencing Mary by expanding on the guilt of Beale.

Elizabeth prolonged the agony of waiting for the ax to fall for two months, debating and muttering to herself, "Suffer or strike, strike or be struck" (623). Finally, Queen Elizabeth's cousin Mary was beheaded Wednesday, February 8, 1587, in the great hall of Fotheringhay in the presence of three hundred onlookers, some of whom had been and perhaps still were sympathetic to her. After several tries, her head was severed, and the executioner held it aloft and cried, "God save the Queen!" Would not the cry of "God save the King!" from Richard just before his death have stirred memories of the tales of Mary's execution in the minds of at least some of the audience?

The dramatic and theatrical qualities of Shakespeare's characterization of Richard are often noted. Mary recognized the theatrical aspects of her own situation when she warned her persecutors: "Look to your consciences and remember that the theater of the world is wider than the realm of England" (597). As the scaffold was being erected on which she would eventually die, she wrote, "I think they are making a scaffold to make me play the last scene of the Tragedy . . ." (613).

To interpret the figure of Richard, at least in Shakespeare's play, as representing only Queen Elizabeth is to be insensitive to the religious imagery surrounding Richard. This interpretation also fails to explain the pathos of Richard's fall as well as fails to account for the unusual popularity of the play. Elizabeth herself indicated the play "was played 40 times in open streets and houses" (Child xxxii). Child continues: "It is to be presumed also that the deposition scene [which was not printed or performed on the public stage until after Elizabeth's death] had been acted on these occasions [1595-6 at which the earl of Essex was often present with great applause giving countenance and lyking the same] . . . and appeared to have been included in 1601" (xxxiii). Child's conclusion about the figure of Richard conforms to the standard allusion that Richard was a vehicle for criticism of Elizabeth, although he recognizes the religious quality of the play, terming it " . . . a sacramental quality in the agony and death of the sacrificed victim . . . " xvi). He comes very near to seeing Richard II as representing Mary by indicating that "One may catch something of this aspect of his [Richard's] tragedy . . . by remembering the passionate devotion which the memory of Mary, Queen of Scots, inspired until an even later date" (xvii). This passionate devotion to Mary would have been evoked even more readily in Shakespeare's day. The deposition scene in Shakespeare's play seems to have had special significance as evidenced by the censorship and by its popularity. It seems to have been significant in Shakespeare's mind because the scene was original with him, the actual deposition having been accomplished by the signing of a document.

The fact the players at the Globe performed the play just prior to Essex's uprising in February 1601 suggests that someone in the acting troup was sympathic with the cause and willing to take a risk. Leeds Barroll gives most of the evidence showing the risk the players took and then comes to the incredible conclusion there was none. The following is the evidence:

Eight to ten days later three depositions separately describing the *Richard II* performance had been taken. The first two depositions were by two conspirators, while the third was by one of the Lord Chamberlain's players, Shakespeare's fellow actor, Augustine Philips. In aggregate, all three depositions make up the record of the events I have just recounted [the request for and presention of the play].
. . . Four of those associated with the performance were executed, but they had been closely involved in the Essex conspiracy as a whole. The large majority were punished by being fined various sums,

presumably scaled according to their ability to pay, and then were freed within six months. . . . the earl closest to Essex, Southampton (not executed but sentenced to the Tower for life); and two other earls close to Essex and Southampton: the earl of Rutland and the earl of Bedford. Both were spared but paid huge fines. (444-445)

I think is it a fair assumption that any Elizabethan called before the Privy Council to give testimony trembled. The player was the third part of the total number called. The sentences were: execution (the traitor's death), crippling fines, or life imprisonment in the Tower. Shakespeare's patron was the closest to Essex and received the life sentence. I agree with Stephen Greenblatt there was risk involved, especially as the queen specifically singled out the play as being a threat to her. Barroll quotes Jonathan Dollimore's corroboration of Greenblatt: "As Stephen Greenblatt points out, what was really worrying for the queen was both the repeatability of the representation—and hence the multipying numbers of people witnessing it—and the *locations* of these repetitions: 'open streets and houses'" (443).27

The figure of Richard II had been used from 1578 to allude to the extravagance, waste, and taxes that were unpopular, warning Elizabeth she might go the way of Richard II if she did not mend her ways. Shakespeare's *Richard II* has a new focus in that it makes Richard a pathetic figure who elicits the sympathy of the audience for about half of the play. Logic is the only proof that is offered here to suggest that Shakespeare wrote the play in 1595 in support of Essex, drawing upon the emotional appeal of the story of Mary, Queen of Scots, via the role of Richard II to support him. The play was then resurrected in 1601 to rally followers when Essex rebelled against Elizabeth.

---

27 Professor David Bergeron was the first to suggest the abdication scene was never cut from the play. Richard Dutton explains that Bergeron's theory was that the scene was "an addition (following a theatrical revival) to the 1608 Quarto, the title page of which proclaims: 'With new additions of the Parliament Scene, and the deposition of King Richard, as it hath been lately acted by the King's Majesty's Servants at the Globe'" (25). I suggest the special attention the title page draws to the notorious scene is meant to advertise to the buyer that he really will be able to read the details in this particular edition of the play.

Campion, Hotspur, and the Catholic Connection

Paola Pugliatti has drawn attention to the ambivalent nature of *Henry V* which points in two directions, one a "celebrative" reading and another the "contrary" reading (234). The play was just as ambiguous when it was performed in 1599, only ten years after the defeat of the Spanish Armada. Any reference to an English king in the plays had the potential of being interpreted as a comment on the current monarch. The queen would have been acutely attuned to any such possible allusion to her and would likely have identified herself with the glory of Henry, the ideal king, who had so successfully conquered his enemy, as she had recently done. Shakespeare's depiction of Henry V on the eve of the battle of Agincourt was, in addition, a reminder of the queen's appearance before her troops at Tilbury on the eve of the arrival of the Armada. Futhermore, Shakespeare's frequent praise of the Welsh and their language would have appealed to the queen because of her pride in her Welsh ancestry.

A somewhat tenuous connection between the queen and the play is the focus on Catherine of Valois who was the great-great-great-grandmother of Queen Elizabeth. Catherine married Owen Tudor after Henry V's death, thereby becoming the matriarch of the Tudor line. The charming personal portrayal of Catherine would have appealed to the queen's pride in her own ancestry. The theme of patriotism that permeates the play was no doubt interpreted and enjoyed as contemporary patriotism. There are many reasons why Queen Elizabeth would have regarded the play as glorification of herself and her reign.

On the other hand, from an Elizabethan Catholic's viewpoint, the flaws portrayed in the character of Henry V would have reflected parallel flaws in their present queen. References to bastard and usurping monarchs in these plays could have been interpreted as possible criticism of Queen Elizabeth's claim, as well as predictions of the consequences of usurpation. The plays as a group bear a message that the wages of usurpation are civil war and from a Catholic viewpoint serve to warn the queen she, too, may have to pay the price for what some regarded as her unlawful usurpation.

We have previously noted the parallels between the Percy rebellion against Henry IV and the Northern Rebellion of 1569 against Queen Elisabeth. Although the actual Wars of the Roses is generally regarded as the conflict between the Yorkists and the Lancastrians, followers of Richard of York and Henry VI, the dispute had its origins in 1399 when Richard II was deposed.

Peter Milward observes Shakespeare's depiction of the Wars of the Roses between the Yorkists and the Lancastrians fits well with the theory Shakespeare spent his early years in Lancashire (42). He further suggests the rebellion of the archbishop of York in the two parts of *Henry IV* is reminiscent of the Northern Rebellion (82) in which the Catholic lords of the North felt betrayed by Queen Elizabeth. They had supported her in the early stages of her accession, hoping she would declare for Catholicism or would at least allow religious toleration. Instead of toleration, the Catholics faced steadily increasing repression. The Percies who had supported and who later felt betrayed by Henry IV in Shakespeare's play were in a sense precursors of the Northern lords who rebelled in the name of their Catholic religion against a queen who had betrayed them. This recalcitrance in the North became linked to Mary, Queen of Scots, who had been assured by the Northern gentry that in 1566 "the papists in England were ready to rise when she would have them" (Pollard 280). The names of the powerful lords who rebelled against Queen Elizabeth in the Northern Rebellion evoke eerie echoes of the lords who supported Henry IV's "usurpation" of Richard II's throne depicted in Shakespeare's *Henriad*: Northumberland, Lady Northumberland, and the earl of Westmorland (Jenkins 166). Shakespeare's audience must have easily seen parallels between the two times such as the parallel Pollard draws between the two Northumberlands: "When Mary Stuart fled to England he [Northumberland] claimed her custody in virtue of his feudal rights over Workington, where she had landed, just as an earlier rebellious Percy had claimed the custody of other Scottish prisoners in 1403; and when it was refused . . . he grew into great heat and anger, and in the hearing of all men gave me great threatenings with very evil words" (278).

The main objective of the Northern Rebellion was to replace the "usurper," Queen Elizabeth, with the rightful English queen, Mary Stuart. Perhaps Shakespeare intended to prick the queen's conscience about what Catholics regarded as her usurpation of Mary Stuart's place by creating Henry IV as fully aware of his guilt in usurping the throne of Richard II. Shakespeare's Henry IV himself admits to having taken the throne from Richard II, and although he is never aware that the punishment for his crime will be visited upon his grandson, Shakespeare's audience and Queen Elizabeth would have known about the Wars of the Roses which followed. Perhaps Shakespeare intended to show that the consequences of such a usurpation for Queen Elizabeth could be a similar civil war. If Henry IV represented Queen Elizabeth in the plays, Catholics would have considered Mary, Queen of Scots, the counterpart for Richard. Shakespeare's *Richard II* draws a pathethic picture of a deposed monarch which, as has been suggested, seems parallel in many ways to the fall of the Scottish queen.

In summary, the *Henriad* presents a contemporary lesson about friends who had helped a monarch attain the throne only to be betrayed by that monarch. It also draws a parallel between Henry IV and Queen Elizabeth and the punishment which is to follow the betrayal. Consequently, the *Henriad* can be interpreted as a presentation of history from the Catholic point of view with a moral application in Shakespeare's time. An Elizabethan audience watching the *Henriad* would have sensed how uneasily a head wears a crown won at the cost of the life of a sovereign cousin. The second Henry IV play depicted Henry IV's need to atone for the murder of Richard perhaps as an intentional parallel to Queen Elizabeth's responsibility for the execution of Mary. Shakespeare emphasized Henry's need to atone for his crime in Henry's opening speech and again at the end of the play almost as if Mary's ghost were prodding the conscience of the queen and the country.

Alongside the ghost of the martyred Queen Mary, the memory of Edmund Campion, the Catholics' most revered martyr, is called to the stage. The Hotspur eulogized by Lady Percy in *2 Henry IV* has little relevance to Hotspur presented in *1 Henry IV*, but it does strangely recall the description of the youthful Edmund Campion at Oxford. If Shakespeare and Campion were friends, and if Shakespeare was deeply moved by Campion's fate, it is likely he would have wanted to absent himself from felicity a while to tell Campion's story, but it would have been dangerous to do that openly. Shakespeare seems to have taken the opportunity through Lady Percy's speech, a safe and disguised way of praising a friend publicly.

Quite a list of adjectives can be compiled to describe the Hotspur of *1 Henry IV*: fiery, scornful, stubborn, loyal, easily angered, jealous, proud, rash, impetuous, frisky, affectionate, canny, impatient, intolerant, unpretentious, and bordering on rude. There is no mention other young men dressed, spoke, or acted like him as if he were the "mark and glass, copy and book" (2.3.31). The focus in *1 Henry IV* is on the "gallant Hotspur," the "all-praised Hotspur" (3.2.140), the Hotspur who had an interest in the state as Henry IV had had in his youth, who filled fields with harness, led ancient lords and bishops in battle, who held "from all soldiers chief majority / And military title capital / Through all the kingdoms that acknowledge Christ" (3.2.108-110). In contrast to the man just described, Hotspur's widow praises a man whose honor:

... stuck upon him as the sun
In the gray vault of heaven, and by his light
Did all the chivalry of England move
To do brave acts. He was indeed the glass
Wherein the noble youth did dress themselves.
He had no legs that practiced not his gait;
And speaking thick, which nature made his blemish,
Became the accents of the valiant,
For those that could speak low and tardily
Would turn their own perfection to abuse,
To seem like him. So that in speech, in gait,
In diet, in affections of delight,
In military rules, humors of blood,
He was the mark and glass, copy and book,
That fashioned others. And him! O wondrous!
Him! A miracle of men! Him did you leave,
Second to none, unseconded by you,
To look upon the hideous god of war
In disadvantage to abide a field
Where nothing but the sound of Hotspur's name
Did seem defensible. So you left him.
Never, O never, do his ghost the wrong
To hold your honor more precise and nice
With others than with him! *(2 Henry IV* 2.2.18 - 41)

Except for the references to "military rules," "valiant," and "the hideous god of war," very little in this eulogy recalls the Hotspur of *1 Henry IV*. Here is an example of the ambiguous nature of Shakespeare's art. In Elizabethan England, the military terms could have described an actual soldier in battle or a missionary priest. The religious battles of the time were often proclaimed in military terms by both Protestants and Catholics, as exemplified by contemporary Jesuit accounts of the 1580 English mission which used military terms to define what was regarded as a kind of religious battle against heresy. These terms were the current nomenclature for the religious battle.

Lady Percy's eulogy of Hotspur is less fitting for Hotspur than it would have been for Edmund Campion, for it is quite similar to the praise heaped on Campion when he was a student at Oxford. For many in the audience, Shakespeare's praise of Hotspur would have evoked the memory of Campion, who had become a martyred saint by the time Shakespeare wrote the Henry plays, and as has been shown, was probably an acquaintance of Shakespeare's, perhaps someone whose loss Shakespeare mourned deeply. The eulogy could have stirred remorse in some Catholics in the audience who felt chastised for having abandoned Campion on the battlefield with only his famous name as his defense. Among those who abandoned Campion was Philip Sidney, who, of course, had been killed in the battle of Zutphen in 1586 and could not therefore have been chastised in 1595. Sidney had visited Campion in Prague in 1576, promising never to hurt any Catholic in his apparent conformity to the queen's policies. Simpson accuses Sidney of failing to back Campion when he needed help desperately: " . . . and for Father Campion himself he assured him that whereinsoever he could stand him in stead, he should find him a trusty friend, which he performed not, for afterwards, Campion being condemned to death, and the other in most high favour, when he might have done him favour he denied to do it, for fear not to offend" (115). But there were others like Sidney who promised their support of the mission and then backed down in the face of government pressure. The eulogy may have had the dual function of pricking guilty consciences while it reminded the guilty ones of Campion's admirable qualities.

What was there about Campion that would have made such an impression on a young man twenty-four years his junior? If Campion and Shakespeare became friends, and if Shakespeare developed a sort of "hero-worship" of Campion, Shakespeare would probably have learned of Campion's illustrious student days at Oxford. Campion had risen from a humble background to become a famous scholar and orator at Oxford by the time of Mary Tudor's accession in 1553, and he was asked to deliver the welcoming address when Mary entered London to be crowned. Princess Elizabeth accompanied Mary that day and heard Campion speak. Later, Campion was a junior fellow at St. John's College, Oxford, for twelve years where "he was the idol of Oxford, and was followed and imitated as no man ever was in an English University except himself and Newman" and "he was so greatly admired for his grace of eloquence that young men imitated not only his phrases but his gait, and revered him as a second Cicero" (Campbell 136). According to Evelyn Waugh, by 1563, Campion "was already a person of outstanding importance in the University. At the age of seventeen he had become a Fellow of St. John's and almost immediately attracted round him a group of pupils over whom he exerted an effortless and comprehensive influence; they crowded to his lectures, imitated his habits of speech, his mannerisms and his clothes, and were proud to style themselves 'Campionists'" (19).

On September 3, 1566, when Queen Elizabeth visited Oxford, Campion welcomed her in the name of the University and spoke in Latin before her. His dissertation was on the influence of the moon upon the tides, "an early instance of the cult of Elizabeth as Diana, the Virgin Goddess" (Jenkins 136). Perhaps this association between Campion and the moon made the link in Shakespeare's mind with Hotspur's "plucking bright honor from the pale-faced moon" (*1 Henry IV* 1.3.201) and led to the later eulogy evoking Campion in *2 Henry IV*. The queen recommended that both Leicester and

Cecil patronize the brilliant young man, with an eye to grooming him as a leader in her English Church. Cecil and Elizabeth were finding it difficult to get suitable candidates for the ministers of the new church (Waugh 24). After his brief service on the English mission, Campion did indeed dive into the deeps and drag Honor up with dripping locks through his execution. His horrible and bloody death was overshadowed by the honor he merited by it.

After this brilliant career at Oxford under the glittering view of the queen and her favorite, Campion was unable to embrace the Protestant faith. He fled to Ireland for a time where he compiled part of a *History of Ireland* and then escaped to Douai in 1570. From there he went on foot to Rome, and upon arrival in 1572, applied to enter the Jesuit Order. After completing his novitiate, he taught at Prague until 1579 when he was called by Cardinal Allen to return to England on the mission. In response to Allen's call, Campion traveled alternately by foot and by coach to the coast where he embarked for England. Young Shakespeare could have been among those who gathered to greet Campion at Shakespeare's Uncle William Catesby's home where they were regaled with humorous accounts of the disguises the priests had devised to avoid discovery en route.

Parsons recounted some of these stories in his biography of Campion, one of which may have been alluded to by Shakespeare in *1 Henry IV*. In one anecdote, Campion threw a shabby cloak over a piece of buckram, probably not unlike the "cases of buckram" (1.2.201) Poins and Hal masked themselves in to attack Falstaff and crew (1.2.182). Later, Campion's shirt became the focus of ridicule in his trial and immediately prior to his execution. Could it be Shakespeare was reminding the audience of Campion's "sweet robe of durance" like the one Falstaff, the Puritan, scorned (1.2.48)? Is there a second reminder of Campion's attire in *2 Henry IV* when Poins and the Prince again disguise themselves as tapsters by donning "two leathern jerkins" (2.2.190)? At his trial, Campion "was accused of having dissembled his identity, of calling himself 'Hastings,' of wearing a velvet hat and a feather, a buff leather jerkin and velvet venetians" (Waugh 177). The buff jerkin became a focus of attention on December 1, 1581, when Campion was taken from prison to be led to the scaffold. A search was made for the clothes he had been wearing when he was arrested because "it had been decided to execute him in the buff leather jerkin and velvet venetians which had been ridiculed at his trial. But the garments had already been misappropriated, and he was finally led out in the gown of Irish frieze which he had worn in prison" (185). Using his clothing as a tool of scorn in this way was a far cry from Campion's humorous account of his companion's costume recounted by Waugh:

> Parsons, the first Jesuit to invade England, was also the most splendid; he had decided to travel as an officer returning from the Netherlands. His friend, Mr. Chamberlain, living at St Omer, helped

to fit him out. He had 'a very fine suit of a captain's apparel of his own, which was of buff laid with gold and with hat and feather suited to the same.' Such glorious haberdashery brought Campion to life. "He was dressed up," writes Campion, "like a soldier; such a peacock, such a swaggerer, that a man needs must have very sharp eyes to catch a glimpse of any holiness and modesty shrouded beneath such a garb, such a look, such a strut." (185)

In this and an earlier reference to their disguises Campion described Parsons as a "swaggerer." Might this description of the disguised Parsons as a "swaggerer" be the reason Mistress Quickly exclaimed in terror, "If he swagger, let him not come here: no by my faith; I must live among my neighbours; I'll no swaggerers" (2 Henry IV 2.4.79-82). She would willingly admit cheaters and other "honest men," but she literally shook at the mention of swaggerers (2.4.110-14). The buff jerkin and the swaggerer had perhaps become "in" jokes about people who truly did "shake like an aspen leaf" for fear of being arrested by the deputy and scolded by the presumably English Church minister for having admitted such a forbidden swaggerer as Parsons.[28] It can always be argued that Shakespeare merely heard these stories as common gossip and incorporated them into his plays. It is only when they are combined with other clues Shakespeare might have been in contact with both priests that they seem to be more likely first-hand information.

This early association with the Catholic priests involved in the mission might cast a new light on Shakespeare's purchase of the Blackfriars Gatehouse in 1613. Shakespeare's interest in purchasing the Gatehouse is a link between Shakespeare and Campion that has not been fully explored. The fact the Blackfriars Gatehouse was owned by Henry, ninth earl of

---

28 Another possible source for such an "in" joke is recounted by Leys: Frances Burroughs had been adopted by a widow ". . . whose house in Leicestershire was a convenient refuge for priests as it was near the border of Warwickshire. As the lady was a Vaux, she was highly suspect, and searches of her house were frequent. When poursuivants came, Frances was usually sent to open the door; although she was only eleven, she was very clever in handling them. One day the dreaded knock came while Mass was actually being said: Frances ran down with a lady, and found to her dismay that the men had already been admitted and stood with their drawn swords in the hall. She cried out to them, 'Oh, put up your naked swords or else my mother will die for she cannot endure to see a naked sword.' She became a nun and told the story to her fellow nuns who recorded it in the Chronicle of St. Monica's, Louvain" (47). Catholics in the audience who knew this story would have been doubly amused by the hostess's attempt to quell the impending duel with, "Alas, alas! Put up your naked weapons, put up your naked weapons" (2.4.210, 211).

Northumberland, in 1589 suggests the possibility of some connection between him and Campion that might parallel the abandonment of Hotspur by the Northumberland of the play. In addition, the Gatehouse "was a notorious center of Catholic activities" (Mutschmann and Wentersdorf 136). It is further described: "About 1586, a Government informer reported his suspicions regarding Blackfriars House: 'Now there dwells in it one that is a very inconformable man to her Majesty's proceedings. It has sundry backdoors and bye-ways, and many secret vaults and corners. It has been in time past suspected, and searched for papists, but no good done for want of knowledge of the backdoors and bye-ways of the dark corners'" (137). In 1569, Mary Campion Blackwell, "a kinswoman of the famous martyr of the English Counter-Reformation, Edmund Campion," (137) inherited the Gatehouse from her husband who was somehow related to Father George Blackwell, the future archpriest.

After the purchase of the Gatehouse, Shakespeare leased it to John Robinson, a Catholic, who also witnessed Shakespeare's will. John Robinson's father, another John Robinson, had been living in the Gatehouse and was under government surveillance as a Catholic. The Robinsons perhaps have some connection with the John Robinson who is listed as a murder suspect in the death of Thomas Hoghton II (Appendix III). If the older Robinson was the same one whose name appears on the list, this would be an excellent tie between Shakespeare and the Hoghtons. Might Shakespeare have persisted in finally purchasing the Gatehouse, which was a complicated business transaction, because of its sentimental value in connection with Campion?

Campion's service on the mission was short, lasting only one and a half years before he was captured. After prolonged questioning and torture, he was finally dragged through the mud and rain to the scaffold at Tyburn on December 1, 1581. Waugh quoted a contemporary account by Bombinus: "[The witness] . . . followed close at hand and stood by the scaffold. He records how one gentleman, 'either for pity or affection, most courteously wiped [Campion's] face, all spattered with mire and dirt, as he was drawn most miserably through thick and thin; for which charity or haply some sudden moved affection, God reward him'" (185, 186). In a symbolic sense, if the Hotspur eulogy in the play referred to Campion, Shakespeare's gesture was quite similar.

While it may seem far-fetched to modern audiences to see any connection between the eulogy by Lady Percy and the Jesuit martyr Edmund Campion, to an Elizabethan audience, such a reference to a hero of the recent Catholic movement might have been understood both from its 1569 perspective and in the light of the events of 1597 when the play is believed to have been written. One thing is certain: in *1 Henry IV,* Hotspur was not portrayed as "the glass wherein the noble youth did dress themselves"; nor did they practice his gait, nor imitate his speech. He was not shown to be the "mark and glass and copy book that fashioned others" for which he is praised in *2 Henry IV*. On the other hand, at Oxford, Edmund Campion was "followed and imitated." Young men imitated not only his phrases but his gait, and revered him as a second Cicero.

For Elizabethan Catholics, the analogy between Hotspur and Campion as "soldiers" would have been understood, for Campion regarded himself as a soldier on a religious battlefield, as did most Jesuits. The Catholics in the audience could have appreciated the tributes to their martyred hero, and some of them would have found satisfaction in having the queen's betrayal of "them" at least brought before public scrutiny. The queen, on the other hand, could have gloried in Shakespeare's "allusion" to her as the ideal monarch who had vanquished her enemy as a kind of reincarnation of Henry V. The real-life Campion was a closer match to Lady Percy's eulogy than was Hotspur. As Pugliatti noted, the *Henriad* points in two directions.

Puritan vs. Catholic in
Shakespeare's *Twelfth Night*

A major comic element of Shakespeare's *Twelfth Night* is the duping of
Malvolio which results in his donning yellow knitted stockings adorned
with cross garters. Why would this have been a humorous sight in
Shakespeare's day? Cross garters and yellow stockings symbolized the
extreme, opposing religious stands of the Puritans and the Catholics that
plagued Queen Elizabeth's reign. When both the yellow stockings and the
cross garters were forced upon the straight-laced Puritan, Malvolio, he
would have looked ridiculous to an audience who understood the religious
implications. *Twelfth Night* abounds with religious references which are
often overlooked, perhaps because the topical significance has been lost to
modern viewers, as well as because of the fact the skillfully structured plot
woven around mistaken identity captures the attention, so religious allusions pass unnoticed. I suggest religious questions, principally the strife
between Puritans and Catholics, form a primary focus Shakespeare intended his audience to consider. The vocabulary, the disguise of the clown as Sir
Topas or Master Parson, Malvolio's "madness" and his enforced, outlandish
attire convey religious symbolism which serves the dual function of enhanc-
ing the humor while conveying religious messages.

In the Catholic Rebellion of the North in 1569, the color yellow was
worn by retainers and adherents of the duke of Norfolk, who was making
a rather hesitant bid to marry the queen of Scotland with the final objective
of replacing Elizabeth with Mary.[29] The fact that Norfolk chose the color

---

[29] When Norfolk returned to London in January 1566, the feud between
Leicester and Norfolk broke out again. Lord Robert's supporters started wearing blue (or purple) and Norfolk's yellow. 'I am told that Leicester began it, so
as to know who were his friends,' wrote de Silva (Williams 95).

"In the mid-sixties. . . . Leicester had got all his followers to put on blue
stripes or laces; it was both a trial and a show of strength. Norfolk immediately
put his people into yellow" (Dodsworth 15).

yellow, or tawny, may reflect yellow's Catholic and Spanish association, for Queen Elizabeth did not like yellow because it appeared in the flag of Catholic Spain (Hunt 198). The fact Shakespeare was specific about Malvolio's stockings being yellow at least opens the possibility he intended to suggest a religious significance through them.

A notorious story having to do with the stockings of a fugitive Catholic priest, Thomas Holford, must have been circulating around Chester in 1585. If Shakespeare was a player in either the Hoghton or the Hesketh household (both within thirty or forty miles of Chester), Shakespeare could have had a ready-made, topical event in mind when he dressed Malvolio in yellow knitted stockings. Holford, who was captured and imprisoned in May 1585, was described by the bishop of Chester:

> The said Holford is a tall, black, fat, strong man, the crown of his head bald, his beard marquessated [shaven except for hair on lip]; his apparel was a black cloak with murrey lace open at the shoulders, a straw-coloured fustion doublet laid on with red lace, the buttons red, cut and laid under with red taffeta, ash-coloured hose laid on with biliment lace [trimming], cut and laid under with black taffeta. A little black hat lined with velvet in the brim, a falling band and yellow knitted stockings. (Appendix IV)

Holford made a spectacular, but short-lived escape, largely because his jailers deemed him mad when he pulled on one yellow stocking and one white hose and stalked around. Holford's jailers thought he was a lunatic because of his antics with his stockings, just as Malvolio's jailers accused him of being mad because of the peculiar leg attire they tricked him into wearing. The decoration of Malvolio's legs with both Catholic and Puritan symbols was meant to poke fun at the ambiguous nature of Shrewsbury's religion. Catholic yellow stockings on a Puritan Malvolio or cross-garters, a style popular with Puritans (Nelson 391; Hunt 198), on a secret Catholic would have been amusing in itself, but to combine them on one person would have been hilarious to Shakespeare's contemporary audience. The earl of Shrewsbury, proposed here as the model for Malvolio, was "on the fence" in terms of religion, sometimes appearing to be a Puritan and at other times in collusion with Catholics.

It was Maria, the maid/confidante of the Countess Olivia, who dreamed up the trick on Malvolio that caused him to don yellow knitted stockings in the misguided belief that the Countess admired them. It was also Maria who characterized Malvolio as being a "kind of Puritan" (2.3.141). For Maria, being a Puritan was the epitome of all she disliked in a religious sense. However, she sees Malvolio as a "kind" of Puritan and not as a totally committed one. She described him as being "an affectioned ass," as speaking in rolling phrases of statecraft, a man who was in love with himself and thought everyone else loved him (2.3.147-154). Earlier, Countess Olivia, who was otherwise sympathetic with her steward Malvolio, had reproved him for being so scornful of the clown, saying Malvolio was "sick of self-love," tasted with a "distempered appetite," made mountains of mole-hills, and was a discreet man but one who scolded too much (1.5.92-99). In short, Malvolio was a satirical portrait of a Puritan, and his Catholic yellow knitted stockings under his Puritan cross-garters must have been a very funny sight, which hinted that perhaps under Shrewsbury's Puritan exterior lurked a secret Catholic.

The story of the yellow-stockinged Catholic Holford may have served another function in the play. Holford had held a secret and illegal mass in Chester Castle "lately," (App. III), an activity which typified the undercover mission of the Jesuits and Seminary priests at work in England during the 1580s. As has been shown, the priests had to disguise themselves for their own protection as well as for the protection of those who sheltered them. Sometimes they wore very unpriestlike clothes like the fancy clothes Holford was wearing when he was apprehended. They "dissembled" often in order to survive. Shakespeare's clown mimicked these disguises when he "dissembled" himself as Master Parson in the priest's gown[30] when Maria sent him to enlighten Malvolio. The clown hoped he was "the first that ever dissembled in such a gown" (4.1. 4-6). Shakespeare's Sir Topas/Master Parson spoke Latin, a probable sign that he was a Catholic priest who was to convert the lost Puritan, Malvolio, "turned heathen" (3.2. 69), a description of a person who had lost his Christian religion. "Sir Topas" was further identified as "Master Parson" by Sir Toby, and then the clown referred to an "old hermit of Prague, that never saw pen and ink . . . " (4.1).

What was behind this reference to a hermit of Prague, and who was the clown satirizing through his role? Might Shakespeare have been referring to the two Jesuit priests, Edmund Campion and Robert Parsons? The pointed reference to the identity of the clown as "Master Parson" must have had reverberations in an audience that knew of and sometimes participated in the secret activity related to the priests. Campion had spent the years 1574 - 1580 at Prague as a teacher where he had been virtually isolated from the

---

30 Peter Milward, S.J., has clarified the distinction between vestment and gown: "the gown was a symbol not of a Catholic priest but of a Calvinist minister, who would wear no vestments over his gown" (FAX 24 Sept. 1999).

If the gown was a symbol of a Calvinist minister, I should think that a priest who spoke Latin and was called "Parsons" would have looked funny to an Elizabethan audience who knew the meaning of of the Calvinist gown and who knew of the Catholic Father Parsons. This would be a mixing of religions which would parallel the yellow stockings and cross garter's of Malvolio.

religious turmoil in England until he was called to the English mission in 1580. Was *he* the hermit of Prague that Shakespeare had in mind? Both he and Parsons were so notorious throughout the country that Shakespeare might have been aware of them simply because of their notoriety, but we have seen that he was probably acquainted with both of them. Disguised references to Robert Parsons and Edmund Campion as the "Master Parson" clown and the "old Hermit of Prague" would have had connotations to a contemporary audience that are long since forgotten. A dissembling, robed priest (to wear or not to wear vestments was a heated debate of the time), and a priest who had come from Rome as witnessed by his Latin "Bonos Dies," sent to enlighten the Puritan Malvolio, was a humorous staging of the religious debate.[31]

In addition to his role in the enlightenment of Malvolio, another function of the clown is to "catechize" Olivia regarding her dead brother's soul. In the course of the catechism, he repeatedly refers to Olivia as "madonna," a religious term which suggests holiness, akin, perhaps to the Catholic perception of the martyr role of Mary, Queen of Scots. Why should a fool question and instruct his mistress on religious questions such as whether or not her brother's soul is in heaven or hell? Why should a fool argue about sin and virtue in syllogisms in the manner of the religious scholars of the seminaries and vaunt his scholarly knowledge? In sermon-like tones, the clown warns Olivia:

> . . . Anything that's mended is but patched:
> virtue that transgresses is but patched with sin,
> and sin that amends is but patched with virtue. If
> that this simple syllogism will serve, so: if it
> will not, what remedy? (1.5.44-48)

Later, in an attempt to enlighten Malvolio, who has been imprisoned in a dark room as a madman, the fool scolds Malvolio for his refusal to subscribe to the theory of Pythagoras concerning the transmigration of the soul:

> Fare thee well: remain thou still in darkness.
> Thou shalt hold th' opinion of Pythagoras ere I
> will allow of thy wits, and fear to kill a woodcock
> lest thou dispossess the soul of thy grandam. Fare
> thee well. (4.2.58-62)

---

31 At the end of December 1558, a proclamation was published that the Litany, the Epistle, and the Gospel should be read in all churches in the English language (Hayward 13).

There is an interesting connection between Parsons and Campion in regard to the theories of Pythagoras. Simpson quotes Parsons' account of their visit to the archbishop of the English College at Rome immediately before their departure for the English mission. Parsons recounted Campion's contribution to the after-dinner discussion:

> Campion's discourse was very pithy, and fit for the place and the time. He began with Cicero's quotation from Pythagoras, who, perceiving by the light of nature man's difficulty to good, and proneness to vice, said, that the way of virtue was hard and laborious, but yet not void of delectation, and much more to be embraced than the other, which was easy. Which Father Campion applying to a Christian life, showed very aptly both the labours and delights thereof, and that the saying of Pythagoras was much more verifiable in the same than in the life of any heathen philosopher, for that the labours were greater, the helps more potent, the end more high, and the reward more excellent. . . . (Simpson 154)

The catechizing and philosophizing from Shakespeare's fool would have come more appropriately from an actual priest. The clown's Latin observation, "cucullus non facit monachum" (a cowl does not make a Monk) (1.5.87), would have been pointedly humorous if the role of the clown and been played by a real Catholic priest in disguise, a priest who "lived by the church" as the clown did (2.5.5-7). It is not unthinkable a fugitive priest could have played the part of the clown in the first performance of the play. Edmund Campion wrote numerous plays while he was in Prague, and one can imagine him or Robert Parsons participating in a play in addition to performing his priestly functions—both secretly—at the home of a private lord. The date of the first performance is now generally believed to be 6 January 1601 (*Twelfth Night*. Introduction. New Arden ed. xxxiv), and yet the topical religious allusions, if the Campion/Parsons allusions are valid, suggest an earlier date, somewhere between 1585 (the date of the yellow-stockinged Holford) and 1587 (the date of the execution of Mary, Queen of Scots) if what I see as allusions to Mary, Queen of Scots, in the play are valid. If Shakespeare was an actor/playwright in the home of Alexander Hoghton or that of his brother-in-law, Thomas Hesketh, during these years, he would have had in either home an audience receptive to a humorous treatment of fugitive Catholic priests and a pathetic Puritan's being confronted by a Catholic clown.

Religious overtones permeate the dialogue of the play. Olivia confirms the religious theme as she spurns Duke Orsino's message of love Viola/Cesario delivers. Their conventional Petrarchan banter is a façade for their more profound communication. Orsino's bosom is referred to as a book with a "doctrine," a word that connotes religious dogma, and she describes his doctrine as "heresy," which at the time would have meant "denial of the doctrine of the Catholic Church." If the real-life counterparts for Olivia and Orsino held opposing religious beliefs, as for instance, the earl of Leicester's Puritan beliefs would have clashed with the Catholic faith of Mary, Queen of Scots, when he made a bid for her hand in marriage, this type of bantering with religious terms would have made sense.32

An offer of marriage is brought to the countess by a young servant (Cesario/Viola) because the duke thinks the offer is more likely to be accepted if it is delivered by "him" than if it were brought by a serious "nuncio":

> O then unfold the passion of my love,
> Surprise her with discourse of my dear faith;
> It shall become thee well to act my woes;
> She will attend it better in thy youth
> Than in a nuncio's of more grave aspect.
> (1.5.24-28)

Clues to Olivia's religion and perhaps her identity may lie in the fact she rejects the offer of marriage because it is "heresy" and because her renunciation of marriage suggests she is a holy martyr. A basic doctrinal disagreement between Catholics and Puritans had to do with the intercession of the Virgin Mary, a belief dear to Catholics and rejected by Puritans. One deduction from these clues is that Olivia symbolized Roman Catholicism, exactly the role Mary, Queen of Scots, was to play. This Catholic lady also sealed her letters with the impressure of Lucrece (2.5.91). "Lucrece" was a conventional tribute to Mary, Queen of Scots, in France, where she was known as "Helen in beauty; Lucrece in chastity . . . " (Fraser 96). It would indeed have been "sport royal" (2.3.172) to gull whomever Malvolio represented into thinking that a queen could be romantically interested in him. Malvolio seemed delighted that the letter was written by a "sweet *Roman* hand," [emphasis mine] a description that would automatically have signified "Papist" to Shakespeare's audience.

The writing of deceptive and incriminating letters played a large role in the family feud developing in relation to Shrewsbury's guardianship of Mary, Queen of Scots. The feud resulted in a trick on the earl of Shrewsbury that is echoed by the trick played on Malvolio in the play. Bess of Hardwick and her children tried to avert disaster and to free the earl of his sixteen-year-old task of overseeing the safety of Mary while at the same time trying

---

32 When Mary Stuart returned to Scotland in 1563, there were rumors that she intended to marry Henry Darnley. Queen Elizabeth decided that she herself should control Mary's marriage and proposed her own favorite, Robert Dudley, as a suitor for Mary. Elizabeth raised Dudley step-by-step socially to make him worthy of Mary. Just at the same time Elizabeth was proposing Leicester as a mate for Catholic Mary, he seemed to be becoming a stricter Puritan and was considered a sort of leader of the Puritans (Chamberlain. *Elizabeth and Leycester,* 150).

to prevent her escape. In 1584 Bess, Shrewsbury's wife, suspected him of joining in a plot to free Mary, and to ward this off, she and her sons circulated the rumor the earl had fallen victim to Mary's charms and that Mary had produced two of his offspring. The alleged romantic relationship between Shrewsbury and his ward, Mary Stuart, has similarities with the plot concocted to make Malvolio believe Olivia is enamored of him. Shrewsbury's anger and humiliation caused a permanent marital rift even Queen Elizabeth's intercession could not bridge. The earl vacillated between Catholicism and Puritanism, just as he wavered in his allegiance to Mary and Elizabeth. The possibility one of the many plots to free Mary and replace Elizabeth with her would succeed must have seemed real enough that the earl thought it wise to remain in the good graces of both. The plight of the Shrewsburys typifies the entanglement of Shakespeare's contemporaries in the most important question of the time—that of religious/political affiliation, and, indeed, politics and religion were nearly synonymous. The earl of Shrewsbury is an excellent candidate for the actual counterpart of Malvolio.

Shakespeare's pitting of the Puritan against the Catholic in the play is humorous, but it also conveys a topical message. If one is to interpret the play as a taking of sides on his part, it might be said that he disapproved of Malvolio and his Puritan approach to life. It seems certain, however, that the religious rivalry as it is depicted in *Twelfth Night* would have been humorous for Shakespeare's audience beyond what present-day audiences see in it. Because the play pokes fun at the religious extremes with which Queen Elizabeth had to contend and because she would have found it amusing to see the earl of Shrewsbury and Mary, Queen of Scots, parodied, even the queen might have enjoyed the humor of the play. Today's audience finds humor in the confusion caused by the mistaken identities, but the religious implications in the play would have been a major source of humor in Shakespeare's day and would have represented to some Elizabethan Catholics another case of mistaken identity in the character of the disguised priest.

What if You Don't Like It at All?

Two of the major themes of Shakespeare's *As You Like It* are the contrast between court and pastoral life and the Cain theme of one brother's wronging another. The locale of the play is envisioned either as the forests of Arden near Stratford or the Ardennes in France. The introduction to the Arden edition of the play notes: "Scholars have learnedly argued that the setting is clearly in some French duchy and it must be in the Ardennes near the Flanders border" (viii). It is interesting to note that William Allen's college was located at Douai which is near the Ardennes. Many Catholic exiles from Queen Elizabeth's court would have passed through and been sheltered at Douai in the late 1570s and early 1580s when Shakespeare could have been a student there. The play depicts a seeming first-hand knowledge about the life of the exiles a student at Allen's school would have seen frequently. The plot has some parallels with the story of the exiled Thomas Hoghton I who left the country for "conscience's sake" and placed his property in the hands of a brother. Whether the setting Shakespeare had in mind was the Forest of Arden in Warwickshire or the Forest of Ardennes in Flanders, he set the play in a sheltering and comforting forest where those who have been wronged in various ways at the sophisticated, deceptive, and ruthless court find peace, honesty, and brotherly love. There is a strong suggestion, although it is not specifically stated, that those who fled the court actually left the country.

During the long reign of Queen Elizabeth, the majority of Catholics remained in England and survived as best they could, employing the evasive devices we have seen John Shakespeare use. Some could not, for conscience's sake (their terminology), remain in the country and sought refuge abroad, living on the meager incomes they were able to salvage, although a few were granted sinecure offices or small pensions by the king of Spain. Some went to Rome, some to Paris, but the favorite place of refuge was Flanders, where the well-established network of seminaries at St. Omer, Louvain, Rheims, Douai, and Eu could offer assistance to the displaced. In addition to the schools, English convents and monasteries were scattered about the north of France and throughout Belgium where refugees could find shelter. Aside from sympathy with the misfortune of exiles he knew, what else might have motivated Shakespeare to depict on the London stage an idealized and unquestionably unrealistic picture of the life of the exiles abroad? Was the play a kind of travel/vacation brochure intended to attract other disaffected Catholics to join their brethren? To combat the exodus of wealthy citizens from the country, the English government had begun publishing accounts of the destitute lives of the exiles, some of whom had been promised relief by Spain only to find that the promises were empty ones. Whether or not it was Shakespeare's intention, *As You Like It* portrays an apt rebuttal to the government's propaganda, picturing life in exile as an idyllic, Christian antithesis to the duplicitous and dangerous life at court.

By 1585 the government was waging a campaign to dissuade potential exiles from leaving the country. A part of that campaign was a book published in 1585 supporting Don Antonio's claim to Portugal in opposition to Philip of Spain, who was moving to preempt the Portuguese throne. The purpose of the book was to enlist support for Don Antonio's cause, which started with the premise that Philip was automatically a villain. The point of one of the arguments was to dissuade English Catholics from seeking exile abroad under the protection of Spain by drawing a bleak picture of the conditions under which the exiles in Spain and Flanders were living. The substance of the argument came from a private letter written by a man who had served under Philip. The letter was addressed to a Catholic relative who was contemplating going into exile. Strype quotes from the letter:

> That himself being five or six years past in these parts of Flanders subject to the Spanish king, he saw a miserable troop of his unhappy countrymen; some, gentlemen of good houses in England, wandering in poor habits and afflicted gestures, heavily groaning under the burden of extreme and calamitous necessity: on the one side, by their heedless demeanour there, debarred from return into their country; and on the other, overlooked by the proud eyes of disdainful Spaniards: and for want of due regard in that comfortless service, perishing without either pity or relief. (513)

Strype's assessment of this propaganda is interesting: "As the Roman Catholics of this nation made great complaints, and publicly clamoured against the severity used towards them, so it was necessary the state should as publicly be vindicated" (513). Verstegen, the chief agent of the Catholics in Antwerp, "had to admit that 'our miseries are such in truthe as that our Catholique friends in England may thereat be much agreaved.' It was 15 months, he wrote, since any money had come from Spain, in spite of 'lies and deluding promises . . . God comfort us and send us meanes to live withoute depending upon any forraine friends'" (Leys 53). Men, once well-to-do and now too old to work, were forced to beg for bread; some actually died of starvation. Their misfortunes were used as propaganda by the English government; in 1595 a pamphlet was published in London on the 'Usage of the English fugitives by the Spaniard'" (Leys 53). Perhaps Shakespeare's play was a kind of rebuttal to the government propaganda. As there are no quarto editions of the play to help in the dating of it, we must rely on the facts that it was not mentioned by Francis Meres in 1598, but there was an entry in the *Stationers' Register* for August 4, 1600, of a play by that name (Shakespeare, Preface, *AYLI* xiv). Therefore the date of composition probably lies between 1598 and 1600, well beyond the Portuguese problem, but the exodus of exiles from England was still a problem for the English government, prompting arguments to dissuade more from leaving.

The plot of the play was probably not intended to parallel a specific real-life story but rather was intended to explore contemporary problems and to deal with parallel themes. However, it does bear some resemblance to a story about a member of the Hoghton family whom Shakespeare might have known. One of the conscientious objectors who went into exile was Thomas Hoghton I of Lea Hall and Hoghton Tower. If Shakespeare lived with the Hoghtons during the 1580s, he would have known the unhappy story of Thomas Hoghton and the difficulties he had with his brothers. These brothers appear to have taken advantage of his estrangement from England to "play upon him," as he phrased it in his letters to the only relative who remained loyal to him, his half brother, Richard Hoghton of Park Hall. If, on the other hand, Shakespeare's only connection with Lancashire was as a member of Ferdinando Stanley's acting group, Shakespeare perhaps would have heard the story anyway, for as we know, Lord Strange and the Hoghtons were close friends.

If Shakespeare actually had in mind the Hoghton family when he wrote the play, he obviously changed the ages of the actors, but the major change is that characters in the play are not protesting on religious grounds. The play would never have made it to the boards with religious exile as the overt basis of the conflict between the brothers. Instead, the younger brother Orlando protests that his older brother Oliver has denied him the means by which he can advance in society. That, in itself, pointed to a contemporary problem of many young men.

Primogeniture provided for the eldest, but the other brothers had to fend for themselves, in many cases going into the priesthood. However, young Catholic men no longer had that option, and the materialism of the court society shut the door to those who lacked wealth and lands, one of Orlando's problems in the play. Sometimes the rifts between brothers were the result of one brother's religious exile and another's conformance to the English Church; sometimes the motivation was simply greed and power. The disagreement between the Hoghton brothers seemed to be a combination of the two. The story of the Hoghton brothers and Queen Elizabeth's intervention would have been an excellent model for Duke Frederick's treatment of his brother and his usurpation of Oliver's property.

Two possible routes by which Shakespeare could have become acquainted with the Hoghton story have been mentioned. There is yet another possibility. The Hoghton saga occurred exactly when Shakespeare could have been a student in a school abroad in the Ardennes, which might have placed him near the old exile, Thomas Hoghton I. Thomas Hoghton's tribulations ended with his death in June 1580, just at the time Shakespeare would have been ready to return to England to join the Hoghton family, perhaps first going as Campion's guide to Lancashire and then remaining as a schoolmaster and eventually becoming part of the group of actors in the household. Shakespeare would probably have left grammar school to go abroad somewhere between 1576 to 1578 and would have finished his course of study by the age of sixteen in 1580, so his time abroad could have coincided with part of Thomas Hoghton's time there.

Thomas Hoghton I (1518-80) left England without permission in 1569 to go into exile at Antwerp and Liège because he was a Roman Catholic recusant. Before he left, he replaced "the old manor house at Houghton Bottoms" with Hoghton Tower on a ridge six miles southeast of Preston (Gillow, "Thomas Hoghton"). He was a friend of William Allen who attended the opening of the rebuilt Hoghton Tower, and we have already noted that he assisted William Allen in the founding of Douai College. Note the timing of Hoghton's departure in connection with the founding of William Allen's seminaries, which began in 1568. Thomas Hoghton I's son, Thomas, was debarred from the succession to the property because he had gone into exile with his father and, shortly after becoming a priest at Douai, was sent back to England as a missionary. Thomas I's "bad" brothers back in England crossed him and offered a thousand marks "to hinder my licence/ That I should not come home again" (Honigmann 11). Hoghton died 4 June 1580 and was buried at Liège.

The manuscript letters between Thomas Hoghton I and Richard Hoghton of Park Hall from 1576 to 1580 (in the John Rylands Library of the University of Manchester) attest to the financial and legal difficulties that arose between Thomas Hoghton I and the brothers who remained at Hoghton Tower and Lea Hall, the family seats. One of these brothers was Alexander Hoghton, who inherited Lea Hall and the Hoghton estate on the death of Thomas Hoghton I. Alexander died the following year, and it is his 1581 will that gave birth to the speculation William Shakespeare served in the Hoghton home.

The nephew of Thomas I, Sir Richard Hoghton (1570 - 1630), exemplified Elizabeth's technique of wresting sons away from Catholic families to mold them into zealous Protestants. Richard was placed in wardship with Sir Gilbert Gerard, the Master of the Rolls, to be brought up a Protestant. The result was that Richard married Sir Gilbert's daughter, Katherine, and became an active poursuivant of Catholic recusants and High Sheriff of Lancashire in 1598. As his reward for service to the government, he was knighted 28 June 1599 and was named a baron in 1611. The connections between Sir Richard with John Davies, who dedicated *Epigrammes* to him, Peter Legh of Lyme, his brother-in-law, and some of the Lancashire Ardens have already been pointed out.

It has been shown that William Shakespeare possibly knew another Richard Hoghton (of Park Hall in Charnock Richard.) This Mr. Hoghton, who was the illegitimate son of the old grandfather, Sir Richard, and was a half brother to Thomas I and Alexander, managed the business affairs during the exile of Thomas Hoghton I, his eldest brother. Alexander Hoghton and Thomas II later divided their time between Lea Hall and the Tower, as did the younger Sir Richard Hoghton, who was to live there along with his widowed mother. On March 17, 1576, Mr. Richard Hoghton, who remained loyal to Thomas I, obtained a license from Queen Elizabeth to visit the exile in Antwerp to persuade him to obey the queen. "Hoghton was anxious to return, but could not make terms with the Court to retain his religion" and so he remained abroad and died at Liège, June 2, 1580, aged 63" (Gillow, "Thomas Hoghton").

Roger Anderton, Hoghton's butler, who went into exile with his master, seems very like old Adam of the play, who contributes his life savings to finance Orlando's escape from the dangerous court. Roger Anderton's loyalty to his master led him to praise Thomas Hoghton and to tell his sad story in verse, which records Thomas's dying words:

> At Hoghton, where I used to rest
> Of men I had great store,
> Full twenty gentlemen at least,
> Of yeomen good three score!
> And of them all, I brought but two
> With me, when I came thence.
> I left them all ye world knows how
> To keep my conscience! . . .
> When to my brethren I had sent
> Ye welcome that they made
> Was false reports me to present,
> Which made my conscience sad.

My brethren all did thus me cross
And little regard my fall,
Save only one, that rued my loss,
This is Richard, of Park Hall,
He was ye comfort that I had;
I proved his diligence;
He was as just as they were bad,
Which cheered my conscience, . . . (Honigmann 10)

Honigmann speculates that the brothers were afraid they would be incriminated by the presence of their recusant relative and blocked his return by withholding documents he needed.

To obstruct Thomas's return was also to obstruct the will of the queen, who wanted him back in England enough to send his half brother to Europe to retrieve him. In 1576, the same year the correspondence between Thomas and Richard began, the queen signed a license allowing Richard to go to Antwerp "to the intent to advise, persuade and counsel Thomas Hoghton, late of Hoghton, . . . to return unto this our realm" (11).33 Hoghton was declared an outlaw, and possession was taken of his estates (Gillow, "Thomas Hoghton"). Her insecurity about Richard's return is very similar to Duke Frederick's concern about Oliver's trustworthiness when Frederick sends Oliver to find and return with his brother Orlando. In addition to taking possession of his estates, Queen Elizabeth required two sureties be bound with Richard if he failed to return to England within two months. The men posting the money would each lose £200 if Richard did not return. How similar the situation is to Duke Frederick's command to Oliver:

Find out thy brother, whereso'er he is;
Seek him with candle; bring him dead or living
Within this twelvemonth, or turn thou no more
To seek a living in our territory.
Thy lands, and all things that thou dost call thine
Worth seizure, do we seize into our hands
Till thou canst quit thee by thy Brother's mouth
Of what we think against thee. (3.1.5-12)

---

33 The relationship between Brian Jackson "the principal messenger between Thomas I and Richard Hoghton in the 1570s" (Honigmann 13) and John Jackson, a Blackfriar trustee, (Mutschmann and Wentersdorf 135) and the John Jackson on the Richard Hoghton list of those indicted for murder should be researched. This might be another connection between Shakespeare, the Hoghtons, and the theater.

The evil brothers, Duke Frederick and Oliver, are redeemed in the play in an almost "wishful thinking," fairytale type of resolution that the real Thomas Hoghton I would have welcomed. Oliver is redeemed through love, and Duke Frederick is redeemed through a change of religion. In the play, Oliver is willing to forfeit all of his wealth, his evil having been over-powered by the goodness of his brother, Orlando, and his love for Celia. The religious goodness of the new society in the wholesome, pastoral set-ting of the play seems to provide a remedy for each evil of the old society. Orlando exemplifies Christ's teaching to turn the other cheek, shown when he saves the life of Oliver who had so wronged him earlier. The power of this religion is great enough to transform so obstinate and vengeful a man as Duke Frederick into a religious monk:

> Duke Frederick, hearing how that every day
> Men of great worth resorted to this forest,
> Addressed a mighty power, which were on foot
> In his own conduct, purposely to take
> His brother here and put him to the sword;
> And to the skirts of this wild wood he came,
> Where, meeting with an old religious man,
> After some question with him, was converted
> Both from his enterprise and from the world,
> His crown bequeathing to his banished brother,
> And all their lands restored to them again
> That were with him exiled. (5.4.159-170)

The persuasive, old religious man is very like many exiled Catholic priests who roamed northern Europe performing such miracles. Frederick's redemption might have suggested that if enough "Men of great worth resorted to this forest" (5.4.160) of Ardennes, the queen might be so convinced of the sincerity of their convictions and their religion that she would call the exiles home to their restored lands.

There were other exiles whom Shakespeare might have known whether or not he lived with the Hoghtons or the Heskeths, because by 1592, Shakespeare is believed to have been a member of Ferdinando Stanley's, earl of Derby's, group of actors, and there were interesting and dangerous connections between Ferdinando and some of the exiled Catholics. A frag-ile link between the play and Ferdinand may be the name Shakespeare assigned Rosalind as her alias: "Ganymede." Might there have been an obscure connection between Rosalind and Chapman's praise of Ferdinando as "Ganymede" in the second hymn of "Shadow of Night" (1594)? Perhaps Ferdinando took the role of Rosalind in an early performance of the play. It is an androgynous role perhaps suiting a slightly more mature young man than usually played the women's roles. If the play were written to reflect Ferdinando's sympathies, as well as Shakespeare's, this would help explain the positive religious overtones in the forest of Arden (Ardennes) where Touchstone points out, "Here we have no temple but the wood" (3.3), literally true of the exiles, for they had had to leave their temples behind in England. Lord Strange was a Catholic who was connected by family members and friends to Catholic exiles abroad, some of whom backed him as a successor to Queen Elizabeth because of his mother's descent from the sister of Henry VIII.

Shakespeare's Forest of Arden is not tainted with the intrigue of the true picture of the exiles' relationship with the court, yet he surely would have been aware of some of the intrigue if he lived with Thomas Hesketh of Rufford. Richard Hesketh, third son of Thomas, became entangled in a complicated and questionable scheme to put Ferdinando Stanley on the English throne. Through this Richard and a cousin of Ferdinando Stanley, Sir William Stanley (author of the plot), both related to as well as visitors of the Heskeths of Rufford and the Stanleys of Derby, Shakespeare might have encountered a shady character named Jaques who hovered around the wings of much of the subversive activity of the exiled Catholics.

Jaques of the play has some traits in common with the real-life Jaques of the dark side of life in exile. The real Jaques served under Sir William Stanley twice: he was Stanley's lieutenant in Ireland in 1585 and later served under Stanley in the Netherlands (St. John Brooks 260). Sir William Stanley is notorious for his surrender of the city of Deventer to the Spanish as part of his Catholic protest against Queen Elizabeth's effort to Protestantize the Dutch. Stanley also played instrumental roles in both the Babington Plot and in the Richard Hesketh Plot to put Ferdinando Stanley on the English throne (Heywood xiii, xlii). In addition, Stanley was a personal friend of Robert Parsons (Heywood xxx). Stanley was later associated with Catesby, a relative of Shakespeare, in the Gunpowder Plot (liv). William Stanley was related to Ferdinando Stanley, and "the heirs of the two great Stanley houses of Hooton and Lathom were on terms of great and suspicious intimacy" (xlii).[34] Shakespeare could very well have been acquainted with the man, Jaques, through the Stanleys.

A brief biographical sketch of the real Jaques reveals personality traits which perhaps inspired Shakespeare to inject a version of the personality in the utopian world of Arden. Jaques (Jacomo Francisci), commonly called

---

34 Sir William Stanley, who married Alice of Timperley in 1375, had an eldest son, also Sir William Stanley; the latter married Margery of Hooton (Wirral, Cheshire) and founded a co-lateral branch of the family, the Stanleys of Hooton, in which an unbroken line of seven successive Sir William Stanleys led to Sir Rowland Stanley in Queen Elizabeth's time, and his son, Sir William Stanley (1548-1630), contemporary with his namesake William Stanley, sixth earl of Derby, eventually deserted to Spain (Titherley 7, footnote).

Captain Jaques, was a soldier of fortune, born in Antwerp of a Venetian father. He was described as "a dangerous and violent man," and the English spies constantly reported his injurious words, and malevolent, nay treasonable, persuasions and acts" (Pollen 95). He dressed in black satin, had a black beard, and always had a man attending him (St John Brooks 276). His personality comes alive in an account of the interrogation of Edward Windsor, one of the conspirators in the Babington Plot, who complained to Hatton that the government seemed to be strangely lenient toward Captain Jaques. He contended that Jaques had been one of "the chief workers of this conspiracy and to be wholly employed by Ballard to be ready in anything they could do for the assistance of the invasion, the one in the North, the other in Ireland" (278, 279). Windsor asked to see Jaques face to face and was surprised he was allowed to do so. Jaques swore his innocence, "laughing at me, and saying I was drunk, and that I had a devil within me, and how I was a dead man" (279).

The real-life Jaques had affinities with Duke Senior's melancholy Jaques in the play. There is a darkness surrounding Shakespeare's Jaques discordant with the loving and Christian world around him. Shakespeare's Jaques in some ways seems to be an addition to the play, for he is not essential to the plot or any relationship and seems out of tune with the almost naïve goodness of the exiles. He seems haughtily disdainful without cause when he begs Amiens to sing to gratify his own desires but is not really grateful for his service: "Well then, if ever I thank any man, I'll thank you. But that they call compliment is like the encounter of two dog-apes; and when a man thanks me heartily, methinks I have given him a penny, and he renders me the beggarly thanks. Come, sing! and you that will not, hold your tongues" (2.5.23-28). He seems not to like anyone in the play, not even his master, Duke Senior, of whom he says: "And I have been all this day to avoid him. He is too disputable for my company. I think of as many matters as he; but I give heaven thanks and make no boast of them" (2.5.32-35). He is a loner and prefers his own company to that of so likable a person as Orlando, for he says with little provocation, except his intolerance of Orlando's verses: "I thank you for your company; but, good faith, I had as lief have been myself alone" (3.2.252-253). Shakespeare's Jaques, self-consciously aware of the aloof, disdainful, and melancholy personality he has cultivated, could very suitably have dressed in black satin and worn a black beard as the real Jaques did. In a like manner, the real Jaques could have said of himself:

I have neither the scholar's melancholy, which is emulation; not the musician's, which is fantastical; nor the courtier's, which is proud; nor the soldier's, which is ambitious; nor the lawyer's, which is politic; nor the lady's, which is nice; nor the lover's, which is all these: but it is a melancholy of mine own, compounded of many simples, extracted from many objects, and indeed the sundry contemplation of my travels, in which my often rumination wraps me in a most humorous sadness (4.1.10-19).

He seems almost to sneer at Amiens' simple song, a song which could have been an invitation for other disaffected to come join the exiles:

> Who doth ambition shun
> And loves to live i' the sun,
> Seeking the food he eats,
> And pleased with what he gets,
> Come hither, come hither, come hither!
> Here shall he see
> No enemy
> But winter and rough weather. (2.5.36-43)

Jaques makes up his own version of the life the exiles are living and scoffs at their foolish stubbornness:

> If it do come to pass
> That any man turn ass,
> Leaving his wealth and ease
> A stubborn will to please,
> Ducdame, ducdame, ducdame!
> Here shall he see
> Gross fools as he,
> An if he will come to me. (2.5.48-55)

The picture of the real Jaques is of a man who is disdainful of all, committed to his own interests, haughty and aloof. This same descriptions applies to Shakespeare's Jaques. His assessment of all of mankind is a reflection of his own duplicitous nature:

> Why, who cries out on pride
> That can therein tax any private party?
> Doth it not flow as hugely as the sea
> Till that the wearer's very means do ebb?
> What woman in the city do I name
> When that I say the city woman bears
> The cost of princes on unworthy shoulders?
> Who can come in and say that I mean her,
> When such a one as she, such is her neighbor?
> Or what is he of basest function

That says his bravery is not on my cost,
Thinking that I mean him, but therein suits
His folly to the mettle of my speech?
(2.7.73-85)

The ironic picture of Jaques at the end of the play, abandoning the
world to join the convertites, from whom there was much to be learned
(5.4.190), and acknowledging the worth of each of the other characters
before his departure, is another fairytale ending that would have been
humorous to those who knew the real Jaques.

The conviviality of Rosalind and Celia is in marked contrast to Jaques'
jaded, lone demeanor. In some respects their sudden decision to disguise
themselves and flee from the court seems unrealistic. This is not very different, however, from the story of two young ladies who actually lived such
an adventure. Simpson tells of Anne Dimocke, a maid of honour to the
queen, who had learned from the court preachers that there was no hell,
"but only a certain remorse of conscience for him that did evil, which was
to be understood for hell, and that all the rest were but bugbears to fright
children" (241). Obviously this was a reference to the Protestant ban on references to Purgatory. Simpson recounts her attempts to find out the truth
about hell by going to Robert Parsons, "under whose instructions she at
once became Catholic, and afterwards left the court and the world" (241).
She and one of Lord Vaux' s daughters followed Parsons to Rouen where
Anne entered a convent.

In England, legally, these two girls were traitors, just as Rosalind and
Celia become traitors in the play: "If she [Rosalind] be a traitor, / Why, so
am I [Celia]!" (1.3.75,76). Rosalind has done nothing to merit the accusation she is a traitor, and the very fact Shakespeare used the term and then
had the girls disguise themselves for their departure must have suggested
to the audience instances of just such flights by friends and relatives. The
plan of the girls could also have served as a "how to" guide for those who
were contemplating leaving but needed direction in how to accomplish an
escape. Peter Milward observed that "The unjust accusation of treason
commonly made against Catholics in Elizabethan England, and particularly against all priests since the harsh penal laws of 1585, is interestingly
reflected in quite a number of plays" (71). In particular, Milward sees a reference to Lord Burghley in Duke Frederick's response to Rosalind's protesta-
tions of innocence: "Thus do all traitors; If their purgation did consist in
words, They are as innocent as grace itself" (1.3.54-56). Milward suggests his
words seem to echo those of Lord Burghley himself, in his self-justifying pamphlet on *The Execution of Justice in England* (1583): "It hath been in all ages and
in all countries a common usage of all offenders for the most part, both great
and small, to make defence of their lewd and unlawful facts by untruths and
by colouring and covering their deeds (were they never so vile) with pretences

of some other causes of contrary operations or effects" (Milward 71). Milward then contrasts this to the contemporary complaint of a Catholic against Elizabethan judges: "It is ordinary with them to call Catholics traitors, and to proceed against them in their judgements as on cases of treason, notwithstanding that the case be directly conscience" (71, 72).

For those like Anne Dimocke, the Vaux daughter, and Thomas Hoghton I, to be called traitors must have been particularly puzzling. Certainly not all exiles belonged in one category, so not all treason laws should have applied to all exiles. There is little question that Sir William Stanley, and perhaps Richard Hesketh, were engaged in treasonous plots that were a great danger to the queen. There were enough like Stanley to make it imperative the government take action against them. The majority, however, left the country for genuine religious beliefs—a move that required courage and steadfastness in the face of great misery and deprivation. The play softens the hardship of life in exile to make it seem bearable in a manner parallel to Edmund Campion's attitude about life in exile. Campion glorified the simple life and contrasted it with court life in a letter he wrote to novices at Brunn, after he had taken his vows and had returned to the college at Prague:

> Believe me, my dearest brethren, that your dust, your brooms, your chaff, your loads, are beheld by angels with joy, and that through them they obtain more for you from God than if they saw in your hands sceptres, jewels, and purses of gold. Would that I knew not what I say; but yet, as I do know it, I will say it; in the wealth, honours, pleasures, pomps of the world, there is nothing but thorns and dirt. The poverty of Christ has less pinching parsimony, less meanness, than the emperor's palace. (Simpson 97)

And again he wrote from Prague (1575):

> Which of us would have believed, unless He had called him and instructed him in this school, that such thorns, such filth, such misery, such tragedies, were concealed in the world under the feigned names of goods and pleasures? Which of us would have thought your kitchen better than a royal palace: your crusts better than any banquet? your troubles than others' contentment? . . . . One sigh of yours for heaven is better than all their clamours for this dirt; one colloquy of yours, where the angels are present, is better than all their parties and debauched drinking-bouts, where the devils fill the bowls. One day of yours consecrated to God is worth more than all their life, which they spend in luxury. (100)

The sad truth is many exiles died of starvation and in great penury. Some, like Thomas Hoghton I, were replaced by men like his nephew, Richard Hoghton, who turned Protestant and inherited all of the wealth and property Thomas Hoghton had renounced for his conscience's sake. Richard Hoghton made doubly sure he was secure in his position by becoming a renowned hunter of Catholic recusants. A few, it is true, were a real threat to the English government because of their subversive activity. The contrast Shakespeare drew between life at the English court and the pastoral life of the exile is persuasive although heavily slanted. It would have beckoned to Catholics to live their religion abroad for their consciences' sake. On a larger scale, the play was a plea to English Christians, Protestants and Catholics alike, to reconcile their differences in Christian forgiveness and love.

Conclusions

Shakespeare's Lancashire connection is the missing link between Stratford and the London stage. It is the essential piece of the puzzle which completes the picture of a man who was raised in a very Catholic home, who may have been educated in a Catholic school, who was patronized by Catholics, whose plays reflect and were intended to elicit sympathy for Catholics, and who "died a papist." It explains the route by which William Shakespeare entered the theater world and the controversial themes he treated in the plays.

The various environments in which he lived provided opportunities for him to meet young priests active in the Catholic mission, many of whom were executed, died in prison, or were banished. He was raised in a Catholic family that appears to have had ties with the Catholic missionaries and, on the mother's side, engaged in Catholic plots against the government. Stratford itself had its share of young men who returned to England as priests—young men Shakespeare may have gone to school with either in Stratford or abroad. Additionally, William Allen appears to have served in Stratford as a schoolmaster in 1563, and through him, the Shakespeares may have learned of the plan for Catholic seminaries abroad and an English mission largely centered in the northern shires of England. William Shakespeare could have become acquainted with the two leaders of the mission, Robert Parsons and Edmund Campion, through his father's apparent connection with them soon after their arrival, or at school abroad, or in the Hoghton home. Additional conjectural ties to Lancashire, derived from circumstantial evidence, are that Shakespeare may have received his secondary education in one of Catholic seminaries or colleges abroad, and upon completing the course, he returned to England as a guide for

Edmund Campion in 1580. Shakespeare's family had direct dealings with Campion, a route by which Shakespeare and Campion could have become acquainted and subsequently good friends. Shakespeare had interesting ties with both men, for his writing at times reflected specific works by both Campion and Parsons, and this association is strengthened by John Speed's suggestion Shakespeare was a spokesperson for Parsons in some way. These environments would have acquainted him with the subversive activity and the anguish of those who suffered under the charge of treason or of the predicament of Catholic exiles abroad, topics which his plays mirror from the point of view of an Elizabethan Catholic. Shakespeare's sympathy with Catholics and their suffering explains apparent references in his plays to Mary, Queen of Scots, as a Catholic martyr as well as the focus for the controversial topics of usurpation, assassination, and religious controversy.

Shakespeare's first step into the professional theater world was made in Lancashire, probably in the earl of Derby's acting group, and Shakespeare maintained his Lancashire ties to his death. Two of the trustees for the building of the Globe Theater, Savage and Leveson, were from Lancashire. John Robinson, the tenant of the Blackfriar's Gatehouse and a close friend of Shakespeare who was with him at his death and witnessed his will, was perhaps related to the John Robinson listed on the murder list in Richard Hoghton's possession.

Shakespeare's relationship to the Ardens of Cheshire needs further investigation, for it is clear that a Robert Ardern who lived there was acquainted with the Hoghtons and Heskeths, and both families are associated with a resident player named William Shakshafte, who might really have been William Shakespeare. Also, the bequest of Altcar to Shakespeare's great-Uncle Robert Arden of Park Hall needs further study to determine if Ardens settled in Altcar. Evidence has been presented here to show a probable relationship between the Hathaway family and the Gyllom family, perhaps an important connection by which William Shakespeare and Fulke Gyllom became associated. A friendship among the Gyllom, Hathaway, and Shakespeare families could explain why William "Shakeshafte" is mentioned together with Gyllom in the 1581 will of Alexander Hoghton.

Additionally, Shakespeare's patron and distant relative, Henry Wriothesley, the earl of Southampton, was acquainted with Campion and sympathetic to the missionary activity. The Essex rebellion in 1601 relied to some extent on Catholic support from Southampton and several of Shakespeare's Park Hall relatives. The fact that Shakespeare's patron, friends, and relatives were participants in the rebellion, combined with the fact that Shakespeare's *Richard II* was played specifically to rally support for the rebellion, make it appear Shakespeare was a participant to some degree. New evidence presented here is the important link between Robert Devereux (Essex) and the Park Hall Ardens.

The three contemporary statements about Shakespeare by Beeston, Davies, and Speed indicate Shakespeare was a Catholic, and each report can be substantiated to a degree. The combined import of these statements is that he was a Catholic throughout his life. This close look at Shakespeare's family, friends, and environment corroborates and strengthens the three contemporary reports about Shakespeare's Catholic faith: that he was a schoolmaster in a Catholic home in the country, he represented some of Robert Parson's ideas in his plays, and he died a papist. A reading of many of Shakespeare's plays from the Catholic position can sometimes reverse the traditional interpretation.

Appendix I Will of Robert Arden.
("Lancaster and Chester" 138)

THE WILL OF ROBERT ARDERN.[1]

———

[1] No date of probate.

IN Dei noïe Amẽ 22 Oct. 1540 32 Hen. VIII. I Robert Ardern dredyng detho &c. my body to be buryed in the pische churche wher as hyt shall ffortune me to dept I beqwethe to a wele disposyt pryst sadde and of vertuose cōdycōns xijli to syng masses......saule iij yeres in the churche were yt shall please God that my body or bones shall lye and the seyde p̃st shall have xs to fynde hym bredde and wyne and all other thyngẹ......ary and the sede pryst one yere of the seyde iij yers shall seye a trentall of Seynt ......ory wyt that at longẹ yrto and the seyde prist shall begynne the trentall at the next......at̃ my deptyng and so foloyng the utas of evy feast and also the sayde pryst shall seye evy Tuysdaye......se of requiẽ and dyrge and comẽdacōn on nyght afor and the seyde pryst shall p̃y for the [soul]s of my father and my moder and Sr Perys Leght knyght and pryst as he doyth for my saw. ....the seyde pryst to helpe to do devyne s̃vyce in the churche on holy dayes and evens yf he [be req]uyryt Also I wyll that all suche peplo as helpe to bryng me fourthe shall be taken to......se and have bredde and ale by tho dyscretyon of my executers Also I wyll that ther be xl......to sexe score of the poryst howses wtin Stokport and Manchast̃ pysches wtin xij dayes......my decesse and thaye and thayr meyny[?] to be requiret to p̃y for my saule Also I wyll have......e masse and a dyrge of the qwere were hyt shall fortune me to be buryed at my buryall......jth surgys to be sett ovr me and othyr lyghtẹ by the dyscretyon of my exccutors and also I wyll that my executors shall cause that daye and wtin viij dayes at̃ a trentall of masse[s to be] seyde for my saule To the repacōn of Stockport churche xls To our lady s̃vyce xs To seynt Petr s̃vyce viijs To seynt Antonye s̃vyce......iiijd To the repacyon of Wynwhyck churche xxs To the byldyng of Chedull churche or steple or repayryng of the same vjs viijd To the.... .ryng of Denton chapell vjs viijd To the chapell of seynt Stephen of Alvandley xls To Norden churche vjs viijd To Dedysbury churche ......js iiijd To the repacyon of Glossoppe churche vjs viijd To [the] maryage of my eldest doght̃r Alyce xli To our lady chapell of Dystele vjs viijd to be sette in the boke of broderhode Also where as I was executor to my mr l Syr Perys Leght knyght and prest I take yt opon my charge as I shall answare afor God that I have no mañ of goodes of hys gold ner sylvur except as her at̃ foloys that ys to wyt iij yardes of black fryce at̃ vijd a yarde x knottẹ of blew threde ye prce iiijd viij knottẹ of whyte threde ye prce iiijd a nold leysthe[2] a

Appendix I Will of Robert Arden continued

case of leydur to cary a glasse in a gaftlyn hedde³ in money vjˢ viijᵈ
also halfe a pownde and a quarteron of greyse a hert gratter of wode
also a leyde mall [? mallet] Iᵗ ij twytfyn baskyttᵉ⁴ yᵉ pᵣᶜᵉ xijᵈ I
have hade more then these bot not past the value of xijᵈ thes goodes
Maystᵣ Perys Leght of Bradley oghe to have bot he doyth oghe me
for more then thys To Annes the wyffe of Rauffe Robynson in
Denton xxˢ To Annes Lauder of Alderley xiijˢ iiijᵈ To Merget
Byrchall the doghtᵣ of Uyrn Byrchall dwellyng in Assheton in
Wynwhyck poche in Lancashyre xiijˢ iiijᵈ I wyll that all suche
that be owyng money to me whyche the names be in a bylle [hav]yng
thyt merk P be pardnut as myche as the scyde merke shall stande a
nendℓ and not......es To the makyng or upholdyng of Penkefurthe
brygge vjˢ viijᵈ Iᵗ to the makyng of Frodsam brygge vjˢ viijᵈ Also
I wyll that one be hyryt to go for me......scynt Truyons in Scot-
lande and offer [for] me a bende placke whyche ys in my purse Also
I wyll that one go on pylgᵣmache for me wᵗ a bend crossyt grote and
a mette of wax wᵗ v lytyll ᵍchys brenyng at evñsonge over nyght
and at matens and masse on the other daye to oure Lady of Wal-
syngliᵐ To Robert Ardern my neyvew my tawne saten boublet
[doublet] I wyll that my executors shall paye any thyng that canne
be provyt that I oghe and make a mendes to any mā that I have
hurte that can be provyt be ryght To Thomas Handley my black
gowne My other apparell for my bodye shall be delt emonge my
teñntes in Stockport pych..... to Hughe Geffronson in Weryngton
pysche I gyffe my borde clothe of twylle the one halfe to Denton
chapell to be auter clothe and the other halfe to the chapell of seynt
Stephyn of Alvandley To my neyvew Rychart Hollonde thre of my
best sylvur spones and to my cosyn John Ardernne two sylvur
spones and my best cofur To my dohtᵣ Alyce my omber beydes
The rest that shall lefe over my wyll fulfyllyt shall be put in a cofur
in a sure kepyng by my executors at the oversyght of my supvysurs
and they to kepe the keye and so to delyvur yt at the tymes
necessary for my doghtᵣ Alys proffet and yff yt fortune her to decesse
afor she have receyvyt thes goodes then myn executors wᵗ the over
syght of my supvysors shall dyspose hytᶦ in almes dedes for my
sawle and my fryndes saules To Alyce my doghtᵣ my bedde And
I make Rychart Hollande of Denton esquyer John Ardern of
Ardeyne esquyer and Thomas Davēport of Dysley chaplyn my executors and I wyll that yechon of theym shall have xˢ for theyr
payne over and besyde theyre costes To Sᵣ Roger Warde xˢ to p̄y
for me and to be a caller on that thys my wyll be fulfyllyt.

¹ Sir Peter Legh of Lyme, created a knight banneret at the siege of Berwick 22
Edward IV., died at Lyme 11th August 1527, having appointed Robert Ardern
one of the executors of his will. — See Beamont's *Warrington in* 1465, note, pp.
xiii., xiv.
² ....

(Chetham Society, Lancashire and Cheshire Wills. Vol. 51, 138-141)

A NOTE ON THE ILLUSTRATIONS

THE six engravings, which are here reproduced, were published from copper plates in the first edition of the Italian translation of this book, printed at Macerata in 1583. I have not found them in any subsequent editions. They represent to us the usual course of the persecution, rather than the history of any particular martyr, though Campion is mentioned once. We are shown how the Catholics were arrested, mocked, led off to prison, examined, tortured, drawn and executed.

It is quite possible that these plates were originally engraved for Father Persons's well-written and popular Latin tract, entitled *De Persecutione Anglicana*, which made a great impression abroad, and which treated of the sufferings of the English Catholics in this general way.

The connection of the plates with the *De Persecutione* may further be argued from the striking incident of the flogging at the cart's tail, and the branding of John Typet (also written Typper), in plate 3. This brave youth, after his courageous confession, became a Carthusian monk, and rose to high office in that Order. Allen, however, does not allude to him at all. So the inspiration must have come from elsewhere.

These pictures give the earliest representations of the sufferings of the English martyrs, and as Allen's book was the seed, as it were, of the subsequent martyrologies, so these pictures afforded ideas to various subsequent artists. The first and chief of these was Niccolo Circiniani (the eldest of three painters who have called themselves Dalle Pomerancie), who was employed in 1583-1584 in painting frescoes of the martyrdoms in the church of the English Martyrs at Rome, which frescoes were engraved by Giovanni Battista Cavalieri and published under the title, *Ecclesiae Anglicanæ Trophæa*, Rome, 1584. The plates regarding the English Martyrs were reprinted by Father John Morris.

Circiniani has evidently based his plates 31, 32, 33 (Morris, plates 5, 6, 7) on our plates 4, 5, 6; while his 34 (Morris, 8) draws from both 2 and 3 of our series. Whilst our plates give us realistically the costume of the day,

Circiniani has represented all but the martyrs in classical attire (or in classical absence of attire). Except that he corrects the gallows into the "triple tree" of Tyburn (probably the earliest representation of it known), his treatment is really inferior to that of our plates.

Richard Verstegan, in his *Theatrum Crudelitatis Hæreticorum nostri tempori*, Antwerp, 1592, in his plates on pp. 71, 73, 79, has used our plates 2, 4, 3; while his p. 83 takes in our 5 and 6. He has also borrowed from Circiniani.

The frontispiece is taken from a very rare plate at the British Museum (P. II, c. iv, 2 sub.) The inscription is in Latin.

Father Persons, in the unfinished *Life and Martyrdom of Father Edmund Campion*, c. xiv, thus described him, when he came to Rome from Germany, "And surely I remember he came after so venerable a manner as might move devotion. For he came in grave priests [gown] with long [beard and] hair, after the fashion of Germany," It is in this dress that Campion is represented here. The exceedingly high collar of the German habit has the effect of making the neck look abnormally short. When this is allowed for, the portrait, though of course not drawn from nature, corresponds fairly with the sub-contemporary portrait formerly at the Gesù (*Lives of the English Martyrs*, ii, 357).

The print is German sixteenth century. A copy of Bromley's *Catalogue of British Portraits* has this note on it, "£8 8s. 0d. Extremely rare. I never saw another copy."

Appendix II From Cardinal William Allen's *A True Report of the Death and Martyrdom of E. Campion Jesuite and Priest.*

Appendix III

A List of Attackers in a Night Skirmish of 1598 in Which Thomas
Hoghton I Was Killed
To prove murder.
1. Theyr pretensed purpose to execute an unlawfull thinge:
2. The extraordynary number of them assembled to do the same:
3. Theyr unusuall furniture and povision lyke unto preparaton for
wars:
4. The maner of theyr marchinge and devidinge theyr companies into
two parts:
5. The time of theyr entry into the place which was aboute one of the
clock afte mydnighte:/
6. Theyr refusall to show the cause of theyr comynge being demended
the same curtiously by the owner of the grounde. [The remainder of
the numbers are not visible on the page.]

The generall pre momuringe of theyr watchworde the crow is white
invented and agree upon before with pretense to use the same at
theyr first assalte:/
The shooting of a piece before any Encounter:
Theyr speches publyshed in the fighte before mr Houghton was
slayne: kille hym, kill that Houghton: downe with him:/
The calling for new supplies of theyr devided companye, and
theyr coming over and breakinge down pales and
hedges to assiste theyr felowes to kylle mr Houghton:/
The maner of his dethe and who kylled hym:/
The speches uttred after he was slayne, I am sure he is
slayne, I have bene in his bowells:/
Theyr flyeng away to avoyde theyr tryall by lawe:/

_ _ _ _ _ _ _ _ _ _ (illegible)   Symon Dalton alredy endyted of murder
                                   Thomason Singleton: _ _ _ _ (illegible)
                    Jul: 33 A: Hughe Anderton::/ not endyted:/.
                                 John: Halton a_: Halton:/
_. Jo: Halton as he taketh it:/
Bradshaw .52: for weapons:/.

Murder _____ (illegible)
1 Mathew Paladay
2 John Gryme:
3 Symon Dalloy
4 Barnaby Thornby:
5 John Weaver
6 w [will]: Hynde:
7 w: Platte:
8 w Rudynge
9 Andr: Singleton
10 Will: Clyfton:
11 Edm: Toogood:
12 w: Parke:
13 Evans Stiloe:
   Manslaughter.

14 Tho: Langton:	Fa: Gregson:	Rob Southworth:
15 Th: Singleton:	Rob: Hendley:	Rob. Martyn
16 w: Anderton:	He: Burch	Math: Styrroppe:
17 Jo: Clyfton:		

——— —— ———   Ry Wood__orks:7 28   Ph: Langton de Cat_
[not numbered]

Jo: Langton	Frances Langton	Jo: Pendlebury:
	Jo: Robinson:	He: Byrom:

19 Jo: Pendlebury:	
20 Cuthb: Clyfton:	Leon: Seried:
21 Jarvys Clyfton:	Edw: Corkshatts:
22 Hughe Anderton:	Rog: Healmesley:
23 w: Charburne:	Edw: _____
Hugh Arden	He Singleton:
Edm: Estham:	w. Noblett:/
Geo: Estham:	Ge: Cott—:/—;/
24 Tho: Batson:	Edm ___ Darwen
Edm: Kellett Ge: Darwen:	
Law: Charneley:	Tho Guerden
Tho: _____ 27	Ry: Sevient:
w: Bateson: Edw: Esthang:	
25 Rogr Darwen	Ro: Darwen
Ha: Caterall: Evan _ Darwen	
Jo: Parks:	Jo: Leighe
Jo: Jackson	w: Leighe:
26 Ry: _raddelle:	Ry: Jacson:
Ja: _____	Ry: Cowpe:
Jo: Halton:	Rob: So__rBu___
Th: Slater	o: Bateson

Th: _oats-   Edm: Tunstall:
Edm: Estham: fol: 46:
Jo: Dawson: Jute: 5:30:
Ja: Woodruf___ 36.5.
H: Bradshaw: 52: 5:

        Hughe Anderton:
_____ ____ _____ (illegible)
Joh: Houghton: 45:.3-4-5
H: Bradshaw: . 52.
NE: Gras__ 58 3:

        for thasselt [and]Shool____go___s and dags:
        Dk_chs Gras__ 5 8:
                that they called for more fresh man/.
                H__t Bradshaw: .55. Jul: is:/.
                H_ch: Grason: 58:/.Ju: cz [?] :/.
                that they had kill Houghton:/
                Jo: Houghton: 48: Jul: 15:1.

[Note: Hugh Arden is listed as is John Jackson. Might Hugh Arden be a relative of Shakespeare and John Jackson the trustee for the purchase of the Gatehouse? A John Robinson was the tenant of the Gatehouse that Shakespeare purchased (see above).]

(Transcribed from English MS 213. "Letters of Richard Hoghton." The John Rylands University Library. University of Manchester.)

Appendix IV
The Original Yellow Knitted Stockings?

Holford, Thomas, was born at Aston, Cheshire (Chalcedon catalogue) in 1541 (CRS, V, 111), his father being a minister. He was schoolmaster to the sons of Sir John Scudmore (including John Scudmore q.v.), of Holme Lacy, Herefords. Here he was reconciled by Richard Davies (q.v.) about 1582 (Chall. 136). He entered the college at Rheims 18 aug 82, was ordained at Laon 9 apr 83 and sent to England 4 may 83. He used the alias of Acton. On 2 nov 84 he was in the house of the Bellamys at Harrow-on-the-Hill, Middlesex with the said Richard Davies when it was raided but they both escaped. Holford went to his native Cheshire, but was apprehended at Nantwich in may 85 (CRS, V, 110) and imprisoned in the castle of West Chester. A number of people were examined in aug about a "mass lately said in Chester castle by Thomas Holford seminary priest lately sent to London". It transpired that there had been a number of masses "about Rogation week" and also at Whitsun (PRO, Chester 23/100/1). There is in my possession an original letter written by Holford, evidently from this prison: "Brother William, whatsoever men report of you, assure yourself that I will love you and trust you as much as one brother can trust another, so long as I find that good nature in you which always I have found. I pray you send or bring unto me my cloak and hose and stockings and scarf that I may make money of them. I would gladly speak with you and I will bear your charges. Let not my things be brought into the castle but left safe in the town whither I may send for them. Commend me unto my good Nicholas, my host and hostess and thank them for their tokens. Once again farewell.

Always one
Tho: Holforde."

He was examined by the bishop of Chester, admitted that he was a priest and that he came to England to persuade H.M's subjects to the catholic faith "saying that he will not depart the realm but that either Tyburn or Boughton shall have his carcass." The bishop sent his examination to London together with his own description: "The said Holford is a tall, black, fat, strong man, the crown of his head bald, his beard marquessated [shaven except for hair on lip]; his apparel was black cloak with murrey lace open at the shoulders, a straw-coloured fustion doublet laid on with red lace, hose laid on with biliment lace [trimming], cut and laid under with black taffeta. A little black hat lined with velvet in the brim, a falling band and yellow knitted stockings."

Holford was conducted to London by two pursuivants. They lodged at an inn in the Strand. The pursuivants drank liberally, and at five in the morning Holford rose, pulled a yellow stocking on one leg and a white boot-hose on the other and walked up and down the chamber. One of his keepers awoke, saw him still there and went to sleep again. He next hood-winked the innkeeper and a catholic gentleman who took him for a lunatic and thus escaped. He pulled off his stocking and boot and ran bare-footed eight miles to Harrow. His feet and legs were badly scratched as he had run through briars, and the two Bellamy daughters, who were soon to suffer so much, bathed his wounds and put him to bed. How well-informed the government was may be seen from the following accusation in a later examination of Richard Bellamy: "Holford alias Acton . . . was harboured there when he fled from the sheriff's men of Cheshire out of the Strand, by the same token that the maiden in Bellamy's house did pick thorns out of his legs gotten with running thither through hedges in the night." Bellamy replies "he knoweth not Holford alias Acton nor of any such, nor never heard of any such man'"(Troub. II, 54).

Holford avoided London for a year, but in 1588 he was recognised by a pursuivant as he was leaving the house of Swithin Wells, in Holborn, where he had said mass, and was arrested. He was sent to Newgate, condemned 26 aug 88 and was martyred at Clerkenwell 28 aug 88. For some account of these executions see under James Claxton. cf. Chall. 136 (a contemporary account); D. 190, 194, 195. (Anstruther 170, 171)

Appendix V
Shakespeare/Priests/Stratford/ Lancashire/Theater Ties

An interesting study would be to search for family connections between Catholic priests, Stratford, Lancashire, Shakespeare, and the theater world. It appears the recurrence of surnames in the various areas is unusually frequent:

Theater	Shakespeare	Stratford	Priests	Lancashire
Allen	Allen	William Allen	Allen	Allen
Beeston	Beeston			Beeston
Blount	Blount	Blount	Blount	
Burbage	Burbage	Burbage		
Byrd	Byrd		Byrd	
	Cotton	Cotton	Cotton	Cotton
Green	Green	Green	Green	
Field	Field	Field		
Heming	Heming	Heming		
Hathaway	Hathaway	Hathaway		
Heywood	Heywood			Heywood
Jones	Jones	Jones	Jones	
Johnson	Johnson	Johnson	Johnson	
Kemp	Kemp		Kemp	
Leveson	Leveson			Leveson
Munday	Munday	Munday		
Nash	Nash	Nash		
Savage	Savage	Savage	Savage	

Obviously, a great amount of biographical information is needed to make this sort of study meaningful. In the foregoing study, the Cotton, Leveson, and Savage ties between Shakespeare, the theater, and Lancashire are substantiated. It also appears from the evidence presented here that the Christopher Beeston, William Beeston, and Hugh Beeston connections are probable. Information about the theater Hathaway and the Shottery Hathaways is hazy, but the playwright, Richard Hathaway, appears to be related to Anne Hathaway. The Burbages, the printer Field, and perhaps the actor Field have been shown to come from Stratford. No information is available about a relationship between the theater Nash and Shakespeare's Stratford friends, the Nash family. No relationship is shown in the DNB between John Heywood (d 1565), court dramatist patronized by Sir Thomas More and Thomas Heywood, who was active in the theater during Shakespeare's life. The DNB shows only that John Heywood was the father of two priests, Jasper and Ellis Heywood, but does not identify the other several children except to show the daughter, Elizabeth, was the mother of John Donne. Perhaps one son was the dramatist that Shakespeare knew in London.

Works Cited

Albright, Evelyn. "Shakespeare's *Richard II* and the Essex Conspiracy." *PMLA*, XLII (1927): 686-720.

Allen, Cardinal William, *Father Edmund Campion & His Companions*, (1582) Reprinted by Rev. J.H. Pollen, S.J. London: Burns and Oates, 1908.

Anstruther, Godfrey, O.P. *The Seminary Priests*. Ware, England: St. Edmund's College P, 1968.

Aveling, Father Hugh, OSB. "The Catholic Recusants of the West Riding of Yorkshire 1558-1790." Proceedings of the Leeds Philosophical and Literary Society. Vol X, June 1962-September 1963. Leeds: W.S. Maney, 1966.

Bagley, J. J. *A History of Lancashire*. Beaconsfield: Darwen Finlayson, 1967.

Baines, Thomas. *Lancashire Past and Present*. London: William Mackenzie, 1867.

Baker, Oliver. *In Shakespeare's Warwickshire and the Unknown Years*. London: Simkin Marshall, 1937.

Barroll, Leeds. "A New History for Shakespeare and His Time." *Shakespeare Quarterly* Winter l988: 441-464.

Bassett, Bernard, S.J. *The English Jesuits*. New York: Herder and Herder, 1968.

Bellew, John. *Shakespeare's Home at New Place, Stratford*. London: Virtue Brothers, 1972.

Bindoff, S. T. *Tudor England*. New York: Viking Penguin, 1985.

Brownlow, E.W. "John Shakespeare's Recusancy: New Light on an Old Document." *Shakespeare Quarterly* Summer 1989: 186-191.

Bruce, John, Esq., F.S.A. *Correspondence of King James VI of Scotland*. Vol. 78. The Camden Society. n.p.: n.p., 1861.

Campbell, Thomas, J., S.J. *The Jesuits 1534-1921*. New York: Encyclopedia P, 1921.

Caraman, Philip. John Gerard: *The Autobiography of an Elizabethan*. New York: Longmans, 1951.

Chamberlain, Frederick. *Elizabeth and Leycester*. New York: Dodd, Mead, 1939.

Chambers, E. K. *The Elizabethan Stage*. Oxford: Clarendon P, 1923; 1967.

—. *Shakespearean Gleanings*. Oxford: Humphrey Milford, 1944.

—. *William Shakespeare: A Study of Facts and Problems*. Oxford: Clarendon P, 1930.

Chetham Society, *Remains Historical & Literary Connected with the Palatine Counties of Lancaster and Chester.* Vol. 51, 59-60.

Child, Harold. "Introduction." *Richard II* by William Shakespeare. Cambridge: UP, 1961.

Chronicles of the English Augustinian Canonesses Regular of the Lateran, at St. Monica's in Louvain, 1548 - 1625. Ed. Dom Adam Hamilton, O.S.B. London: Sands, 1904.

Clare, Janet. *'Art Made Tongue-Tied by Authority.'* Manchester: UP, 1990.

Clark, Eleanor Grace. *Ralegh and Marlowe.* New York: Russell & Russell, 1965.

Craig, Hardin, ed. *The Complete Works of Shakespeare.* Glenview, Ill: Scott, Foresman, 1961.

De Groot, John Henry. *The Shakespeares and "the Old Faith."* Freeport: Books for Libraries P, 1946.

Derby Household Books. The Stanley Papers, Part II. The Chetham Society Vol. 31, 1853.

Devlin, Christopher. *Hamlet's Divinity.* Carbondale: Southern Illinois UP, 1964.

Dictionary of National Biography.

Dutton, Richard. "Shakespere and Marlowe: Censorship and Construction." *Yearbook of English Studies* 23 (1993): 1-29.

Dyce, The Rev. Alexander. Introduction. *Kemps Nine Daies Wonder: Performed in a Daunce.* London: The Camden Society, 1840.

Elton, G. R. *England Under the Tudors.* London: Methuen, 1955.

Fraser, Antonia. *Mary Queen of Scots.* St. Albans: Granada, 1975.

French, George Russell. *Shakespeareana Genealogica*, Parts I and II. London: Macmillan, 1869.

Fripp, Edgar L. *Shakespeare: Man and Artist.* Oxford: Humphrey Milford, 1938.

—-. *Shakespeare's Stratford.* Oxford: Clarendon P, 1928.

Frye, Roland Mushat. *The Renaissance Hamlet.* Princeton: UP, 1984.

Gillow, Joseph. *Bibliographic Dictionary of English Catholics.* London: Burns & Oates, 1885-1902.

Greenblatt, Stephen. *Shakespearean Negotiations.* Berkeley: U of Cal P, 1988.

Greg, W. W. "The Handwritings of the Manuscript." *Papers by Alfred W. Pollard, W.W. Greg, E. Maunde Thompson, J. Dover Wilson, and R.W. Chambers.* Cambridge: UP, 1923.

Hamilton, Donna B. *Shakespeare and the Politics of Protestant England.* Lexington, Kentucky: UP, 1992.

Hayward, Sir John, Knight. *Annals of the Reign of Queen Elizabeth.* Vol 7. London: Camden Society, 1839.

Heydt, Bruce. "The Many Shakespeares." *British Heritage* X, Oct/Nov 1991: 53-58.

Heywood, Thomas. ed. Introduction. *Cardinal Allen's Defence of Sir William Stanley's Surrender of Deventer.* Vol 25. The Chetham Society, 1851-52.

Hoghton, Thomas. "Letters." English ms 213. The John Rylands Library. University of Manchester.

Honigmann, E. A. J. *Shakespeare: the 'Lost Years.'* Manchester: UP, 1985.

Hosking, G. L. *The Life and Times of Edward Alleyn*. London: Jonathan Cape, 1951.

Howard, Jean. "The New Historicism in Renaissance Studies." Reprinted from *English Literary Renaissance*, 16 (1986): 13-43.

Hughes, Ted. *Shakespeare and the Goddess of Complete Being*. London: Faber and Faber, 1992.

Hunt, Maurice. "The Religion of *Twelfth Night*." *CLA Journal* Dec. l993: 189-203.

Hutchinson, Harold. *The Hollow Crown*. London: Eyre and Spottiswoode, 1961.

Jenkins, Elizabeth. *Elizabeth the Great*. London: Granada, 1958.

Jory, Colin. Address to the St. Thomas More Society, Sydney Australia, 22 June 1999, anticipated publication, November 1999.

—. E-mail 5 October 1999.

"Lancashire and Cheshire Wills." The Chetham Society 51, 1844.

Leys, M. D. R. *Catholics in England, 1559 - 1829; A Social History*. New York: Sheed and Ward, 1961.

Marc'hadour, Germain, Abbé. "S. Edmund Campion et S. Thomas More." *Moreana* XIX, 75 - 76 (Nov 1982): 201 - 104.

Marcus, Leah. *Puzzling Shakespeare*. Berkeley: U of Cal P, 1988.

McCoog, Thomas M., S. J. "'The Flower of Oxford': The Role of Edmund Campion in Early Recusant Polemics." *Sixteenth Century Journal* Winter 1993: 901-913.

Merriam, Thomas. "Did Shakespeare Model Camillo in *The Winter's Tale* on Sir Thomas More?" *Moreana* XIX (Nov 1982): 74-76, 91-101.

—. E-mail 14 October 1999.

Milward, Peter, S.J. FAX 24 September 1999.

—. *Shakespeare's Religious Background*. Bloomington: Indiana UP, 1973.

Morey, Andrew. *The Catholic Subjects of Elizabeth I*. Totawa, NJ: Rowman and Littlefield, 1978.

Mullaney, Steven. "Mourning and Misogyny." *Shakespeare Quarterly* Summer 1994: 139 - 162.

Mutschmann, H. and K. Wentersdorf. *Shakespeare and Catholicism*. New York: AMS P, 1969.

Nelson, Thomas, ed. *The Works of William Shakespeare*, V 2. New York: Thomas Nelson, n. d.

Newdigate, Bernard. *Michael Drayton and his Circle*. Oxford: Shakespeare Head P, 1941.

Omerod. *History of Cheshire* Vol 2.

Paulet, Sir Amias. *The Letter-Books of Sir Amias Poulet, Keeper of Mary Queen of Scotts*. Ed. John Morris. London: Burns and Oates, 1962.

Peck, D. C. "Government Suppression of Elizabethan Catholic Books: the Case of *Leicester's Commonwealth*." *The Library Quarterly* April 1977: 163 - 177.

Pollard, A. F. , M.A. *The History of England.* N Y: Greenwood P, 1969.

Pollen, Father J.H. *Mary Queen of Scots and the Babington Plot.* Edinburgh: UP, 1922.

Pugliatti, Paola. "The Strange Tongues of *Henry V.*" *The Yearbook of English Studies* 3 (1993): 235-253.

Reed, Robert Rentoul, Jr. *Crime and God's Judgment in Shakespeare.* Kentucky: UP, 1984.

Remnick, David. "A Reporter at Large; Hamlet in Hollywood." *The New Yorker* 20 November 1995: 66-81.

Rowse, A. L. *Shakespeare's Southampton.* New York: Harper & Row, 1965.

St. John Brooks, Eric. *The Life of Hatton.* London: Jonathan Cape, 1947.

Sams, Eric. *The Real Shakespeare.* New Haven: Yale UP, 1995.

Savage, Richard, transcriber. *Minutes and Accounts of the Corporation of Stratford-upon-Avon and other Records 1553-1620.* Introduction and notes by Edgar I. Fripp. Vol. 1 1553-1566. Dugdale Society, 1921.

Saxton, Christopher. "Lancashire," "Shropshire," "Yorkshire" maps. Shrewsbury: Chatsworth Library, 1992.

Schoenbaum, S. *William Shakespeare, a Compact Documentary Life.* Oxford: UP, 1987.

Shakespeare, William. *As You Like It.* Ed. Louis B. Wright and Virginia A. LaMar. Folger Library. New York: Washington Square P, 1959.

—. *Hamlet.* Ed. Edward Hubler. Signet ed. New York: Penguin, 1963.

—. *1 Henry IV.* Ed. Maynard Mack. Signet ed. New York: Sylvan Barnet, 1963.

—. *Richard II.* Ed. G. B. Harrison. New York: Harcourt Brace, 1948.

—. *2 Henry IV.* Ed. John Russell Brown. Signet ed. New York: Sylvan Barnet, 1963.

—. *Twelfth Night.* Ed. J. M. Lothian and T.W. Craik. Arden ed. New York: Routledge, 1975.

"Shakespeare's Britain," *National Geographic*, May 1964.

Simpson, Richard. *Edmund Campion, a Biography.* London: John Hodges, 1896.

Speed, John. London: *The History of Great Britaine Under the Conquest of the Romans, Saxons, Danes, Normans* . . . . [Imprinted by W. Hall and I Beale] and to be solde by I Sudbury and G. Humble, 1611.

Stopes, Charlotte. *Shakespeare's Family.* London: Elliot Stock, 1901.

—. *Shakespeare's Warwickshire Contemporaries.* Stratford: Shakespeare Head P, 1908.

—. *Third Earl of Southampton.* Cambridge: UP, 1922.

Strype, John. *Annals of the Reformation and Ecclesiastical Memorials.* Vol. III, Pt. 1. Oxford: UP, 1820.

Thoms, William J., F.S.A. "Shakespeare in Germany I. Three Notelets on Shakespeare." London: John Russell Smith, 1865.

Titherley, Arthur, Walsh. *Shakespeare's Identity*. Winchester: Wykeham P, 1952.

Trevelyan, G.M. *A Shortened History of England*. Baltimore: Penguin, 1959.

Waugh, Evelyn. *Edmund Campion*. Garden City: Image Books, 1956.

"What Was the Religion of Shakespeare?" *The Rambler, a Catholic Journal and Review*. New Series IV. n. p.: n. d., 1858.

Whitfield, Christopher. "Some of Shakespeare's Contemporaries at the Middle Temple." *Notes and Queries* 211 (1966): 122, 283, 363, 443.

Wilkes, G. "Shakspeare and Father Campion." *Catholic Progress* iv (1877): 202, 203.

Williams, Nevill. *Thomas Howard, Fourth Duke of Norfolk*. London: Barrie and Rockliff, 1964.

Wilson, Ian. *Shakespeare: the Evidence*. New York: St. Martin's P, 1993.

Wilson, John Dover. *The Essential Shakespeare, a Biographical Adventure*. Cambridge: UP, 1932; 1942.

Index

Asbies, 54, 55, 60
Ashcroft, Mr. Philip, 78
Aspinall, Alexander, 36
Aubrey, John, 77
Audley, John, 52
Aveling, Father Hugh, 73
Babington (Babyngton), Anthony, 21, 92, 122
Babington Plot, 18; 20-22; 35; 38; 92-94; 122; 153; 154;
    government list of conspirators in, 92
Bagley, J. J., map, 83
Baines, Thomas, 48
Baker, Oliver, 41, 73
Ballard, John, 92
Bardell, George, 60
Barnewell, Robert, 92
Barroll, Leeds, 75, 128, 129
Bassett, Bernard, 87
Beeston, Christopher, 77, 78, 83, 161, 170
Beeston, Hugh 78, 170
Beeston, William, 75, 78, 79
Bellamy, Elizabeth (listed later as Katherine), 92
Bellamy, Jerome, 92
Bellamy, Richard, 169
Bellew, John, 51
Bergeron, David, 129
Bess of Hardwick, 144, 145
Bilson, Bishop, 116
Bindoff, S. T., 3, 4, 8-10, 16, 27, 29, 112, 126
Blackfriars' Gatehouse, 136, 137, 151, 160
Blackwell, George, 33, 137
Blackwell, Mary Campion, 137
"Bloody question, The," 30
Blount, Charles, Lord Mountjoy, 102, 106, 114, 115
Blundell, Richard, 79
Boleyn, Anne, Queen of Henry VIII (1507-36); portrait, 6; 8; 9
Bolingbroke, 119, 120-123, 126, 127
Bond of Association, 20, 30
Borromeo, Cardinal, 53
Borromeo testament, 54, 66
Bothwell, earl of: *see* Hepburn, James
Bromley, Lord Chancellor, 124
Brooke, Henry, 111
Brookesby, Edward, 92
Browne, Henry, 54, 94, 108

Brownlow, F. W., 47
Bruce, John, Esq., F. S. A., 112, 114
Bull of Excommunication, 15, 16, 19, 25, 29
Burghley, Lord: *see* Cecil, William
Burroughs, Frances, 136
Camden, 122
Campbell, Thomas J., S. J., 134
Campion, Edmund, S.J., (1540-81), 22; 25-27; 32; 35; 45; 47; 50-55; 76;
    77; 81; 84; 87-89; 95-103; 108; 109; and Henry plays, 130-138; his
    execution, 135, 137; 141; 143; 149; 157; 159; 164
Caraman, Philip, 28, 29, 36
Catan, Anne, 81
Catesby, Anne, 54, 56, 108
Catesby family, 4
Catesby, John, 70
Catesby, Robert, 36, 54, 56, 70, 95, 96, 107, 108
Catesby, Sir William, 35, 52-54, 67, 70, 94-96, 135
Catherine de Medici, Queen of France (1519-89), 16
Catherine of Aragon, Queen of Henry VIII (1485-1536), 9, 99
Catherine of Valois, 130
Catholic seminaries in France and Belgium, map, 86
Cecil, Sir Robert (1560-1612), 105-107, 111, 112, 115-117, 119
Cecil, William, Lord Burghley (1520-98), 4, 12, 23, 34, 79, 83, 108, 110,
    111, 115-117, 134, 156
Chamberlain, Frederick, 144
Chamberlain's Men, 43, 78, 101, 105, 128
Chambers, E. K., 39-41, 73, 79, 82, 92
Charnock, John, 92
Cheney, Bishop of Gloucester, 48
Chester, Robert, 94
Child, Harold, 121, 128
Clare, Janet, 44, 46, 111
Clark, Eleanor Grace, 119
Clement VII, pope at Avignon, 122
Clopton House, 36, 66
Coat of Arms (Shakespeare) 48-51, 63, 67
Cobham, Lord, 111
Coke, Attorney General, 107
Communion, 3, 26, 29
Como, Cardinal, 27
Conference about Succession to the Crown, A, 119
Cottam, John, 36, 68, 82, 88
Cottam, Thomas, 82, 88, 103
Craig, Hardin, 51, 110

20; and theater, 41; and *Henry VI*, 45; and Wars of the Roses, 63; fear of aging, 111; problem of her successor, 111; and Essex, 112 -118; and *Richard II*, 119 - 128; parallels with Bolingbroke, 121; effect of execution of Mary, Queen of Scots, 124 - 128; responsibility for death of Mary, Queen of Scots, 126, 127;

Elton, G. R., 3, 9, 33, 37

Emerson, Ralph, 98

Englefield, Sir Francis, 44

English Mission of Counter-Reformation, 25-31, 35-38, 101, 108, 109, 133, 141, 159

Equivocation, 30, 31, 36

Essex, earl of: *see* Robert Devereux

Essex Rebellion, 18, 75, 95, 104-109, 125, 128, 160

Exorcism, 38

Falstaff, Sir John, 43, 101, 135

First Part of the Life and Reigne of King Henrie Fourth, a book by Sir John Haywood, 106

Fitton, Anne, 96

Fitton, Mary, 76-78, 97

Fitton, Sir Edward, 97

Fitton, William, 76

Fitzherberts, 88

Fortinbras, 115

Francis II, King of France (1550-60), 11

Fraser, Antonia, 17, 20-22, 120, 122, 124-126, 144

French, George Russell, 37, 51, 57, 61-64, 66, 67, 77, 79, 80, 97, 107, 108

Fripp, Edgar L., 35-37, 49, 50, 58, 66, 107

Frye, Roland Mushat, 116

Fulwood, John, 36, 37

Fulwood, Richard, 36, 37

Gage, Robert 92

Ganymede, 152

Garnet, Henry, 30, 31, 36, 64

Gerard, Balthasar, 19

Gerard, John, 30, 36

Gerard, Katherine (wife of young Richard Hoghton), 150

Gerard, Sir Gilbert, Master of the Rolls, 150

Gerard (Gerrard), Sir Thomas, 92

Gibbes, George, 55

Gifford, Gilbert, 21, 92

Gilbert, George, 38, 88, 92

Gilbert, William, 49

Gillow, Joseph, 75, 88, 92, 95, 96, 100, 109, 149

Globe Theater, 21, 76, 93, 94, 128, 129, 160

Henry VII, King of England (1485-1509), 54, 68, 69, 112

Henry VI, a play by William Shakespeare, 42

Hepburn, James, earl of Bothwell, 115, 122

Herbert, Philip, earl of Montgomery, 76, 77

Herbert, William, earl of Pembroke, 42, 76, 77

Hesketh, Bartholomew, 36, 79

Hesketh, Janet, 93

Hesketh, Richard, 68, 153, 157

Hesketh, Sir Thomas, 68, 77, 78, 80, 84, 86, 93, 143, 153

Heydt, Bruce, 51

Heywood, Jasper, 29

Heywood, John, 170

Heywood, Thomas, 49, 86, 153

Hill, Agnes, 37, 76

Hilliard portrait (thought to be of William Shakespeare), 66

History of Ireland by Edmund Campion, 98, 135

Hoby, Sir Edmund, 105

Hoghton, Adam de, 63

Hoghton, Alexander, 25, 35, 36, 40, 52, 72, 73, 77-79, 82, 100, 143,
144, 149, 155, 160

Hoghton, John, 167

Hoghton, Margaret 71

Hoghton, Mrs. Anne, 79

Hoghton, Richard (of Park Hall), 76, 79, 83, 97, 98, 100, 148-151, 160

Hoghton, Sir Otnell, 71

Hoghton, Sir Richard, nephew of Thomas I, 71, 150, 152, 158

Hoghton, Sir Richard de, 100, 150

Hoghton, Thomas I, 71,83, 85, 100, 146-151, 158, 165

Hoghton, Thomas II, 71, 78, 79, 137

Hoghton Tower, 63, 67, 68, 70, 71, 73, 81, 100, 148, 149

"Hoghton, William" 102

Holcroft, Alice, 77, 78

Holford, Thomas, 140, 141, 143, 168, 169

Holinshed, 98

Holliday, William, 96

Honigmann, E. A. J., 36, 40, 41, 52, 63, 68, 73, 76-79, 81, 82, 85, 93, 94,
96, 149, 151

Hooper, Humphrey, 55

Hosking, G. L., 111

Hotson, Leslie, 93

Hotspur, 129-138

Howard, Jean, 41

Howard, Lord Henry, 88

Howard, Thomas, 4th duke of Norfolk, 12-17, 106, 117, 118, 139

Hughes, Ted, 42, 43
Hulton, William, 79
Hunt, Maurice, 140
Hunt, Simon, 35
Hutchinson, Harold, 123
Isabella, Infanta, 33, 59, 106, 112, 119
Jackson, Brian, 151
Jackson, Jo (John?), 151, 166, 167
Jac[k]son, Ry (Richard?), 166
James VI, King of Scots (1567-1625) and James I of England (1603-25),
    1-7, 18, 23, 33, 34, 96, 106, 107, 111, 112, 115-118
Jaques, 153-156
Jay, Thomas, 92
Jenkins, Elizabeth, 13, 15-17, 20, 23, 24, 26, 27, 29, 30, 131, 134
Jesuit colleges, 49, 102
Jesuits, 19, 30, 33, 40, 52, 60, 138, 141
John of Gaunt, 23, 122
Jones, Edward, 21, 92
Jones, Richard, 21
Jordan, John, 53
Jory, Colin, 52, 60
Judas, 121
Julius Caesar, 22, 23
Julius Caesar, a play by William Shakespeare, 22, 23, 24
Kemp, Will, 97, 98
King John, a play believed to be in part by William Shakespeare, 102
King Lear, a play by William Shakespeare, 35, 38, 113
Knolleys, Lettice, 107
Knowsley, 68, 70, 83, 92
Lambert, Edmund, 54, 55
Lathom Hall, 68, 70, 83, 153
Lea Hall, 68, 148, 149
Leigh (or Legh), Sir Peter, of Lyme, 71, 72
Leveson, 77, 160
Leveson, Elizabeth Arden, 77
Leveson, Sir Richard, 76
Leveson, Walter, 77
Leveson, William, 76
Leys, M. D. R., 1, 2, 30, 31, 87, 136, 148
Life of Sir John Oldcastle, The, 43, 101
"Little John" *see* Owens, Nicholas
Longworth, Clara, 53
"Lucrece," 42, 144
Lucy, Sir Thomas, 58, 66, 94

Luther, Martin, 110
Macbeth, a play by William Shakespeare, 31, 40
Malone, Edmond, 53
Malvolio, 139-145
Manchester, 68, 71, 149
Marc'hadour, G., 101
Marcus, Leah, 42
Marie de Guise, 11
Mary, Countess of Southampton, 54, 108
Mary, Queen of England (1553-8), 2, 4, 8, 11, 87, 111, 134
Mary, Queen of Scots (1542-67), 4; portrait, 7 ; 8; 9; 11-24; and Treaty
    of Edinburgh, 11; plots to free her, 12, 25; Catholic Association, 17;
    18; and the Babington Plot, 18, 20 - 22; imprisonment in England,
    19, 20; conviction under Bond of Association, 20, 22, 30; trial, 22 -
    23, 124; her role as a Catholic martyr, 22, 24; parallels with Richard
    II, 23, 24, 45, 119 -129; death, 23, 25, 26; 32; 106; 112; 115-119;
    121-123; 142; 144; and *Julius Caesar*, 24;138; relationship with son
    James, 117; and the Northern Rebellion, 131, 132; 138; allusions
    to in *Twelfth Night*, 142-145; known as "Lucrece," 144;155
Mass (Catholic), 26, 41
Mayne, Cuthbert, 87
McCoog, Thomas M., S. J., 88
Measure for Measure, a play by William Shakespeare, 59
Mendoza, Spanish Ambassador, 87
Mercurian, Father, 87
Meres, Francis, 110, 148
Merriam, Thomas, 49, 101
Milward, Peter, S.J., 14, 30, 35, 38, 40, 46, 47, 49, 52, 60, 68, 113-115,
    131, 141, 156, 157
Monteagle, Lord, 105
Montgomery, earl of: *see* Herbert, Philip
Montrose, Louis, 41
More, Sir Thomas,100, 101
More, Sir Thomas, a play by Anthony Munday and others, 101
Morey, Andrew, 29-32, 38, 96
Mosley, Joseph, 53
Mountjoy, Lord: *see* Blount, Charles
Mowbray, 123
Mulberry tree, 100
Mullaney, Steven, 111
Munday, Anthony, 101
Mutschmann, H., 27, 28, 35-37, 40, 41, 47, 48, 50, 52, 53, 56, 58, 60,
    64, 66, 77, 94, 95, 99, 106-109, 137
National Geographic, map, 74

Pollard, A. F., 2, 12-14, 17, 28, 29, 87, 112, 131
Pollen, Father J. H., 17, 19, 20, 89, 154
Polonius, 110, 115, 116
Pound, Thomas, 88, 92, 94, 108, 109
Pugliatti, Paola, 104, 111, 130, 138
Pythagoras, 142, 143,
Raleigh, Sir Walter, 105, 106
Recusant, defined, 48; concealment of property, 55
Reed, Robert Rentoul, Jr., 110, 117
Remnick, David, 110
Richard II, a play by William Shakespeare, and Richard II, King of
    England (1377-1399), 14, 22-24, 27, 45, 75, 104-107, 115, 119-129;
    131, 132, 160
Ridolfi Plot, 16, 17
Ridolfi, Roberto (1531-1612), 16
Rivers, Anthony, 111
Robinson, John (Father); Robinson, John (son), 137, 160, 166
Rowse, A. L., 37, 108
Rufford Hall, 68, 70, 73, 78, 79, 82, 93, 153
St Bartholomew, Massacre of (1572), 16, 17
St. John Brooks, Eric, 153, 154
Salisbury, John, 94
Salisbury (Salysburye), Thomas, 92, 94
Sams, Eric, 62
Sandys, Edwin, 37
Savage, John, 21, 91-94
Savage, Richard, 49, 93
Savage, Sir John, 92
Savage, Thomas, 21, 93
Saxton, map, 70, 73, 83
Schillings, A., 102
Schoenbaum, S., 39, 47, 49, 50, 54, 62, 75, 77, 101
Shakeshafte, William, 40, 41, 52, 73, 77-81, 83, 93, 94, 97, 160
Shakespeare Coat of Arms, 48-51, 67
Shakespeare, Edmund (Edward), 54, 55
Shakespeare, John, 47; and religion, 47-61; application for coat of arms
    and civic career, 48-50, 67; court summons in 1584, 48; retirement
    from civic life, 48-61, 87; Catholic will, 52; 53, 54, 66; evidence of
    Catholic recusancy, 55, 58-61, 88, 146; relation to Somerville Plot, 80;
Shakespeare, Mary Arden, 36, 62, 68, 70, 96, 97
Shakespeare, Richard, 95
Shakespeare, William, 33, 34; and mission priests 35-38; and
    Southampton, 37, 42, 94, 104-109, 120, 160; religion a factor in
    understanding the plays, 39; Catholic upbringing, 44-59;

speculations on education, 59, 76, 86, 102, 159; acquaintance with Park Hall Ardens, 66-67; speculation on membership in Lord Strange's group of actors, 68, 75, 77, 79; and Robert Parsons, 102

Shallow, Justice, 66

Shaw, Francis, 36

Shaw, Gabriel, 36, 79

Shaw, Henry, 36

Shaw, Juline, 36

Shaw, Rafe, 36

Shrewsbury, earl of: see Talbot, George

Sidney, Philip, 134

Simpson, Richard, 27, 54, 87, 88, 97, 98, 100, 143, 156, 157

Somerville, John, 36, 64, 66

Somerville Plot, 18, 36, 64, 66

Somerville, William, 36, 66, 67, 71

Southampton, 3rd earl of: see Wriothesley, Henry

Southwell, Robert, 30

Spanish Armada, 23, 26, 32, 119, 130

Speed, John, 75, 102, 103, 112, 160, 161

Stanley, Ferdinando, Lord Strange,19, 41, 68, 76-79, 82, 148, 152, 153

Stanley, Henry, 79, 94

Stanley, Sir Edward, 82, 83

Stanley, Sir Thomas, 82

Stanley, Sir William, 153, 157

Stokport, 70, 71

Stoners, 88

Stopes, Charlotte, 37, 49, 54, 58, 62, 63, 67, 69, 70, 75, 81, 95, 107, 108

Storey, Dr., 87

Strype, John, 26, 50, 147

Stuart, Esmé, duke of Lennox, 18

Stuart, Henry, Lord Darnley (1545-67), 12, 21, 115, 122, 144

Sugar, John, 35

Talbot, George, earl of Shrewsbury (1528?-90), 13, 19, 20, 124, 140, 144, 145

Tarnacre, 81

Tempest, The, a play by William Shakespeare, 37, 43

Thoms, William, 98

Throckmorton, Catherine, 95

Throckmorton, Clement, 107

Throckmorton family, 88, 95, 96

Throckmorton, Margaret, 95

Throckmorton, Mary, 95, 107

Throckmorton Plot, 18

Throckmorton, Robert, 95, 96